Graphical User Interfaces in C++

& Object-Oriented Programming

MARK GOODWIN

PUBLISHING FOR THE TWENTY-FIRST CENTURY

Copyright © 1990 by Management Information Source, Inc.
P.O. Box 5277
Portland, Oregon 97208-5277
(503) 282-5215

Second Printing

ISBN 1-55828-032-4 (Book)
ISBN 1-55828-053-7 (Book and Disk)

All rights reserved. Reproduction or use, without express permission, of editorial or pictorial content, in any manner, is prohibited. No patent liability is assumed with respect to the use of the information contained herein. While every precaution has been taken in the preparation of this book, neither the publisher nor the author assumes responsibility for errors or omissions. Neither is any liability assumed for damage resulting from the use of the information contained herein.

Ami is a trademark of Samna Corporation.
AutoCAD is a registered trademark of Autodesk, Inc.
IBM is a trademark of International Business Machines Corporation.
Lotus and 1-2-3 are registered trademarks of Lotus Development Corporation.
Microsoft, MS, and MS-DOS are registered trademarks of Microsoft Corporation.
PageMaker is a registered trademark of Aldus Corporation.
Ventura Publisher is a trademark of Ventura Software, Inc.

Printed in the United States of America

To Dee Dee: the most wonderful person in the world.

ACKNOWLEDGMENTS

I would like to express my sincere thanks to Zortech, Inc. of Arlington, MA. Without their generous contribution, this book would not have been possible.

TABLE OF CONTENTS

Introduction xv

Section I: The GWINDOWS Toolbox

Chapter 1: IBM PC Graphic Displays 3
MS-DOS Video Functions 4
ROM BIOS Video Functions 4
Direct Memory Access Techniques 7
    Color Graphics Adapter's Video Modes 8
    Enhanced Graphics Adapter's Video Modes 9
Reading and Writing Graphic Displays 9
    Graphic Coordinates 10
    CGA Graphic Pixels 11
    EGA Graphic Pixels 17
    Displaying Text Characters 26
    GWINDOWS Method for Displaying Input/Output 31

Chapter 2: Low-Level Assembly Language Functions 33
Function and Variable Names 34
Parameter Passing 34
Returning to the Calling Program 35
Other Assembly Language Interfacing Requirements 36
The 80286 and Others 38
Source Listing 2.1: graphics.asm 38
    Function Description: graphinit 68
    Function Description: egamode 68
    Function Description: resetmouse 69
    Function Description: showmouse 69
    Function Description: hidemouse 69
    Function Description: readmouse 69
    Function Description: cursoron 70
    Function Description: ucursoron 70
    Function Description: cursoroff 71
    Function Description: ucursoroff 71
    Function Description: cursorcolor 71
    Function Description: displaychar 71
    Function Description: displaystring 72

Function Description: clearwindow 73
Function Description: fillwindow 74
Function Description: underline 74
Function Description: savewindow 75
Function Description: restorewindow 76
Function Description: movewindow 77
Function Description: keypressed 78
Function Description: waitkey 78
Function Description: getfontvectors 78
Function Description: setfontvectors 79
Function Description: fig_vid_ptr 79
Function Description: font_tab_ptr 79
Function Description: disp_char 79
Function Description: bit_planes 80
Function Description: read_mask 80
Function Description: write_mask 80

Chapter 3: C++ Input/Output Function 81
Header File Listing 3.1: gwindows.hpp 82
Source Listing 3.2: lowlevel.cpp 88
    Constructor Description: environment::environment 91
    Destructor Description: environment::~environment 91
    Constructor Description: font::font 91
    Destructor Description: font::~font 91
    Function Description: font::open 91
    Function Description: font::close 92
    Function Description: setcurpos 92
    Function Description: getcurpos 92
    Function Description: displaycenter 92
    Function Description: drawborder 93

Chapter 4: Pointing Devices 95
Microsoft Mouse Driver Functions 97
Source Listing 4.1: pointer.cpp 97
    Constructor Description: pointer::pointer 99
    Destructor Description: pointer::~pointer 99
    Function Description: pointer::on 99
    Function Description: pointer::off 99
    Function Description: pointer::read 99
    Function Description: pointer::x 99
    Function Description: pointer::y 100

Function Description: pointer::row 100
Function Description: pointer::col 100
Function Description: pointer::lbutton 100
Function Description: pointer::rbutton 100
Object Description: mouse 100

Chapter 5: Dynamic Window Functions 101
Display Screen Window 102
C++ Dynamic Memory Management Operators and Functions 103
Source Listing 5.1: windows.cpp 107
    Constructor Description: window::window 113
    Destructor Description: window::~window 113
    Function Description: window::draw 113
    Function Description: window::open 114
    Function Description: window::close 114
    Function Description: window::setcurpos 114
    Function Description: window::cls 115
    Function Description: window::clreol 115
    Function Description: window::scroll 115
    Function Description: window::print 116
    Function Description: window::println 117
    Function Description: window::printat 117
    Function Description: window::printlnat 118
    Function Description: window::horizontal_bar 118
    Function Description: window::vertical_bar 118

Chapter 6: Menu Functions 119
Source Listing 6.1: menus.cpp 120
    Function Description: hotstring 120
Pop-Up Menus 121
Source Listing 6.2: popup.cpp 121
    Function Description: popup::get 124
Dialog Box Menus 126
Source Listing 6.3: dialog.cpp 127
    Function Description: dialog::get 131
Pull-Down Menus 133
Source Listing 6.4: pulldown.cpp 135
    Function Description: pulldown::display 141
    Function Description: pulldown::get 141

Chapter 7: GWINDOWS Data Entry Functions 147
  Source Listing 7.1: idate.cpp 148
    Function Description: date_string 150
    Function Description: date_func 150
    Function Description: display_date 152
    Function Description: input_date 152
  Source Listing 7.2: idollar.cpp 152
    Function Description: dollar_func 155
    Function Description: display_dollar 157
    Function Description: input_dollar 157
  Source Listing 7.3: inumber.cpp 157
    Function Description: number_func 159
    Function Description: display_number 160
    Function Description: input_number 160
  Source Listing 7.4: iphone.cpp 160
    Function Description: phone_string 163
    Function Description: phone_func 163
    Function Description: display_phone 165
    Function Description: input_phone 165
  Source Listing 7.5: issn.cpp 165
    Function Description: ssn_string 168
    Function Description: ssn_func 168
    Function Description: display_ssn 170
    Function Description: input_ssn 170
  Source Listing 7.6: istring.cpp 170
    Function Description: string_func 171
    Function Description: display_string 172
    Function Description: input_string 172

Chapter 8: FONTEDIT 173
  Source Listing 8.1: fontedit.cpp 174
    Function Description: main 186
    Function Description: editfont::csfont 187
    Function Description: editfont::erase 187
    Function Description: editfont::erasecharacter 188
    Function Description: editfont::fillcharacter 188
    Function Description: editfont:copycharacter 188
    Function Description: editfont::display 188
    Function Description: editfont::setchar 188
    Function Description: editfont::toggle 189
    Function Description: editfont::drawgridbox 189

Function Description: new_func 189
Function Description: lf_func 190
Function Description: sf_func 190
Function Description: ga_func 190
Function Description: cs_func 191
Function Description: ep_func 191
Function Description: ec_func 191
Function Description: fc_func 191
Function Description: cc_func 191
Function Description: copysysfont 191
Function Description: displayerror 192
Source Listing 8.2: sanscga.cpp 192
Source Listing 8.3: sansega.cpp 198

Section II: The Reference Guide

Chapter 9: GWINDOWS Reference Guide 207
Standard Data Types 209
    boolean 209
    date 209
    MENU 209
    MENU_HEAD 210
    phone 210
    ssn 211
Objects 211
    dialog 211
    environment 211
    font 212
    menucolors 212
    pointer 213
    popup 213
    pulldown 214
    window 214
Functions 215
    background 216
    clearcolumn 216
    clearrow 217
    clearwindow 218
    cursorcolor 219
    cursoroff, cursoron 219
    date_string 220

dialog::get	221
display_date	222
display_dollar	223
display_number	224
display_phone	225
display_ssn	226
display_string	227
displaycenter	228
displaychar	228
displaystring	229
drawborder	230
egacolor	230
egamode	231
fillcolumn	232
fillrow	233
fillwindow	234
font::close	234
font::getptr	235
font::open	236
getcurpos	237
getfontvectors	237
hidemouse	238
hotstring	239
input_date	240
input_dollar	241
input_number	241
input_phone	242
input_ssn	243
input_string	244
keypressed	245
max	246
menucolors::color	247
menucolors::highlight	247
menucolors::setcolor	248
menucolors::sethighlight	249
min	250
movewindow	251
phone_string	251
pointer::col	252
pointer::lbutton	253
pointer::off	254
pointer::on	255

pointer::rbutton 255
pointer::read 256
pointer::row 258
pointer::x 258
pointer::y 259
popup::get 260
pulldown::display 262
pulldown::get 263
readmouse 268
resetmouse 270
restorewindow 270
savewindow 271
setcurpos 272
setfontvectors 273
showmouse 274
ssn_string 274
ucursoroff, ucursoron 275
underline 276
waitkey 277
window::close 277
window::clreol 278
window::cls 279
window::curcol 279
window::currow 280
window::draw 281
window::horizontal_bar 281
window::open 282
window::p_col 283
window::p_row 284
window::print 284
window::printat 285
window::println 286
window::printlnat 287
window::scroll 287
window::setcurpos 289
window::vertical_bar 289

Chapter 10: IBM PC and EGA ROM BIOS Video Services **291**
Set Video Mode (Function 00H) 293
Set Cursor Type (Function 01H) 295
Set Cursor Position (Function 02H) 297

Read Cursor Values (Function 03H) 299
Read Light Pen Values (Function 04H) 301
Select Display Page (Function 05H) 303
Scroll Window Up (Function 06H) 305
Scroll Window Down (Function 07H) 307
Read Character/Attribute Pair (Function 08H) 309
Write Character/Attribute Pair (Function 09H) 311
Write Characters (Function 0AH) 313
Set Color Palette (Function 0BH) 315
Write Graphics Pixel (Function 0CH) 317
Read Graphics Pixel (Function 0DH) 319
Write Character in Teletype Mode (Function 0EH) 321
Get Video Mode (Function 0FH) 323
Set Palette Register (Function 10H, Subfunction 00H) 325
Set Border Color (Function 10H, Subfunction 01H) 327
Set All Palette Registers and the Border Color (Function 10H,
  Subfunction 02H) 329
Toggle Blink/Intensity Flag (Function 10H, Subfunction 03H) 331
Load User Font (Function 11H, Subfunction 00H) 333
Load ROM BIOS 8-by-14 Font (Function 11H, Subfunction 01H) 335
Load ROM BIOS 8-by-8 Font (Function 11H, Subfunction 02H) 337
Select Character Generator RAM Block (Function 11H,
  Subfunction 03H) 339
Load User Font (Function 11H, Subfunction 10H) 341
Load ROM BIOS 8-by-14 Font (Function 11H, Subfunction 11H) 344
Load ROM BIOS 8-by-8 Font (Function 11H, Subfunction 12H) 346
Set the Upper Font Table Pointer (Function 11H, Subfunction 20H) . 348
Set Font Table Pointer (Function 11H, Subfunction 21H) 350
Set Font Table Pointer to ROM BIOS 8-by-14 Font (Function 11H,
  Subfunction 22H) 352
Set Font Table Pointer to ROM BIOS 8-by-8 Font (Function 11H,
  Subfunction 23H) 354
Get Font Information (Function 11H, Subfunction 30H) 356
Get Configuration Information (Function 12H, Subfunction 10H) ... 358
Select Alternate Screen Print Routine (Function 12H,
  Subfunction 20H) 360
Write String in Teletype Mode (Function 13H) 362

Chapter 11: The Microsoft Mouse Driver Routines **365**
Reset the Mouse Driver (Function 00H) 367
Turn On the Mouse Pointer (Function 01H) 369

Turn Off the Mouse Pointer (Function 02H) 371
Get Button Status and Pointer Position (Function 03H) 373
Set Pointer Position (Function 04H) 375
Get Button Press Status (Function 05H) 377
Get Button Release Status (Function 06H) 379
Set Horizontal Limits (Function 07H) 381
Set Vertical Limits (Function 08H) 383
Set Graphic Shape (Function 09H) 385
Set Text Pointer Type (Function 0AH) 387
Get Motion Count (Function 0BH) 389
Set User-Defined Event Handler (Function 0CH) 391
Turn On Light Pen Emulation (Function 0DH) 394
Turn Off Light Pen Emulation (Function 0EH) 396
Set Mickey:Pixels Ratios (Function 0FH) 398
Set Exclusion Area (Function 10H) 400
Set Double Speed Threshold (Function 13H) 402
Swap User-Defined Event Handlers (Function 14H) 404
Get Mouse Status Buffer Size (Function 15H) 406
Save Mouse Driver Status (Function 16H) 408
Restore Mouse Driver Status (Function 17H) 410
Set Alternate Event Handler (Function 18H) 412
Get Alternate Event Handler's Address (Function 19H) 415
Set Sensitivity (Function 1AH) 417
Get Sensitivity (Function 1BH) 419
Set Interrupt Rate (Function 1CH) 421
Set Pointer Display Page (Function 1DH) 423
Get Pointer Display Page (Function 1EH) 425
Disable Mouse Driver (Function 1FH) 427
Enable Mouse Driver (Function 20H) 429
Reset Mouse Driver (Function 21H) 431
Set Language (Function 22H) 433
Get Language Code (Function 23H) 435
Get Mouse Information (Function 24H) 437

Chapter 12: Compiling the GWINDOWS Toolbox 439
The Zortech C++ Compiler 440
Other C++ Compilers 440
    graphics.asm 441
    lowlevel.cpp 441
    fontedit.cpp 441
    Other Programs 441

Graphical User Interfaces in C++ and Object-Oriented Programming gives C++ programmers the most advanced techniques for writing graphical application programs. This specifically means using graphics programming routines for

- opening and closing dynamic display screen windows
- pull-down menus
- pop-up menus
- dialog boxes
- on-line help

Introduction

A special feature is the unique interface toolbox called **gwindows.lib** (GWINDOWS). A graphical user interface with state-of-the-art techniques appears when GWINDOWS functions are applied. The use of low-level graphics programming is necessary when writing a C++ graphical user interface toolbox. This book provides guidance for quick and easy implementation of graphical interface techniques for IBM PCs and compatibles.

Programmers have the opportunity to create customized, self-written graphical interface toolboxes by performing minor changes to the toolbox's low-level functions. Instead of using the generic one-size-fits-all commercial toolbox packages, a graphical user interface toolbox can be tailored to meet an application program's individual needs.

Most application programs intermix text display modes with graphic display modes to construct a user interface. For example, many word processing programs edit text while using a text display mode and offer a page preview feature for graphically depicting a printed page. Although text-based user interfaces are still the norm, many application programs are implemented using graphical user interfaces. These graphically oriented programs include: desktop publishing programs (PageMaker and Ventura Publisher), CAD programs (AutoCAD), word processing programs (AMI), and spreadsheet programs (Microsoft Excel).

Most compilers are equipped with library functions for drawing a variety of graphic figures. Unfortunately, most compiler libraries can't perform simple operations, such as displaying multiple text strings with more than one background color. To compensate for a compiler library's deficiencies, application programmers rely heavily on graphical user interface toolboxes that provide ready-made functions for implementing common graphical user interface features. Generic functions supplied in most commercial interface toolboxes aren't always the best choice for all programs.

USER REQUIREMENTS

Using the programs in this book requires you to have an IBM PC or compatible, the Zortech C++ compiler or equivalent, and a Microsoft Macro Assembler (MASM) or equivalent. Although GWINDOWS provides extensive support for a Microsoft-compatible mouse, using a mouse is optional. An intermediate level of programming knowledge is helpful for using this book. However, even a novice C++ programmer can easily incorporate GWINDOWS routines into an application program.

CHAPTER OVERVIEWS

This book is divided into two sections. Section I, *The GWINDOWS Toolbox*, consists of Chapters 1 through 8. These chapters explain the various C++ and video functions and offer routines for implementing them. Section II, *The Reference Guide,* is composed of Chapters 9 through 12.

Chapter 1 explains the MS-DOS video functions, the IBM PC ROM BIOS video functions, and the EGA ROM BIOS video functions, and it tells you how to use direct memory access techniques to perform display input/output.

Chapter 2 offers routines for low-level assembly language, including:
- displaying single characters
- displaying text strings
- filling portions of the display screen with a specific character
- clearing portions of the display screen
- moving a portion of the display screen to a different location
- saving a portion of the display screen in a memory buffer
- redisplaying a previously buffered screen display
- retrieving keyboard input
- displaying the cursor
- underlining characters
- performing a wide variety of low-level mouse functions

Chapter 3 presents low-level C++ functions, including:
- initializing the GWINDOWS operating environment
- drawing a single-lined or a double-lined border around a portion of the display screen
- positioning the cursor
- implementing a class of font objects

Chapter 4 presents routines for implementing a class of pointer objects.

Chapter 5 presents routines for implementing a class of dynamic window objects.

Chapter 6 presents routines for constructing three distinct classes of menu objects.

Chapter 7 presents routines for displaying and retrieving dates, dollar values, numeric values, telephone numbers, Social Security numbers, and strings.

Introduction

Chapter 8 presents FONTEDIT, a computer-assisted software engineering (CASE) tool that produces C++ source code files for user-defined font tables. Additionally, FONTEDIT illustrates using the GWINDOWS toolbox to build an actual application program.

Chapter 9 contains a complete reference guide for the GWINDOWS toolbox. Each GWINDOWS function is provided with a description explaining the function's purpose, a syntax summary, and a coding example.

Chapter 10 contains a reference guide for the IBM PC and EGA ROM BIOS video functions.

Chapter 11 contains a reference guide for the Microsoft mouse driver functions.

Chapter 12 explains compiling the GWINDOWS toolbox using the Zortech C++ compiler. It also tells you where to modify the GWINDOWS programs to build the GWINDOWS toolbox when using a non-Zortech C++ compiler.

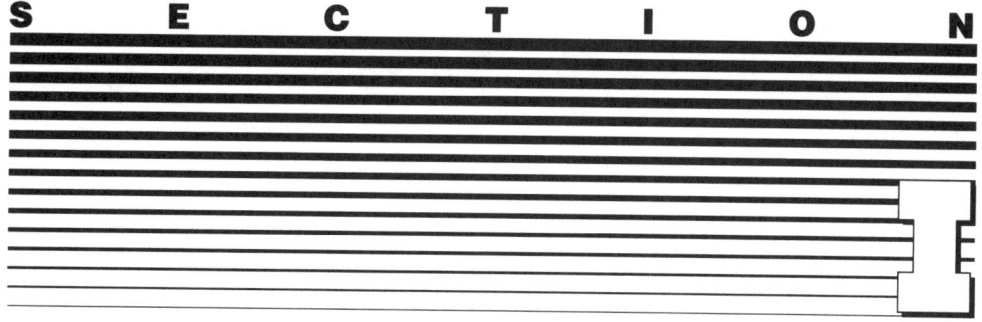

THE GWINDOWS TOOLBOX

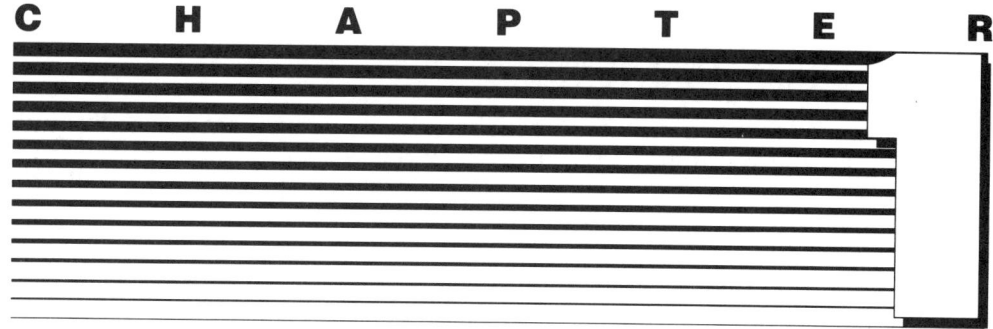

IBM PC GRAPHIC DISPLAYS

This chapter discusses display input/output performed by the GWINDOWS toolbox. All three IBM PC display methods, which allow reading from and writing to the display screen, are examined. Included are the MS-DOS video functions, the ROM BIOS video functions and direct memory access techniques. Program portability, speed, and ease of programming are evaluated for each display method.

1 IBM PC Graphic Displays

MS-DOS VIDEO FUNCTIONS

The MS-DOS video functions offer the highest degree of program portability and compatibility for any computer that runs the MS-DOS operating system. Because the MS-DOS video functions are called as MS-DOS function calls (calls to INT21H), they are considered easy to use.

The MS-DOS video functions lack functions for display reading, drawing and erasing graphic pixels, and cursor control; therefore, they are unsuitable for implementing a graphical user interface such as the GWINDOWS operating environment (a graphic pixel is an individual dot that is used to construct a graphic display). Many high-level languages use the MS-DOS video functions to implement generic display output commands (i.e., C++ and C printf functions, Pascal Writeln procedure, and BASIC PRINT statement).

The highly compatible MS DOS video functions are excellent for writing portable programs, but their lack of speed and versatility make them unsuitable for a graphical windowing environment, such as GWINDOWS. With the exception of their use by a C++ compiler's run-time library, the MS-DOS video functions are not used by a GWINDOWS application program.

ROM BIOS VIDEO FUNCTIONS

The ROM BIOS video functions offer a variety of routines to meet the demands of application programs. They are limited in program portability to IBM PCs and other compatibles, but offer speed and versatility required by today's application programs. Because of a strong commitment by IBM and other manufacturers to maintain ROM BIOS compatibility, all of today's PC compatibles have ROM BIOSes that are upwardly compatible with the original IBM PC's ROM BIOS. Therefore, use of the ROM BIOS video functions does not impose problems in transporting a program from an IBM PC to another compatible computer.

IBM PC Graphic Displays 1

Function Name	Function Code
Set Video Mode	00H
Set Cursor Type	01H
Set Cursor Position	02H
Read Cursor Values	03H
Read Light Pen Position	04H
Select Display Page	05H
Scroll Window Up	06H
Scroll Window Down	07H
Read Character/Attribute Pair	08H
Write Character/Attribute Pairs	09H
Write Characters	0AH
Set Color Palette	0BH
Write Graphics Pixel	0CH
Read Graphics Pixel	0DH
Write Character in Teletype Mode	0EH
Get Video Mode	0FH

Figure 1.1 IBM PC, ROM BIOS video functions.

1 IBM PC Graphic Displays

Function Name	Function Code
Set Palette Register	1000H
Set Border Color	1001H
Set All Palette Registers and the Border Color	1002H
Toggle Blink/Intensity Flag	1003H
Load User Font	1100H
Load ROM BIOS 8-by-14 Font	1101H
Load ROM BIOS 8-by-8 Font	1102H
Select Character Generator RAM Block	1103H
Load User Font	1110H
Load ROM BIOS 8-by-14 Font	1111H
Load ROM BIOS 8-by-8 Font	1112H
Set Upper Font Table Pointer	1120H
Set Font Table Pointer	1121H
Set Font Table Pointer to ROM BIOS 8-by-14 Font	1122H
Set Font Table Pointer to ROM BIOS 8-by-8 Font	1123H
Get Font Information	1130H
Get Configuration Information	1210H
Select Alternate Screen Print Routine	1220H
Write String in Teletype Mode	13H

Figure 1.2   EGA, ROM BIOS video functions

Using a ROM BIOS video function involves simply loading a few parameters into the CPU registers and making a call to INT 10H. Figure 1.1 outlines the ROM BIOS functions on all IBM PCs and compatibles. Figure 1.2 outlines the ROM BIOS functions available on IBM PCs and compatibles that have an EGA display adapter available. Chapter 10 provides a complete description of the IBM PC and EGA ROM BIOS video functions. The following code fragment illustrates using the ROM BIOS **Set Cursor Position** function to move the cursor to the upper left corner of the display screen:

IBM PC Graphic Displays

```
.
.
.
mov    bh,0      ;BH = Video page
mov    dh,0      ;DH = Row position
mov    dl,0      ;DL = Column position
mov    ah,2      ;Set the new
int    10h       ; cursor position
.
.
.
```

As shown in the above program fragment, a ROM BIOS function's code is always passed in register AH. Additionally, many of the EGA ROM BIOS functions require that a subfunction code be passed in register AL. If a video page number is required by a ROM BIOS function, it is frequently passed in register BH. Instead of the two separate statements used in the above example, a **mov dx,0** statement could have been used to pass the new cursor location. An **xor dx,dx** statement would be a more efficient method to pass the Row 0, Column 0 cursor location. Any number **xor**ed with itself always produces a zero result. Thus, **xor**ing the DX register with itself results in the correct cursor position being passed to the ROM BIOS video function.

The ROM video functions do not provide adequate speed for constructing an effective graphical user interface, and they are not the best techniques for implementing the GWINDOWS toolbox. Direct memory access techniques provide the required speed and response times.

DIRECT MEMORY ACCESS TECHNIQUES

Most GWINDOWS video functions use direct memory access techniques and are written in assembly language to provide the necessary lightning-fast response times. Directly accessing a display adapter's memory for a Color Graphics Adapter (CGA) and an Enhanced Graphics Adapter (EGA) is discussed.

Both of these display adapters are memory-mapped devices. When a graphics display adapter is a memory-mapped device, programs read directly from and write to the display adapter's memory by simply using a specific area of the computer's memory. Figure 1.3 presents a simple memory map for the IBM PC and the two graphics display adapters mentioned previously. As this illustration indicates, the CGA uses 16K of memory starting at 0B8000H (B800:0000H) and the EGA uses 256K of memory starting at 0A0000H (A000:0000H).

1   IBM PC Graphic Displays

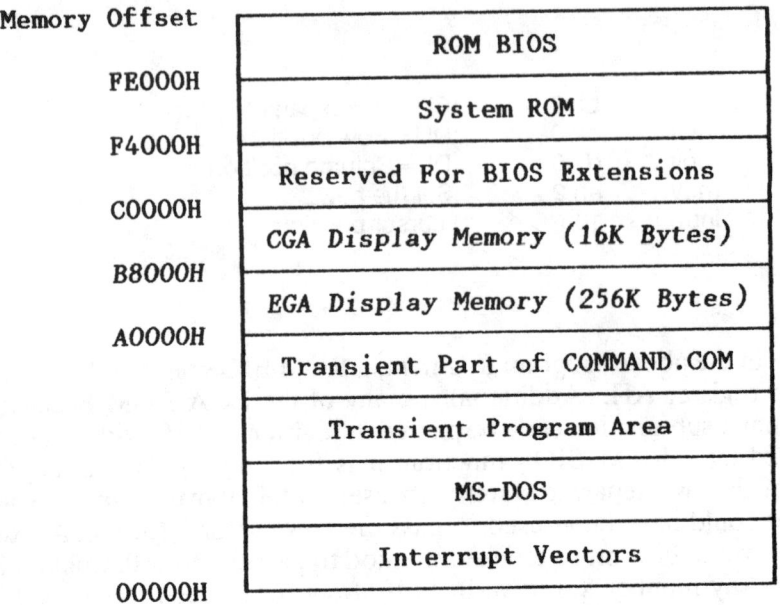

Figure 1.3   IBM PC Memory Map.

Color Graphics Adapter's Video Modes

The CGA offers four text modes, including:
- 40-column by 25-row, black-and-white
- 40-column by 25-row, color
- 80-column by 25-row, black-and-white
- 80-column by 25-row, color.

Three graphics modes are available through the CGA, including:
- 320-horizontal-pixel by 200-vertical-pixel, four-color graphics.
- 320-horizontal-pixel by 200-vertical-pixel, four-color graphics (without color burst).
- 640-horizontal-pixel by 200-vertical-pixel, two-color graphics.

Since a high resolution is most desirable for building a graphical user interface, the CGA's 640-by-200, two-color graphics mode is the only CGA mode supported by the GWINDOWS operating environment.

IBM PC Graphic Displays 1

Enhanced Graphics Adapter's Video Modes

The five text modes and seven graphics modes of the EGA are discussed below. The EGA offers the following text modes:

- 40-column by 25-row, black-and-white
- 40-column by 25-row, color
- 80-column by 25-row, black-and-white
- 80-column by 25-row, color
- 80-column by 25-row, monochrome

Additionally, the EGA provides the following graphics modes:

- 320-horizontal-pixel by 200-vertical pixel, four-color graphics
- 320-horizontal-pixel by 200-vertical pixel, four-color graphics (without color burst)
- 640-horizontal-pixel by 200-vertical-pixel, two-color graphics
- 640-horizontal-pixel by 350-vertical-pixel, monochrome graphics
- 320-horizontal-pixel by 200-vertical-pixel, sixteen-color graphics
- 640-horizontal-pixel by 200-vertical-pixel, sixteen-color graphics
- 640-horizontal-pixel by 350-vertical-pixel, sixteen-color graphics.

As with the CGA, the highest resolution video mode is the most desirable for building a graphical user interface. Therefore, the EGA's 640-by-350 sixteen-color graphics mode is the only EGA mode supported by the GWINDOWS operating environment.

READING AND WRITING GRAPHIC DISPLAYS

While in a text mode, a text character can be displayed by simply placing the character's ASCII code in an appropriate location of the display adapter's memory. Unfortunately, displaying a text character in a graphics mode is not as simple. Text characters on a graphics display must be written to the display screen pixel-by-pixel. Writing an individual graphic pixel to the display will be discussed. Retrieving a graphic pixel's value from video memory and preserving large sections of the display screen in other areas of the computer's memory will be explained.

1 IBM PC Graphic Displays

Graphic Coordinates

Figure 1.4 illustrates the graphic coordinate system used by the CGA's 640-by-200 graphics mode. Figure 1.5 shows the graphic coordinate system used by the EGA's 640-by-350 graphics mode. As shown in these illustrations, a graphic display screen has horizontal coordinates called x-coordinates and has vertical coordinates called y-coordinates. By using appropriate (x,y) coordinates, any of the display screen's individual graphic pixels can be located. For example, the graphic pixel in the upper left corner of the display screen is located at coordinate (0,0) for both the CGA and EGA graphics modes. The graphic pixel in the center of the display screen is located at (320,100) for the CGA graphics mode and (320,175) for the EGA graphics mode. The graphic pixel in the lower right corner of the display screen is located at coordinate (639,199) for the CGA graphics mode and (639,349) for the EGA graphics mode.

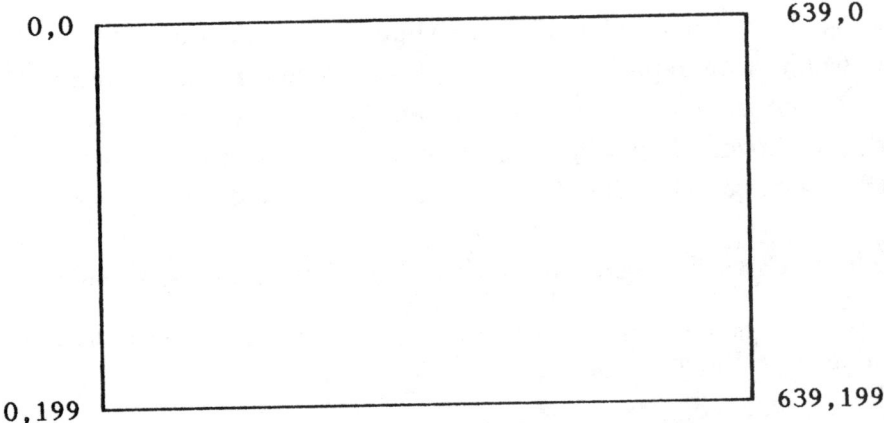

Figure 1.4 CGA 640-by-200 graphic coordinates.

IBM PC Graphic Displays 1

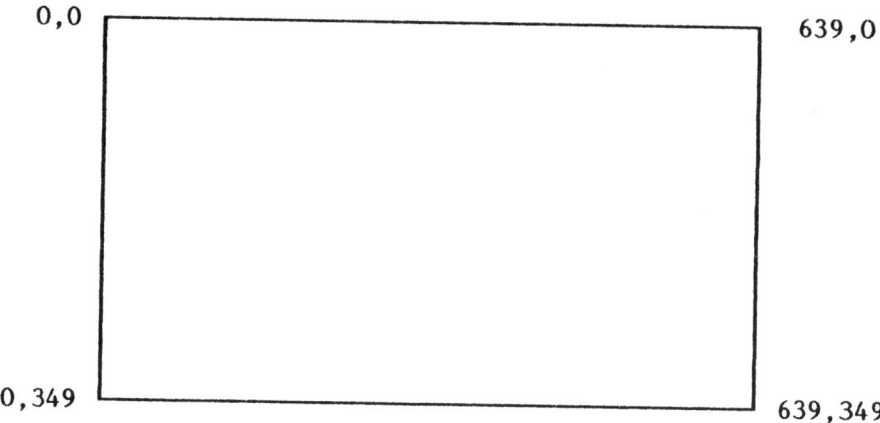

Figure 1.5   EGA 640-by-350 graphic coordinates.

CGA Graphic Pixels

The CGA's video memory and location of graphic pixels are analyzed. Algorithms and subroutines provide instructions about the following areas:

- Determining a graphic pixel's video memory offset
- Constructing a bit mask
- Setting a CGA graphic pixel
- Resetting a CGA graphic pixel
- Testing the state of a CGA graphic pixel

Each bit of video memory represents a corresponding graphic pixel. Accordingly, a graphic pixel will be lit if its matching video memory bit is equal to 1. Otherwise, a graphic pixel will be turned off to represent a video memory bit equal to 0. Because each byte of video memory has eight bits, a byte of video memory is capable of representing eight graphic pixels. Figure 1.6 shows that the first byte of video memory is used to represent graphic pixels (0,0) to (0,7). As this illustration depicts, the most significant bit of the video memory byte represents the left-most graphic pixel. The least significant bit of the video memory byte represents the right-most graphic pixel.

1 IBM PC Graphic Displays

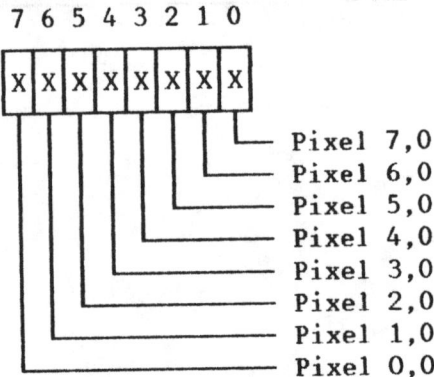

Figure 1.6 First byte of CGA video memory.

Since a horizontal line is composed of 640 graphic pixels and a byte of video memory represents eight graphic pixels, then each horizontal line of the display screen requires 80 bytes of video memory (640 horizontal pixels / 8 pixels per byte = 80 bytes of video memory). Therefore, it would be logical to assume that the video memory location for graphic pixel (0,1) occurs 80 bytes away from graphic pixel (0,0)'s video memory location. Unfortunately, this assumption is incorrect. The CGA's video controller scans all even lines of the display screen before scanning the display screen's odd lines. Consequently, the video memory location for graphic pixel (0,2) is found 80 bytes away from the video memory location for graphic pixel (0,0). The video memory location for graphic pixel (0,1) exists 2000H bytes away from the video memory location for graphic pixel (0,0).

Thus, a graphic pixel's video memory offset can be determined by using the following algorithm:

Construct a CGA Video Memory Offset Algorithm

1. Figure the row offset by dividing the y-coordinate by 2 and multiplying the result by 80. (Row offset = y / 2 * 80).

2. If the y-coordinate is odd, add in the memory interlace offset. (Row offset = Row offset + 2000H).

3. Figure the column (byte) offset and add the result to the row offset. (Video memory offset = Row offset + x / 8).

IBM PC Graphic Displays

The following assembly language subroutine shows a practical use for the above algorithm:

```
;
; Figure CGA Video Memory Offsets Routine
;
; Entry:
; Register    Contents
; cx          x-coordinate
; dx          y-coordinate
;
; Exit:
; Register    Contents
; di          video memory offset
;
cga_offsets     proc
                push    ax              ;Save
                push    cx              ; the
                push    dx              ; registers
                shr     dx,1            ;DX = y / 2, Carry flag = Even/Odd
                pushf                   ;Save the flags
                mov     ax,80           ;AX = Number of bytes per row
                mul     dx              ;AX = Row offset
                popf                    ;Restore the flags
                jnc     cga_offsets1    ;Jump if y wasn't odd
                add     ax,2000h        ;Adjust the offset for the interleave
cga_offsets1:   shr     cx,1            ;Figure
                shr     x,1             ; the
                shr     cx,1            ; column offset
                add     ax,cx           ;A = Video memory offset
                mov     di,ax           ;Put it into DI
                pop     dx              ;Restore
                pop     cx              ; the
                pop     ax              ; registers
                ret                     ;Return
cga_offsets     endp
```

To read or to write the graphic pixel's corresponding video memory bit, a bit mask must be constructed. The following algorithm describes constructing a bit mask:

1   IBM PC Graphic Displays

Construct a Graphic Bit Mask Algorithm

1. Set the starting bit mask to 80H. (Bit mask = 80H)

2. Determine the loop counter by figuring the remainder of the x-coordinate divided by 8. (Loop counter = x MOD 8)

3. If the loop counter is equal to 0, the bit mask is completed and go to 6.

4. Shift the bit mask right one position. (Bit mask = SHR(Bit mask)).

5. Decrement the loop counter and go to 3.

6. The algorithm is complete.

The following assembly language subroutine shows a practical use for the above algorithm.

```
;
; Figure Bit Masks Routine
;
; Entry:
; Register      Contents
; cx            x-coordinate
;
; Exit:
; Register      Contents
; al            bit mask
;
bit_masks       proc
                push    cx                      ;Save CX
                mov     al,80h                  ;AL=Starting bit mask
                and     cx,7                    ;CX=x MOD 8
                jcxz    bitmasks2               ;Jump if done
bit_masks1:     shr     al,1                    ;Shift the bit mask
                loop    bit_masks1              ;Loop till the bit mask is complete
bit_masks2:     pop     cx                      ;Restore CX
                ret                             ;Return
bit_masks       endp
```

Using the above two subroutines, a variety of graphic operations can be performed easily. A graphic pixel can be set (turned on) by ORing the value of its bit mask with the value already stored in its video memory location. The following assembly language subroutine can be used to set a CGA graphic pixel:

IBM PC Graphic Displays 1

```
;
; SET CGA Graphic Pixel Routine
;
; Entry:
; Register     Contents
; cx           x-coordinate
; dx           y-coordinate
;
set_cga       proc
              push     ax              ;Save
              push     cx              ;  the
              push     di              ;  registers
              push     es              ;
              call     cga_offsets     ;DI = Video memory offset
              call     bit_masks       ;AL = Bit mask
              mov      cx,0b800h       ;CX = Video memory segment
              mov      es,cx           ;Put it in ES
              or       es:[di],al      ;Set the graphic pixel
              pop      es              ;Restore
              pop      di              ;  the
              pop      cx              ;  registers
              pop      ax              ;
              ret                      ;Return
set_cga       endp
```

A graphic pixel can be reset (turned off) by ANDing the inverse of its bit mask with the value already stored in its video memory location. The following assembly language subroutine can be used to reset a CGA graphic pixel:

```
;
; RESET CGA Graphic Pixel Routine
;
; Entry:
; Register     Contents
; cx           x-coordinate
; dx           y-coordinate
;
reset_cga     proc
              push     ax              ;Save
              push     cx              ;  the
              push     di              ;  registers
              push     es              ;
              call     cga_offsets     ;DI = Video memory offset
              call     bit_masks       ;AL = Bit mask
              not      al              ;Invert the bit mask
              mov      cx,0b800h       ;CX = Video memory segment
```

continued...

1 IBM PC Graphic Displays

```
                mov     es,cx                   ;Put it in ES
                and     es:[di],al              ;Reset the graphic pixel
                pop     es                      ;Restore
                pop     di                      ; the
                pop     cx                      ;  registers
                pop     ax                      ;
                ret                             ;Return
reset_cga       endp
```

A graphic pixel's on/off status can be determined by simply ANDing its bit mask with the value stored in its video memory location. If a non-zero result occurs, the graphic pixel is on. Otherwise, a zero result will indicate a turned off graphic pixel. The following assembly language subroutine can be used to test the state of a CGA graphic pixel:

```
;
; TEST CGA Graphic Pixel Routine
;
; Entry:
; Register       Contents
; cx             x-coordinate
; dx             y-coordinate
;
; Exit:
; Register       Contents
; ax             0000H - if graphic pixel isn't set
; ax             FFFFH - if graphic pixel is set
;
; Flag
; Zero           Z - if graphic pixel isn't set
;                NZ - if graphic pixel is set
;
test_cga        proc
                push    cx                      ;Save
                push    di                      ; the
                push    es                      ;  registers
                call    cga_offsets             ;DI = Video memory offset
                call    bit_masks               ;AL = Bit mask
                mov     cx,0b800h               ;CX = Video memory segment
                mov     es,cx                   ;Put it in ES
                and     al,es:[di]              ;Test the graphic pixel
                mov     ax,0                    ;AX = Pixel not set return value
                jz      test_cga1               ;Jump if the pixel wasn't set
                dec     ax                      ;AX = Pixel was set return value
```

continued...

```
test_cga1:      pop     es              ;Restore
                pop     di              ; the
                pop     cx              ;  registers
                ret                     ;Return
test_cga        endp
```

EGA Graphic Pixels

The EGA's video memory requires at least four bits to represent a single graphic pixel. The color requirements of the EGA's graphic mode is discussed. The EGA color planes' video memory is analyzed, and the video memory location for graphic pixels is identified.

Algorithms and subroutines are provided for guidance in the following areas:

1. Determining an EGA pixel's video memory offset.

2. Setting an EGA graphic pixel to a particular color.

3. Setting write-only bit masks.

4. Setting map masks.

5. Setting a graphic pixel's color value.

6. Retrieving a graphic pixel's color value.

7. Setting the read map select register.

The EGA's 640-by-350 graphics mode is able to represent graphic pixels in 16 distinct colors. Four bits are required to represent 16 distinct values (0 to 15); therefore, an EGA graphic pixel must use at least four bits of video memory to represent a corresponding color value. A byte of EGA video memory can represent eight individual graphic pixels because the EGA uses four color planes to hold a graphic pixel's video memory representation. Figure 1.7 illustrates the construction of the EGA's four color planes. As this figure shows, each of the EGA's color planes represents a unique color value: blue, green, red, or intensified. Figure 1.8 demonstrates blending the colors from these four color planes to form the EGA's 16 available colors. Adjusting a graphic pixel to a certain color, requires the corresponding video memory bit be set to an appropriate value in each of the four color planes. For example, a light blue graphic pixel has a corresponding video memory bit set in the blue color plane, reset in the green color plane, reset in the red color plane, and set in the intensified color plane.

1 IBM PC Graphic Displays

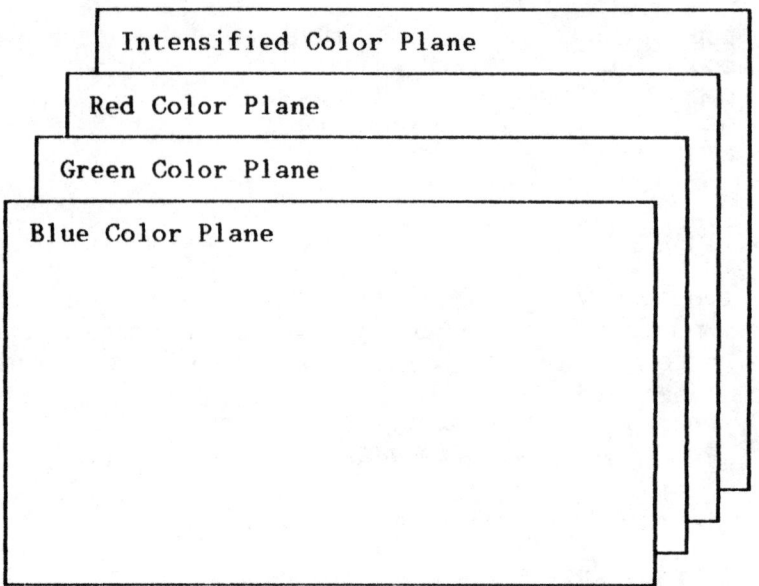

Figure 1.7   EGA Color Planes.

I	R	G	B	Hex	Pixel Color
0	0	0	0	00	Black
0	0	0	1	01	Blue
0	0	1	0	02	Green
0	0	1	1	03	Cyan
0	1	0	0	04	Red
0	1	0	1	05	Magenta
0	1	1	0	06	Brown
0	1	1	1	07	White
1	0	0	0	08	Dark Gray
1	0	0	1	09	Light Blue
1	0	1	0	0A	Light Green
1	0	1	1	0B	Light Cyan
1	1	0	0	0C	Light Red
1	1	0	1	0D	Light Magenta
1	1	1	0	0E	Yellow
1	1	1	1	0F	Intense White

Figure 1.8   EGA Color Values.

IBM PC Graphic Displays 1

Because each byte of an EGA color plane's video memory represents eight individual graphic pixels, each horizontal line requires 80 bytes of video memory (640 horizontal pixels / 8 pixels per byte = 80 bytes of video memory). Unlike the scanning method used by the CGA where the video controller scans all of the display screen's even lines and then all of the odd lines, the EGA's video controller scans the display screen's horizontal lines in order. Accordingly, the video memory location for graphic pixel (0,1) is 80 bytes away from the video memory location for graphic pixel (0,0). Thus, an EGA graphic pixel's video memory offset can be determined by using the following algorithm:

Construct an EGA Video Memory Offset Algorithm

1. Figure the row offset by multiplying the y-coordinate by 80. (Row offset = y * 80)

2. Figure the column (byte) offset and add the result to the row offset. (Video memory offset = Row offset + x / 8)

The following assembly language subroutine shows a practical use for the algorithm:

```
;
; Figure EGA Video Memory Offsets Routine
;
; Entry:
; Register     Contents
; cx           x-coordinate
; dx           y-coordinate
;
; Exit:
; Register     Contents
; di           video memory offset
;
ega_offsets  proc
             push    ax              ;Save
             push    cx              ; the
             push    dx              ;  registers
             mov     ax,80           ;AX = Number of bytes per row
             mul     dx              ;AX = Row offset
             shr     cx,1            ;Figure
             sr      cx,1            ; the
             shr     cx,1            ;  column offset
             add     ax,cx           ;AX = Video memory offset
```

continued...

1 IBM PC Graphic Displays

```
            mov    di,ax          ;Put it into DI
            pop    dx             ;Restore
            pop    cx             ; the
            pop    ax             ;  registers
            ret                   ;Return
ega_offsets endp
```

Bit masks for EGA graphic pixels can be determined using the same algorithm that was used to determine CGA bit masks. Unfortunately, setting a graphic pixel to a certain color on the EGA isn't as straightforward as setting a graphic pixel on the CGA. The following is an algorithm for setting an EGA graphic pixel to a particular color:

Set an EGA Graphic Pixel's Color Algorithm

1. Figure the video memory offset.

2. Figure the bit mask.

3. Set the graphic controller's write-only bit mask.

4. Turn on all color planes.

5. Turn off all bits.

6. Turn on the graphic pixel's color planes.

7. Turn on all of the color planes' bits.

8. Turn on all color planes.

9. Set the write-only mask for all bits on.

The above algorithm employs two techniques that are very important to the EGA graphics programmer. These techniques involve setting the EGA graphic controller's, write-only, bit mask and enabling the EGA's color planes. Figure 1.9 illustrates using the EGA graphic controller's write-only, bit mask. As this figure shows, only the write-only, bit mask's bits that are equal to 1 will allow their corresponding bits in video memory to be changed. A write-only, bit mask bit with a value of 0, prevents any corresponding video memory bits from being modified by a write operation. Setting the write-only, bit mask is accomplished by sending a value of 08H to port 03CEH and then sending the appropriate bit mask value to port 03CFH. The following short program can be used to set write-only, bit masks:

IBM PC Graphic Displays 1

```
;
; Set the EGA Write-Only Mask Routine
;
; Entry:
; Register    Contents
; ah         write-only mask
;
write_mask  proc
            push    ax              ;Save the
            push    dx              ; registers
            mov     al,8            ;Select
            mov     dx,03ceh        ; the write-only
            out     dx,al           ;  mask register
            inc     dx              ;Set
            mov     al,ah           ; the
            out     dx,al           ;  write-only mask
            pop     dx              ;Restore
            pop     ax              ; the registers
            ret                     ;Return
write_mask  endp
```

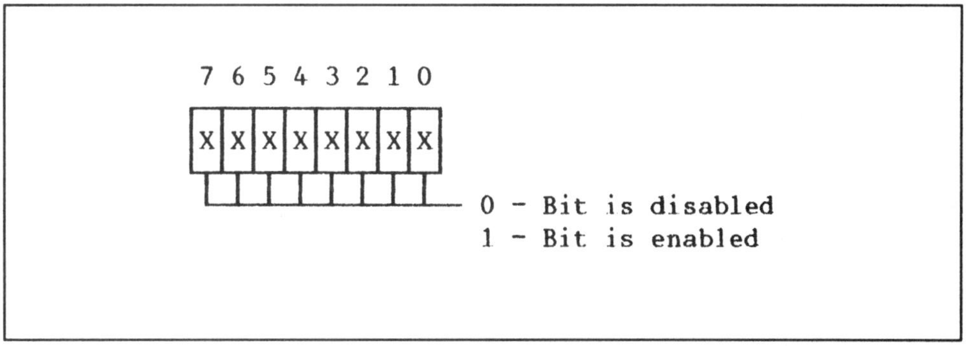

```
         7 6 5 4 3 2 1 0
        ┌─┬─┬─┬─┬─┬─┬─┬─┐
        │X│X│X│X│X│X│X│X│
        └─┴─┴─┴─┴─┴─┴─┴─┘
         │ │ │ │ │ │ │ │
         └─┴─┴─┴─┴─┴─┴─┴── 0 - Bit is disabled
                           1 - Bit is enabled
```

Figure 1.9   EGA write-only bit mask register.

1 IBM PC Graphic Displays

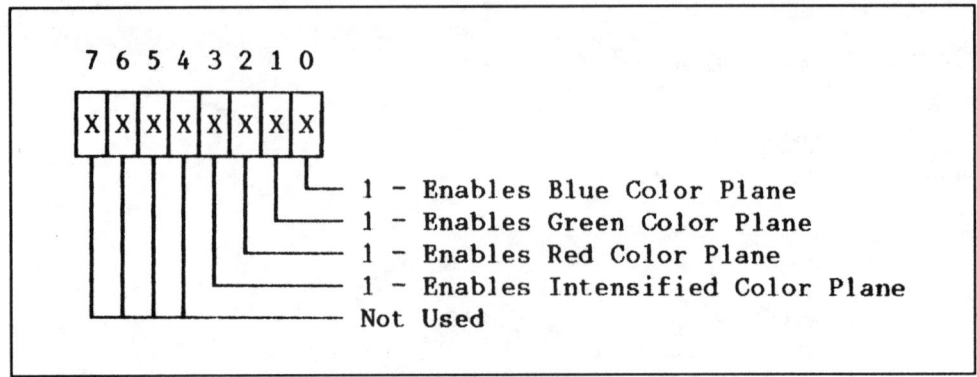

Figure 1.10 EGA map mask register.

Figure 1.10 illustrates using the EGA controller's map mask register. As this figure depicts, a color plane is enabled if a corresponding bit in the EGA controller's map mask is equal to 1. Setting the map mask is effected by sending a value of 02H to port 03C4H and sending the color plane mask value to port 03C5H. The following short program can be used to set map masks:

```
;
; Set the EGA Map Mask Routine
;
; Entry:
; Register    Contents
; ah          map mask
;
map_mask    proc
            push    ax                  ;Save the
            push    dx                  ; registers
            mov     al,2                ;Select
            mov     dx,03c4h            ; the map
            out     dx,al               ;  mask register
            inc     dx                  ;Set
            mov     al,ah               ; the
            out     dx,al               ;  map mask
            pop     dx                  ;Restore
            pop     ax                  ; the registers
            ret                         ;Return
map_mask    endp
```

By using the above subroutines and algorithms, the following assembly language subroutine demonstrates setting an EGA graphic pixel's, color value:

IBM PC Graphic Displays 1

```
;
; SET EGA Graphic Pixel Routine
;
; Entry:
; Register    Contents
; al          color
; cx          x-coordinate
; dx          y-coordinate
;
set_ega       proc
              push    ax              ;Save
              push    di              ; the
              push    es              ;  registers
              call    ega_offsets     ;DI = Video memory offset
              push    ax              ;Save AX
              mov     ax,0a000h       ;AX = Video memory segment
              mov     es,ax           ;Put it into ES
              call    bit_masks       ;AL = Write-only bit mask
              mov     ah,al           ;Set the
              call    write_mask      ; write-only bit mask
              mov     ah,0ffh         ;Enable all
              call    map_mask        ; color planes
              mov     al,es:[di]      ;Latch the data
              xor     al,al           ;Reset
              mov     es:[di],al      ; the pixel
              pop     ax              ;AL = Color value
              mov     ah,al           ;Enable the
              call    map_mask        ; color planes
              mov     al,es:[di]      ;Latch the data
              mov     al,0ffh         ;Set
              mov     es:[di],al      ; the pixel
              mov     ah,0ffh         ;Enable
              call    write_mask      ; all bits
              call    map_mask        ;  and color planes
              pop     es              ;Restore
              pop     di              ;the
              pop     ax              ;  registers
              ret                     ;Return
set_ega       endp
```

The following algorithm demonstrates retrieving an EGA graphic pixel's, color value:

1   IBM PC Graphic Displays

Retrieve an EGA Graphic Pixel's Color Value Algorithm

1. Figure the video memory offset.

2. Figure the bit mask.

3. Zero the result (Result = 0).

4. Set the loop counter to 3 (Loop counter = 3).

5. Shift the result one place to the left (Result = SHL(Result).

6. Enable the loop counter's color plane.

7. If the pixel's bit is set (Color plane byte AND Bit mask), set bit 0 of the result (Result = Result OR 01H).

8. Decrement the loop counter and go to 5 while the loop counter is still positive.

The above algorithm requires the EGA graphic controller's read map select register be set to enable the appropriate color plane. Figure 1.11 illustrates the EGA graphic controller's read map select register. To set the EGA graphic controller's read map select register, first send a value of 04H to port 03CEH and then send the color plane's value (00H to 03H) to port 03CFH. The following short program can be used to set the read map select register:

```
;
; Set the EGA Read Mask Routine
;
; Entry:
; Register     Contents
; ah           read mask
;
read_mask   proc
            push    ax              ;Save the
            push    dx              ; registers
            mov     al,4            ;Select
            mov     dx,03ceh        ; the read
            out     dx,al           ;  mask register
            inc     dx              ;Set
            mov     al,ah           ; the
            out     dx,al           ;  read mask
            pop     dx              ;Restore
            pop     ax              ; the registers
            ret                     ;Return
read_mask   endp
```

IBM PC Graphic Displays 1

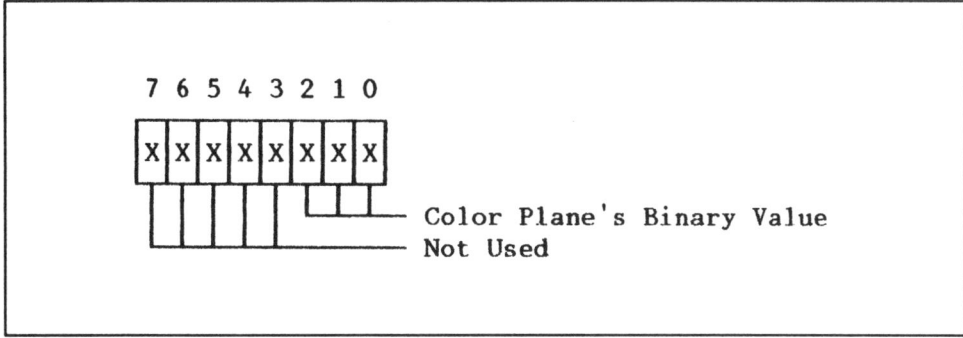

Figure 1.11   EGA read map select register.

By using the above subroutines and algorithms, the following assembly language subroutine demonstrates retrieving an EGA graphic pixel's color value:

```
;
; TEST EGA Graphic Pixel Routine
;
; Entry:
; Register    Contents
; cx          x-coordinate
; dx          y-coordinate
;
; Exit:
; Register    Contents
; ax          color
;
test_ega    proc
            push    cx              ;Save
            push    di              ; the
            push    es              ;  registers
            call    ega_offsets     ;DI = Video memory offset
            mov     ax, 0a000h      ;AX = Video memory segment
            mov     es, ax          ;Put it into ES
            call    bit_masks       ;AL = Bit mask
            mov     ah, 0           ;AH = Starting result
            mov     cl,3            ;CL = Loop counter
```

continued...

1 IBM PC Graphic Displays

```
test_ega1:      shl     ah, 1           ;Shift the result
                push    ax              ;Save AX
                mov     ah, cl          ;Enable the
                call    read_mask       ; color plane
                pop     ax              ;Restore AX
                test    al, es:[di]     ;Jump if the
                jz      test_ega2       ; pixel isn't set
                inc     ah              ;Bump the result
test_ega2:      dec     cl              ;Loop
                jns     test_ega1       ; till done
                mov     al, ah          ;AL = Color value
                xor     ah,ah           ;AX = Color value
                pop     es              ;Restore
                pop     di              ; the
                pop     cx              ;  registers
                ret                     ;Return
test_ega        endp
```

Displaying Text Characters

A text character is displayed as a collection of graphic pixels. The text characters of the CGA and EGA graphics modes are analyzed. The display coordinates of the GWINDOWS toolbox are identified. The benefits of implementing the GWINDOWS toolbox by displaying a character's graphic pixels a byte at a time are explained. Algorithms for displaying CGA and EGA text characters are provided.

A text character is displayed as a collection of graphic pixels. In the 640-by-200 CGA graphics mode, a text character is constructed from an 8-by-8 matrix of graphic pixels which yields a display screen of 80 columns (640 pixels / 8 pixels = 80 columns) by 25 rows (200 pixels / 8 pixels = 25 rows). Figure 1.12 illustrates constructing the letter A in an 8-by-8 CGA character matrix. In the 640-by-350 EGA graphics mode, a text character is constructed from an 8-by-14 matrix of graphic pixels which yields a display screen of 80 columns (640 pixels / 8 pixels = 80 columns) by 25 rows (350 pixels / 14 pixels = 25 rows). Figure 1.13 demonstrates constructing the letter B in an 8-by-14 EGA character matrix.

Figure 1.14 illustrates the display coordinates that the GWINDOWS toolbox uses for displaying text. As this figure depicts, the text character in the upper left corner of the display screen is located at coordinate (1,1) and the character in the lower right corner of the display screen is located at coordinate (25, 80).

IBM PC Graphic Displays 1

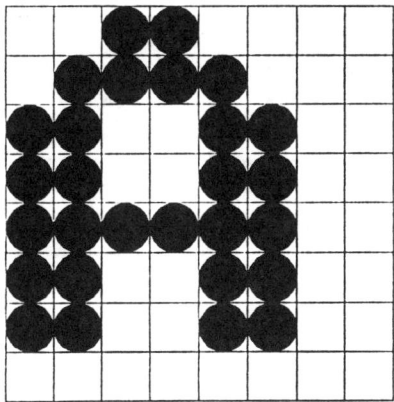

Figure 1.12   CGA Letter "A"

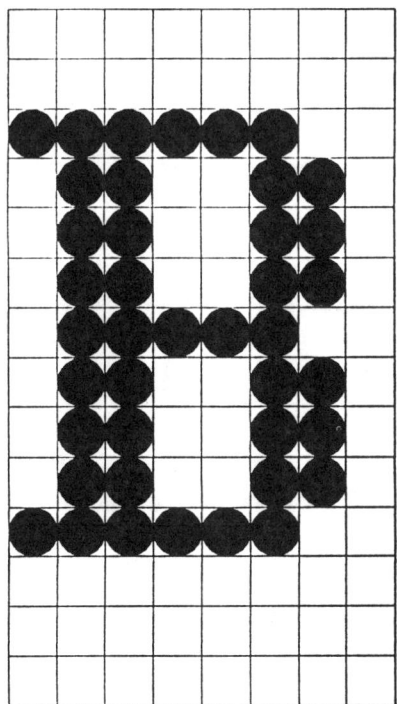

Figure 1.13   EGA Letter "B"

1 IBM PC Graphic Displays

Note: *The ROM BIOS routines use a coordinate of (0,0) for the upper left corner of the display screen and (24,79) for the lower right corner of the display screen. The coordinate system used in figure 1.12 is the most commonly used by high-level programming languages and is the most desirable method for implementing the GWINDOWS toolbox.*

Figure 1.14   GWINDOWS text coordinates.

A character is eight graphic pixels wide and each byte of CGA and EGA video memory represents eight horizontal graphic pixels. Therefore, a text character can be displayed by simply setting the character's graphic pixels a byte at a time instead of setting each individual graphic pixel a bit at a time. This method greatly simplifies implementing the GWINDOWS toolbox. Furthermore, displaying a text character a byte at a time is many times faster than displaying the same character a bit at a time. Displaying a character in the CGA's 640-by-200 graphics mode can be accomplished by using the following algorithm:

Display a CGA Text Character Algorithm

1. Figure the video memory pointer.

2. Figure the font table pointer.

3. Set the loop counter to half of the character height (Loop counter = 4).

4. Get the byte mask from the font table (Byte mask = Font table byte).

5. If the character is a white-on-black character, put the byte mask into the current video memory location. Go to 7.

6. Put the inverse of the byte mask into the current video memory location.

7. Point the font table pointer to the next byte mask (Font table pointer = Font table pointer + 1).

8. Get the byte mask from the font table (Byte mask = Font table byte).

9. If the character is a white-on-black character, put the byte mask into the current video memory location + 2000H. Go to 11.

10. Put the inverse of the byte mask into the current video memory location + 2000H.

11. Point the font table pointer to the next byte mask (Font table pointer = Font table pointer + 1).

12. Point the video memory pointer to the text character's next line (Video memory pointer = Video memory pointer + 80).

13. Decrement the loop counter and go to 3 until the loop counter is equal to 0.

The algorithm's video memory pointer, shown above, can be calculated by applying the formula ((row - 1) * 320 + (column - 1)) to the text character's GWINDOWS coordinates. The font table pointer is calculated for text characters with ASCII codes of 00H to 7FH as (Lower font table pointer + (character code * 8)) and for text characters with ASCII codes of 80H to FFH as (Upper font table pointer + (character code - 80H) * 8). The CGA's lower font table pointer is stored in the computer's INT 43H interrupt vector, and the CGA's upper font table pointer is stored in the computer's INT 1FH interrupt vector.

Displaying a character in the EGA's 640-by-350 graphics mode can be accomplished by using the following algorithm:

Display an EGA Text Character Algorithm

1. Figure the video memory pointer.

2. Figure the font table pointer.

3. Turn on all of the color planes.

1 IBM PC Graphic Displays

4. Set the loop counter for the character's height (Loop counter = 14).

5. Save the video memory pointer.

6. Turn off all of the current video memory location's pixels.

7. Adjust the video memory pointer for the next line (Video memory pointer = Video memory pointer + 80).

8. Decrement the loop counter and go to 6 until the loop counter is equal to 0.

9. Restore the video memory pointer.

10. Turn on the background color's color planes.

11. Save the video memory and font table pointers.

12. Set the loop counter for the character's height (Loop counter = 14).

13. Get the byte mask from the font table (Byte mask = Font table byte).

14. Put the inverse of the byte mask into the current video memory location.

15. Adjust the video memory pointer for the next line (Video memory pointer = Video memory pointer + 80).

16. Adjust the font table pointer for the next byte mask (Font table pointer = Font table pointer + 1).

17. Decrement the loop counter and go to 13 until loop counter is equal to 0.

18. Restore the video memory and font table pointers.

19. Turn on the foreground color's color planes.

20. Set the loop counter for the character's height (Loop counter = 14).

21. Get the byte mask from the font table (Byte mask = Font table byte).

22. Set the EGA graphic controller's write-only, bit mask to the value of the text character's byte mask.

23. Save the byte mask in the current video memory location.

24. Adjust the video memory pointer for the next line (Video memory pointer = Video memory pointer + 80).

25. Adjust the font table pointer for the next byte mask (Font table pointer = Font table pointer + 1).

26. Decrement the loop counter and go to 21 until loop counter is equal to 0.

27. Set the EGA graphic controller's write-only, bit mask to enable all bits.

28. Enable all color planes.

The algorithm's video memory pointer, provided above, can be calculated by applying the formula ((row - 1) * 1120 + (column - 1)) to the text character's GWINDOWS coordinates. The font table pointer is calculated as (Font table pointer + (character code * 14)). The EGA's font table pointer is stored in the computer's INT 43H interrupt vector.

GWINDOWS Method for Displaying Input/Output

The advantages and disadvantages of the three basic methods for displaying text in a graphics mode by the GWINDOWS operating environment are analyzed.

The MS-DOS video functions do not provide sufficient speed and versatility. ROM BIOS video functions have sufficient versatility, but their lack of speed limits their usefulness for implementing an efficient graphical user interface. Consequently, the GWINDOWS operating environment uses a mixture of ROM BIOS video functions and direct memory access techniques. Functions, such as display initialization and cursor positioning, will use the ROM BIOS video functions. Other operations, such as reading from and writing to large segments of the display screen, filling large segments of the display screen with one particular character, and displaying strings, will be handled by direct memory access techniques. Consequently, the GWINDOWS operating environment uses a mixture of the available tools for the best blend of speed and programming ease.

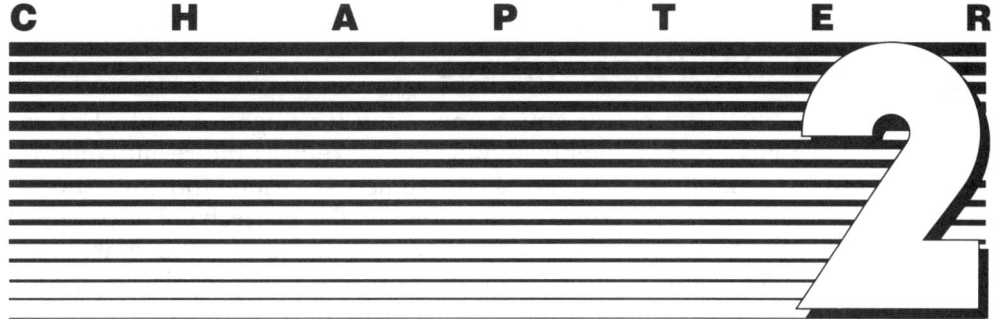

LOW-LEVEL ASSEMBLY LANGUAGE FUNCTIONS

This chapter explains selecting an appropriate function or variable name and the process of using a stack frame to pass parameters to an assembly language function. The memory needs of GWINDOWS application programs and the GWINDOWS toolbox, which require a Zortech C++ compiler's large memory model, are also discussed. Allocating variable space from the stack frame and other assembly language interfacing requirements are explained for 80286 and other microprocessors. Chapter 2 contains all low-level assembly language functions for GWINDOWS.

2 Low-level Assembly Language Functions

FUNCTION AND VARIABLE NAMES

Selecting a C++ function or variable name is fairly straightforward. For example, a C++ function that adds two integers and returns the result could be named **addints**. The name **addints** could be assumed as a useful tool for a similar assembly language function's name. Unfortunately, the Zortech C++ compiler requires a leading underscore character (_) be prepended to an assembly language function's name. For example, **_addints** would be an appropriate name for an assembly language **addints** function.

Besides complying with the C++ compiler's naming conventions, an assembly language function or variable name must be made global before a C++ program can call either the function or reference the variable. Therefore, all global assembly language function and variable names are declared **public**. Using a **public** declaration, allows the user to correctly link assembly language functions and variables to any C++ functions utilizing them.

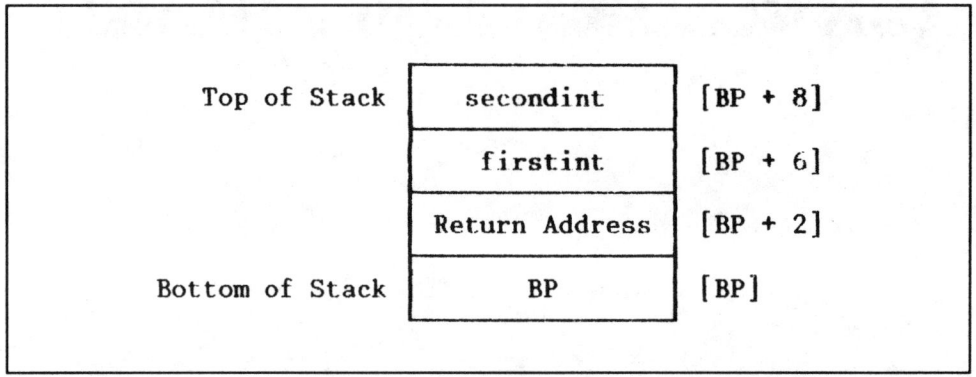

Figure 2.1 The addints stack Frame.

PARAMETER PASSING

To pass parameters to an assembly language function, a C++ program builds a stack frame. Upon entry to the assembly language function, the stack frame consists of a return address (two bytes for **near** calls or four bytes for **far** calls) followed by the first parameter and the last parameter. Because the GWINDOWS operating environment requires an extensive amount of dynamic memory for buffering display screen windows, The GWINDOWS toolbox and all GWINDOWS application programs must be compiled using the Zortech C++ compiler's large memory model. Consequently, all calls to an assembly language

Low-level Assembly Language Functions 2

function are **far** calls and require a four-byte return address. An example stack frame for the **addints** function is presented in Figure 2.1. This stack frame assumes that **addints** is to be used with a compact or large memory model program and has a function prototype of **int addints(int firstint, int secondint);**. Because **addints** is accessed with a **far** call, the C++ compiler puts a four-byte return address on the bottom of the stack. To reference the passed parameters, the assembly language function first saves and then points register BP to the bottom of the stack, as follows:

```
        .
        .
        .
_addints proc    far
         push    bp              ;Save BP
         mov     bp, sp          ;Point it to the stack
         .
         .
         .
```

With register BP pointing to the bottom of the stack frame, **firstint** can be referenced by using the offset 6[bp]. Remember, register BP was pushed onto the stack below the four-byte return address; therefore, the first parameter is located six bytes from the bottom of the stack. Additionally, **secondint** can be referenced by using an offset of 8[bp]. By accessing the parameters as register BP offsets, the coding of the **addints** function can be continued, as follows:

```
        .
        .
        .
        mov     ax,6[bp]        ;AX = First integer
        add     ax,8[bp]        ;Figure the result
        .
        .
        .
```

RETURNING TO THE CALLING PROGRAM

Finally, the **addints** function has performed its intended task, but the calculated result must be returned to the calling program. With Zortech C++, a value is returned to the calling program by placing the return value in a CPU register or combination of CPU registers. The **addints** function's integer result is returned in the AX register. Because the **addints** function's result is already in register

2 Low-level Assembly Language Functions

AX, no further steps are necessary to return the value to the calling program. However, if the result ended up register BX instead of register AX, then the value is returned to the calling program by the **addints** function executing a **mov ax,bx** instruction, before returning control to the calling C++ program.

The **addints** function not only prepares the return value but also cleans up the stack before returning to the calling program. Because register BP was pushed onto the stack, this register must be retrieved with a **pop bp** instruction. Retrieving register BP from the stack restores the stack to its entry condition. Therefore, the **addints** function can return to the calling program by simply executing a **ret** instruction. The following program illustrates the remainder of the **addints** function's code:

```
                    .
                    .
                    .
            pop     bp              ;Restore BP
            ret                     ;Return
_addints    endp
                    .
                    .
                    .
```

OTHER ASSEMBLY LANGUAGE INTERFACING REQUIREMENTS

Many assembly language functions will require memory space for local variables although this is not required by the **addints** function. Local variable space is allocated by subtracting the required number of bytes from the stack pointer. If the **addints** function had required local variable space for two integers (*row* and *col*), then the **addints** function's entry code would be revised to allocate the necessary local variable space:

```
                    .
                    .
                    .
_addints    proc    far
            push    bp              ;Save BP
            mov     bp,sp           ;Point it to the stack
            sub     sp,4            ;Reserve local variable space
                    .
                    .
                    .
```

Low-level Assembly Language Functions 2

With the necessary local variable space allocated, the local variables can be referenced as negative offsets to the BP register. Thus, *row* and *col* could be referenced by the offsets -2[bp] and -4[bp]. Which of the two locations selected for a variable does not matter; however, a variable's location must remain constant after being assigned.

The stack pointer is moved by the local variable space allocation. Therefore, the assembly language function must deallocate the local variable space before restoring register BP. Deallocation of local variable space is accomplished by a simple **mov sp,bp** instruction. Recall that before the local variable space was allocated, register BP and SP were pointing to the same memory location. Consequently, loading register SP with the pointer in register BP effectively removes the local variable space from the stack. The following code fragment shows the modified **addints** function deallocating its local variable space before returning to the calling program:

```
            .
            .
            .
            mov     sp,bp       ;Restore the stack pointer
            pop     bp          ;Restore BP
            ret                 ;Return
_addints    endp
            .
            .
            .
```

Zortech C++ requires that certain CPU registers remain unaltered by an assembly language function. Therefore, any unalterable registers used in an assembly language function must be saved on the stack at the start of the function and retrieved from the stack before returning to the calling C++ program. Functions that do not require a local variable space allocation should save the necessary registers just after the stack frame pointer has been set with the **mov bp,sp** instruction. Saved registers must be retrieved before register BP is restored during the function's exiting routine. Functions requiring a local variable space allocation should save the required registers after the local variable space allocation has occurred. Accordingly, the saved registers must be retrieved before the assembly language function deallocates the local variable space. If the local variable space is deallocated first, the registers' contents will be lost and erratic program execution is likely.

2 Low-level Assembly Language Functions

THE 80286 AND OTHERS

The 80286, 80386, 80486, V20, and V30 microprocessors all have additional assembly language instructions for handling stack frames. These instructions are **enter** and **leave**. **Enter** automatically sets up register BP as the stack frame pointer and will allocate any necessary local variable space. **Leave** will deallocate any previously allocated local variable space and will restore the original value to register BP. Because the **enter** and **leave** instructions use less memory and are faster than their equivalents, they should be used whenever the computer has a supporting microprocessor; furthermore, using **enter** and **leave** greatly simplifies the implementation of the stack frame coding requirements. The following program fragment illustrates rewriting the **addints** function to take advantage of the **enter** and **leave** instructions:

```
           .
           .
           .
_addint    proc     far
           enter    0,0           ;Set up the stack frame
           mov      ax,6[bp]      ;AX = First integer value
           add      ax,8[bp]      ;Figure the result
           leave                  ;Restore the stack
           ret                    ;Return
_addints   endp
           .
           .
           .
```

The code in the previous example does not allocate any local variable space. To allocate local variable space with **enter**, the programmer indicates the required number of bytes with the first value in the **enter** instruction's operand field. Thus, four bytes of local variable space could be allocated with an **enter 4,0** instruction.

SOURCE LISTING 2.1: graphics.asm

Listing 2.1, **graphics.asm**, contains all of the low-level GWINDOWS assembly language functions including: mouse, keyboard, and video functions.

```
;
; graphics.asm    For the GWINDOWS Toolbox
;                 (Low-Level Assembly Language Routines)
;
```

   continued...

Low-level Assembly Language Functions 2

```
                ifdef   cpu286
                .286
                endif

ufont           equ     1fh*4
lfont           equ     43h*4

DGROUP          group   _DATA
_DATA           segment word public 'DATA'
                assume  ds:DGROUP
                public  _mouse_x,_mouse_y
                public  _mouse_row,_mouse_col
                public  _left_button,_right_button

_mouse_x        dw      0
_mouse_y        dw      0
_mouse_row      dw      0
_mouse_col      dw      0
_left_button    dw      0
_right_button   dw      0
egaflag         dw      1
displayseg      dw      0a000h
numlines        dw      14
bytesrow        dw      1120
undoff          dw      960
c_color         dw      0
c_flag          dw      0ffffh
uc_flag         dw      0ffffh
c_buffer        db      0,0,0,0,0,0,0,0
m_flag          dw      0

_DATA           ends

GRAPHICS_TEXT
                segment para public 'CODE'
                assume  cs:GRAPHICS_TEXT

                public  _graphinit,_egamode,_resetmouse
                public  _showmouse,_hidemouse,_readmouse
                public  _cursoron,_ucursoron,_cursoroff,
                public  _ucursoroff,_cursorcolor,_displaychar
                public  _displaystring,_clearwindow,_fillwindow
                public  _underline,_savewindow,_restorewindow
                public  _movewindow,_keypressed,_waitkey
                public  _getfontvectors,_setfontvectors
```

continued...

2 Low-level Assembly Language Functions

```
;
; graphinit function
;
_graphinit      proc    far
                mov     ah,15                   ;Get the
                int     10h                     ; video mode
                cmp     al,6                    ;Jump if it's
                je      graphinit1              ; already set for CGA
                mov     ah,12h                  ;Check
                mov     bl,10h                  ; for
                int     10h                     ;  EGA
                cmp     bl,10h                  ;Jump
                jne     graphinit2              ; if EGA
                mov     ah,0                    ;Set mode
                mov     al,6                    ; for 640 x 200
                int     10h                     ;  2-color graphics
graphinit1:     mov     egaflag,0               ;Flag CGA
                mov     displayseg,0b800h       ;Set the display segment address
                mov     numlines,8              ;Set the number of lines per row
                mov     bytesrow,320            ;Set the number of bytes per row
                mov     undoff,2000h+240        ;Save the underline offset
                jmp     short graphinit3        ;Jump
graphinit2:     mov     ah,0                    ;Set mode
                mov     al,10h                  ; for 640 x 350
                int     10h                     ;  16-color graphics
graphinit3:     ret                             ;Return
_graphinit      endp

;
; egamode function
;
_egamode        proc    far
                mov     ax,egaflag              ;AX=1 for EGA, 0 for CGA
                ret                             ;Return
_egamode        endp

;
; resetmouse function
;
_resetmouse     proc    far
                xor     ax,ax                   ;Reset the
                int     33h                     ; mouse driver
                mov     m_flag,ax               ;Save the driver's status
                ret                             ;Return
_resetmouse     endp
```

continued...

Low-level Assembly Language Functions 2

```
;
; showmouse function
;
_showmouse      proc    far
                mov     ax,1            ;Turn on the
                int     33h             ; mouse pointer
                ret                     ;Return
_showmouse      endp


;
; hidemouse function
;
_hidemouse      proc    far
                mov     ax,2            ;Turn off the
                int     33h             ; mouse pointer
                ret                     ;Return
_hidemouse      endp


;
; readmouse function
;
_readmouse      proc    far
                mov     _left_button,0  ;Flag left button not pressed
                mov     _right_button,0 ;Flag right button not pressed
                mov     _mouse_x,0      ;Set the dummy x-coordinate
                mov     _mouse_y,0      ;Set the dummy y-coordinate
                mov     _mouse_row,0    ;Set the dummy row
                mov     _mouse_col,0    ;Set the dummy column
                cmp     m_flag,0        ;Jump if
                je      readmouse3      ; no mouse
                mov     ax,3            ;Read the
                int     33h             ; mouse values
                test    bx,1            ;Jump if the left
                jz      readmouse1      ; button isn't being pressed
                inc     _left_button    ;Flag left button pressed
readmouse1:     and     bx,2            ;Jump if the right
                jz      readmouse2      ; button isn't being pressed
                inc     _right_button   ;Flag right button pressed
readmouse2:     mov     _mouse_x,cx     ;Save the mouse's x-coordinate
                mov     _mouse_y,dx     ;Save the mouse's y_coordinate
                shr     cx,1            ;Figure
                shr     cx,1            ; the
                shr     cx,1            ; column
                inc     cx              ;  position
```

continued...

2 Low-level Assembly Language Functions

```
                    mov     _mouse_col,cx       ;Save the column position
                    mov     ax,dx               ;AX = Mouse y_coordinate
                    mov     dl,byte ptr numlines ;DL = Number of lines per row
                    div     dl                  ;Figure
                    xor     ah,ah               ; the row
                    inc     ax                  ;  position
                    mov     _mouse_row,ax       ;Save the row position
readmouse3:         ret                         ;Return
_readmouse          endp

;
; cursoron function
;
_cursoron           proc    far
                    push    di                  ;Save
                    push    si                  ; the registers
                    cmp     c_flag,0            ;Jump if the
                    je      cursoron1           ; cursor is already on
                    inc     c_flag              ;Bump the cursor flag
                    jz      cursoron2           ;Jump if the cursor isn't on
cursoron1:          jmp     cursoron8           ;Jump if don't turn the cursor on
cursoron2:          call    _hidemouse          ;Turn the mouse pointer off
                    mov     ah,3                ;Get
                    mov     bh,0                ; the
                    int     10h                 ;  cursor position
                    mov     al,dh               ;AL = Cursor row position
                    xor     ah,ah               ;AX = Cursor row position
                    inc     ax                  ;Adjust it
                    mov     bl,dl               ;BL = Cursor column position
                    xor     bh,bh               ;BX = Cursor column position
                    inc     bx                  ;Adjust it
                    call    fig_vid_ptr         ;ES:DI = Video memory pointer
                    add     di,undoff           ;Adjust it for the correct line
                    cmp     egaflag,0           ;Jump
                    je      cursoron5           ; if CGA
                    mov     si,offset DGROUP:c_buffer  ;SI = Cursor buffer
                    push    di                  ;Save the video memory offset
                    mov     cx,2                ;CX = Number of lines
cursoron3:          mov     ah,3                ;AH = Starting bit mask
cursoron4:          mov     al,ah               ;Set the color plane's
                    call    read_mask           ; read enable mask
                    mov     al,es:[di]          ;AL = Color byte
                    mov     [si],al             ;Save it
                    inc     si                  ;Bump the buffer pointer
                    dec     ah                  ;Loop for
```

continued...

42

Low-level Assembly Language Functions 2

```
                jns     cursoron4           ; all bit planes
                add     di,80               ;Bump the offset to the next line
                loop    cursoron3           ;Loop till both lines are saved
                pop     di                  ;Restore the video memory offset
                push    di                  ;Resave it
                mov     al,0fh              ;Turn on
                call    bit_planes          ; all bit planes
                xor     al,al               ;AL = All pixels off value
                mov     ah,es:[di]          ;Latch the data
                mov     es:[di],al          ;Turn off the line
                add     di,80               ;Bump the offset to the next line
                mov     ah,es:[di]          ;Latch the data
                mov     es:[di],al          ;Turn off the line
                pop     di                  ;Restore the video memory offset
                mov     ax,c_color          ;AL = Cursor color
                call    bit_planes          ;Turn on the cursor color's bit planes
                mov     al,0ffh             ;AL = All pixels on value
                mov     ah,es:[di]          ;Latch the data
                mov     es:[di],al          ;Turn on the cursor line
                add     di,80               ;Bump the video memory offset
                mov     ah,es:[di]          ;Latch the data
                mov     es:[di],al          ;Turn on the cursor line
                mov     al,0fh              ;Turn on
                call    bit_planes          ; all bit planes
                jmp     short cursoron7     ;Jump
cursoron5:      mov     al,es:[di]          ;AL = Current 8th line
                mov     c_buffer,al         ;Save the line
                xor     al,al               ;Figure
                cmp     c_color,0           ; the
                je      cursoron6           ;   color
                dec     al                  ;   mask
cursoron6:      stosb                       ;Turn on the cursor line
cursoron7:      call    _showmouse          ;Turn the mouse pointer back on
cursoron8:      pop     si                  ;Restore
                pop     di                  ; the registers
                ret                         ;Return
_cursoron       endp

;
; ucursoron function
;
```

continued...

2 Low-level Assembly Language Functions

```
_ucursoron      proc    far
                mov     ax,c_flag               ;Save the
                mov     uc_flag,ax              ; cursor flag
                mov     c_flag,0ffffh           ;Turn on
                call    _cursoron               ; the cursor
                ret                             ;Return
_ucursoron      endp

;
; cursoroff function
;
_cursoroff      proc    far
                push    di                      ;Save
                push    si                      ; the registers
                cmp     c_flag,0                ;Jump if the
                jne     cursoroff5              ; cursor is already off
                call    _hidemouse              ;Turn the mouse pointer off
                mov     ah,3                    ;Get
                mov     bh,0                    ; the
                int     10h                     ;  cursor position
                mov     al,dh                   ;AL=Cursor row position
                xor     ah,ah                   ;AX=Cursor row position
                inc     ax                      ;Adjust it
                mov     bl,dl                   ;BL=Cursor column position
                xor     bh,bh                   ;BX=Cursor column position
                inc     bx                      ;Adjust it
                call    fig_vid_ptr             ;ES:DI=Video memory pointer
                add     di,undoff               ;Adjust it for the correct line
                cmp     egaflag,0               ;Jump
                je      cursoroff3              ; if CGA
                mov     si,offset DGROUP:c_buffer    ;SI=Cursor buffer
                mov     cx,2                    ;CX=Number of lines
cursoroff1:     mov     ah,8                    ;AH=Starting bit mask
cursoroff2:     mov     al,ah                   ;Turn on
                call    bit_planes              ; the bit plane
                mov     al,es:[di]              ;Latch the data
                mov     al,[si]                 ;AL=Color value
                inc     si                      ;Bump the buffer pointer
                mov     es:[di],al              ;Save it
                shr     ah,1                    ;Loop for the
                jnc     cursoroff2              ; whole line
                add     di,80                   ;Bump the offset to the next line
                loop    cursoroff1              ;Loop till done
                mov     al,0fh                  ;Turn on
                call    bit_planes              ; all bit planes
                jmp     short cursoroff4        ;Jump
```

continued...

Low-level Assembly Language Functions 2

```
cursoroff3:         mov     al,c_buffer         ;AL = Old cursor line
                    stosb                       ;Redisplay the line
cursoroff4:         call    _showmouse          ;Turn the mouse pointer back on
cursoroff5:         dec     c_flag              ;Decrement the cursor flag
                    pop     si                  ;Restore
                    pop     di                  ; the registers
                    ret                         ;Return
_cursoroff          endp

;
; ucursoroff function
;
_ucursoroff         proc    far
                    mov     c_flag,0            ;Turn off
                    call    _cursoroff          ; the cursor
                    mov     ax,uc_flag          ;Restore the
                    mov     c_flag,ax           ; cursor flag
                    ret                         ;Return
_ucursoroff         endp


;
; cursorcolor function
;
_cursorcolor        proc    far
color               equ     <6[bp]>
                    ifdef   cpu286
                    enter   0,0                 ;Set up the stack frame
                    else
                    push    bp                  ;Save BP
                    mov     bp,sp               ;Point it to the stack
                    endif
                    call    _cursoroff          ;Turn the cursor off
                    mov     ax,color            ;AX = New cursor color
                    mov     c_color,ax          ;Save it
                    call    _cursoron           ;Turn the cursor back on
                    ifdef   cpu286
                    leave                       ;Restore the stack
                    else
                    pop     bp                  ;Restore BP
                    endif
                    ret
_cursorcolor        endp
;
; displaychar function
;
```

continued...

2 Low-level Assembly Language Functions

```
_displaychar    proc    far
row             equ     <6[bp]>
col             equ     <8[bp]>
color           equ     <10[bp]>
char            equ     <12[bp]>
                ifdef   cpu286
                enter   0,0                 ;Set up the stack frame
                else
                push    bp                  ;Save BP
                mov     bp,sp               ;Point it to the stack
                endif
                push    di                  ;Save the
                push    si                  ; registers
                call    _hidemouse          ;Turn the mouse pointer off
                call    _cursoroff          ;Turn the cursor off
                mov     ax,row              ;AX=Display screen row
                mov     bx,col              ;BX=Display screen column
                call    fig_vid_ptr         ;ES:DI=Video memory pointer
                mov     ax,char             ;AX=Character value
                push    ds                  ;Save DS
                cmp     egaflag,0           ;CGA?
                pushf                       ;Save the flags
                call    font_tab_ptr        ;DS:SI=Font table pointer
                popf                        ;Restore the flags
                je      displaychar4        ;Jump if CGA
                mov     al,0fh              ;Turn on
                call    bit_planes          ; all bit planes
                push    di                  ;Save the video memory offset
                xor     al,al               ;AL=All pixels off value
                mov     cx,14               ;CX=Number of lines
displaychar1:   mov     ah,es:[di]          ;Latch the data
                stosb                       ;Turn off all pixels
                add     di,79               ;Adjust the offset for the next line
                loop    displaychar1        ;Loop for the whole character
                mov     ax,color            ;Turn on the
                mov     al,ah               ; background color's
                call    bit_planes          ;  bit planes
                pop     di                  ;Restore the video memory offset
                push    di                  ;Resave it
                push    si                  ;Save the font table offset
                mov     cx,14               ;CX=Number of lines
```

continued...

Low-level Assembly Language Functions 2

```
displaychar2:   lodsb                           ;AL = Character bit mask
                mov     ah,es:[di]              ;Latch the data
                not     al                      ;Invert the pixels
                stosb                           ;Turn off all pixels
                add     di,79                   ;Adjust the offset for the next line
                loop    displaychar2            ;Loop for the whole character
                pop     si                      ;Restore the font table offset
                pop     di                      ;Restore the video memory offset
                mov     ax,color                ;Turn on the foreground
                call    bit_planes              ; color's bit planes
                mov     cx,14                   ;CX = Number of lines
displaychar3:   lodsb                           ;Set the write
                call    write_mask              ; enable bit mask
                mov     ah,es:[di]              ;Latch the data
                stosb                           ;Display the new character line
                add     di,79                   ;Adjust the offset for the next line
                loop    displaychar3            ;Loop for the whole character
                mov     al,0ffh                 ;Enable
                call    write_mask              ; all bits
                mov     al,0fh                  ;Turn on
                call    bit_planes              ; all bit planes
                jmp     short displaychar5      ;Jump
displaychar4:   mov     bx,color                ;BX = Character color
                call    disp_char               ;Display the character
displaychar5:   pop     ds                      ;Restore DS
                call    _cursoron               ;Turn the cursor back on
                call    _showmouse              ;Turn the mouse pointer back on
                pop     si                      ;Restore
                pop     di                      ; the registers
                ifdef   cpu286
                leave                           ;Restore the stack
                else
                pop     bp                      ;Restore BP
                endif
                ret                             ;Return
_displaychar    endp

;
; displaystring function
;
_displaystring  proc    far
row             equ     <6[bp]>
col             equ     <8[bp]>
color           equ     <10[bp]>
```

continued...

2 Low-level Assembly Language Functions

```
string              equ     <12[bp]>
                    ifdef   cpu286
                    enter   0,0                 ;Set up the stack frame
                    else
                    push    bp                  ;Save BP
                    mov     bp,sp               ;Point it to th stack
                    endif
                    push    di                  ;Save the
                    push    si                  ; registers
                    call    _hidemouse          ;Turn the mouse pointer of
                    call    _cursoroff          ;Turn the cursor off
                    les     di,string           ;ES:DI = String pointer
displaystring1:     mov     al,es:[di]          ;AL = String character
                    or      al,al               ;Jump if it's the
                    jz      displaystring7      ; end of the string
                    xor     ah,ah               ;AX = String character
                    push    di                  ;Save the
                    push    es                  ; string pointer
                    push    ax                  ;Save the character
                    mov     ax,row              ;AX = Display screen row
                    mov     bx,col              ;BX = Display screen column
                    call    fig_vid_ptr         ;ES:DI = Video memory pointer
                    pop     ax                  ;AX = String character
                    push    ds                  ;Save DS
                    cmp     egaflag,0           ;EGA?
                    pushf                       ;Save the flags
                    call    font_tab_ptr        ;DS:SI = Font table pointer
                    popf                        ;Restore the flags
                    jne     displaystring2      ;Jump if EGA
                    mov     bx,color            ;BX = Character color
                    call    disp_char           ;Display the character
                    jmp     displaystring6      ;Jump
displaystring2:     mov     al,0fh              ;Turn on
                    call    bit_planes          ; all bit planes
                    push    di                  ;Save the video memory offset
                    xor     al,al               ;AL = All pixels off value
                    mov     cx,14               ;CX = Number of lines
displaystring3:     mov     ah,es:[di]          ;Latch the data
                    stosb                       ;Turn off all pixels
                    add     di,79               ;Point to the next line
                    loop    displaystring3      ;Loop for the whole character
                    mov     ax,color            ;Turn on the
                    mov     al,ah               ; background color's
                    call    bit_planes          ;  bit planes
```

continued...

Low-level Assembly Language Functions 2

```
                        pop     di              ;Restore the video memory offset
                        push    di              ;Resave it
                        push    si              ;Save the font table offset
                        mov     cx,14           ;CX = Number of lines
displaystring4:         lodsb                   ;AL = Character bit mask
                        mov     ah,es:[di]      ;Latch the data
                        not     al              ;Invert the pixels
                        stosb                   ;Turn off all pixels
                        add     di,79           ;Adjust the offset for the next line
                        loop    displaystring4  ;Loop for the whole character
                        pop     si              ;Restore the font table offset
                        pop     di              ;Restore the video memory offset
                        mov     ax,color        ;Turn on the foreground
                        call    bit_planes      ; color's bit planes
                        mov     cx,14           ;CX = Number of lines
displaystring5:         lodsb                   ;Set the write
                        call    write_mask      ; enable bit mask
                        mov     ah,es:[di]      ;Latch the data
                        stosb                   ;Display the new character line
                        add     di,79           ;Adjust the offset for the next line
                        loop    displaystring5  ;Loop for the whole character
                        mov     al,0ffh         ;Enable
                        call    write_mask      ; all bits
                        mov     al,0fh          ;Turn on
                        call    bit_planes      ; all bit planes
displaystring6:         pop     ds              ;Restore DS
                        pop     es              ;Restore the
                        pop     di              ; string pointer
                        inc     di              ;Bump the offset
                        inc     word ptr col    ;Bump the column number
                        jmp     displaystring1  ;Loop till done
displaystring7:         call    _cursoron       ;Turn the cursor back on
                        call    _showmouse      ;Turn the mouse pointer back on
                        pop     si              ;Restore
                        pop     di              ; the registers
                        ifdef   cpu286
                        leave                   ;Restore the stack
                        else
                        pop     bp              ;Restore BP
                        endif
                        ret                     ;Return
_displaystring          endp

;
; clearwindow function
;
```

continued...

2 Low-level Assembly Language Functions

```
_clearwindow    proc    far
row1            equ     <6[bp]>
col1            equ     <8[bp]>
row2            equ     <10[bp]>
col2            equ     <12[bp]>
color           equ     <14[bp]>
                ifdef   cpu286
                enter   0,0                     ;Set up the stack frame
                else
                push    bp                      ;Save BP
                mov     bp,sp                   ;Point it to the stack
                endif
                push    di                      ;Save
                push    si                      ; the registers
                call    _hidemouse              ;Turn the mouse pointer off
                call    _cursoroff              ;Turn the cursor off
                mov     ax,row1                 ;AX=Upper screen row
                mov     bx,col1                 ;BX=Left screen column
                call    fig_vid_ptr             ;ES:DI=Video memory pointer
                mov     ax,row2                 ;Figure
                sub     ax,row1                 ; the
                inc     ax                      ;  number
                mov     bx,numlines             ;  of
                mul     bx                      ;   lines
                mov     cx,ax                   ;CX=Number of lines
                mov     dx,col2                 ;Figure
                sub     dx,col1                 ; the number
                inc     dx                      ;  of columns
                cmp     egaflag,0               ;Jump
                je      clearwindow4            ; if CGA
clearwindow1:   push    cx                      ;Save the line counter
                push    di                      ;Save the video memory offset
                mov     al,0fh                  ;Turn on
                call    bit_planes              ; all bit planes
                mov     cx,dx                   ;CX=Number of columns
                xor     al,al                   ;AL=All pixels off mask
clearwindow2:   stosb                           ;Turn off the pixels
                loop    clearwindow2            ;Loop for the entire row
                mov     ax,color                ;Turn on the
                call    bit_planes              ; color's bit planes
                mov     cx,dx                   ;CX=Number of columns
                pop     di                      ;Restore the
                push    di                      ; video offset
                mov     al,0ffh                 ;AL=All pixels on mask
```

continued...

Low-level Assembly Language Functions 2

```
clearwindow3:   mov     ah,es:[di]              ;Latch the data
                stosb                           ;Turn on the pixels
                loop    clearwindow3            ;Loop till the row is down
                pop     di                      ;Restore the video offset
                pop     cx                      ;Restore the line counter
                add     di,80                   ;Adjust the offset for the next line
                loop    clearwindow1            ;Loop till done
                mov     al,0fh                  ;Turn on
                call    bit_planes              ; all bit planes
                jmp     short clearwindow6      ;Jump
clearwindow4:   shr     cx,1                    ;CX = Number of lines / 2
                xor     al,al                   ;Figure
                cmp     word ptr color,0        ; the
                je      clearwindow5            ; color
                dec     al                      ;   mask
clearwindow5:   push    cx                      ;Save the line counter
                push    di                      ;Save the video memory offset
                mov     cx,dx                   ;CX = Number of columns
                rep     stosb                   ;Set the line
                pop     di                      ;Restore the video memory offset
                push    di                      ;Resave it
                add     di,2000h                ;Adjust the video memory offset
                mov     cx,dx                   ;CX = Number of columns
                rep     stosb                   ;Set the next line
                pop     di                      ;Restore DI
                add     di,80                   ;Adjust the video memory offset
                pop     cx                      ;Restore the line counter
                loop    clearwindow5            ;Loop till done
clearwindow6:   call    _cursoron               ;Turn the cursor back on
                call    _showmouse              ;Turn the mouse pointer back on
                pop     si                      ;Restore
                pop     di                      ; the registers
                ifdef   cpu286
                leave                           ;Restore the stack
                else
                pop     bp                      ;Restore BP
                endif
                ret                             ;Return
_clearwindow    endp
```

;
; fillwindow function
;

continued...

2 Low-level Assembly Language Functions

```
_fillwindow  proc   far
row1         equ    <6[bp]>
col1         equ    <8[bp]>
row2         equ    <10[bp]>
col2         equ    <12[bp]>
color        equ    <14[bp]>
char         equ    <16[bp]>
rows         equ    <word ptr -2[bp]>
cols         equ    <word ptr -4[bp]>
colcnt       equ    <word ptr -6[bp]>
             ifdef  cpu286
             enter  6,0                ;Set up the stack frame
             else
             push   bp                 ;Save BP
             mov    bp,sp              ;Point it to the stack
             sub    sp,6               ;Save space for local data
             endif
             push   di                 ;Save
             push   si                 ; the registers
             call   _hidemouse         ;Turn the mouse pointer off
             call   _cursoroff         ;Turn the cursor off
             mov    ax,row2            ;Figure
             sub    ax,row1            ; the number
             inc    ax                 ; of rows
             mov    rows,ax            ;Save the number of rows
             mov    ax,col2            ;Figure
             sub    ax,col1            ; the number
             inc    ax                 ; of columns
             mov    cols,ax            ;Save the number of columns
             mov    ax,row1            ;AX=Upper screen row
             mov    bx,col1            ;BX=Left screen column
             call   fig_vid_ptr        ;ES:DI=Video memory pointer
             mov    ax,char            ;AX=Character value
             push   ds                 ;Save DS
             cmp    egaflag,0          ;EGA?
             pushf                     ;Save the flags
             call   font_tab_ptr       ;DS:SI=Font table pointer
             popf                      ;Restore the flags
             jne    fillwindow1        ;Jump if EGA
             jmp    fillwindow8        ;Jump
fillwindow1: push   di                 ;Save the video memory offset
             mov    ax,cols            ;Set the
             mov    colcnt,ax          ; column counter
```

continued...

Low-level Assembly Language Functions 2

```
fillwindow2:    mov     al,0fh              ;Turn on
                call    bit_planes          ; all bit planes
                push    di                  ;Save the video memory offset
                xor     al,al               ;AL=All pixels off value
                mov     cx,14               ;CX=Number of lines
fillwindow3:    mov     ah,es:[di]          ;Latch the data
                stosb                       ;Turn off all pixels
                add     di,79               ;Adjust the offset for the next line
                loop    fillwindow3         ;Loop for the whole character
                mov     ax,color            ;Turn on the
                mov     al,ah               ; background color's
                call    bit_planes          ;  bit planes
                pop     di                  ;Restore the video memory offset
                push    di                  ;Resave it
                push    si                  ;Save the character pointer
                mov     cx,14               ;CX=Number of lines
fillwindow4:    lodsb                       ;AL=Character bit mask
                mov     ah,es:[di]          ;Latch the data
                not     al                  ;Invert the pixels
                stosb                       ;Turn on the background pixels
                add     di,79               ;Adjust the offset for the next line
                loop    fillwindow4         ;Loop for the whole character
                pop     si                  ;Restore the character pointer
                pop     di                  ;Restore the video memory offset
                push    di                  ;Resave the video memory offset
                push    si                  ;Resave the character pointer
                mov     ax,color            ;Turn on the foreground
                call    bit_planes          ; color's bit planes
                mov     cx,14               ;CX=Number of lines
fillwindow5:    lodsb                       ;Set the write
                call    write_mask          ; enable bit mask
                mov     ah,es:[di]          ;Latch the data
                stosb                       ;Turn on the foreground pixels
                add     di,79               ;Adjust the offset for the next line
                loop    fillwindow5         ;Loop for the whole character
                mov     al,0ffh             ;Enable
                call    write_mask          ; all bits
                pop     si                  ;Restore the character offset
                pop     di                  ;Restore the video memory offset
                inc     di                  ;Bump the offset to the next location
                dec     word ptr colcnt     ;Loop
                jz      fillwindow6         ; for the
                jmp     fillwindow2         ;  whole row
```

continued...

2 Low-level Assembly Language Functions

```
fillwindow6:    pop     di                  ;Restore the video memory offset
                add     di,1120             ;Adjust it for the next row
                dec     word ptr rows       ;Loop
                jz      fillwindow7         ; for the
                jmp     fillwindow1         ;  whole window
fillwindow7:    mov     al,0fh              ;Turn on
                call    bit_planes          ; all bit planes
                jmp     short fillwindow10  ;Jump
fillwindow8:    push    di                  ;Save the video memory offset
                mov     cx,cols             ;CX = Number of columns
fillwindow9:    mov     bx,color            ;BX = Character color
                call    disp_char           ;Display the character
                inc     di                  ;Bump the video memory offset
                loop    fillwindow9         ;Loop for the entire line
                pop     di                  ;Restore the video memory offset
                add     di,320              ;Adjust for the next line
                dec     rows                ;Loop
                jnz     fillwindow8         ; till done
fillwindow10:   pop     ds                  ;Restore DS
                call    _cursoron           ;Turn the cursor back on
                call    _showmouse          ;Turn the mouse pointer back on
                pop     si                  ;Restore
                pop     di                  ; the registers
                ifdef   cpu286
                leave                       ;Restore the stack
                else
                mov     sp,bp               ;Reset the stack pointer
                pop     bp                  ;Restore BP
                endif
                ret                         ;Return
_fillwindow     endp

;
; underline function
;
_underline      proc    far
row             equ     <6[bp]>
col             equ     <8[bp]>
color           equ     <10[bp]>
                ifdef   cpu286
                enter   0,0                 ;Set up the stack frame
                else
                push    bp                  ;Save BP
                mov     bp,sp               ;Point it to the stack
                endif
```

continued...

Low-level Assembly Language Functions 2

```
                push    di                      ;Save DI
                call    _hidemouse              ;Turn the mouse pointer off
                call    _cursoroff              ;Turn the cursor off
                mov     ax,row                  ;AX = Display screen row
                mov     bx,col                  ;BX = Display screen column
                call    fig_vid_ptr             ;ES:DI = Video memory pointer
                add     di,undoff               ;Adjust it for the correct line
                cmp     egaflag,0               ;Jump
                je      underline1              ; if CGA
                mov     al,0fh                  ;Turn on
                call    bit_planes              ; all bit planes
                xor     al,al                   ;AL = All pixels off value
                mov     ah,es:[di]              ;Latch the data
                mov     es:[di],al              ;Turn off the line
                mov     ax,color                ;Turn on the
                call    bit_planes              ; color's bit planes
                mov     al,0ffh                 ;AL = All pixels on value
                mov     ah,es:[di]              ;Latch the data
                mov     es:[di],al              ;Underline the character
                mov     al,0fh                  ;Turn on
                call    bit_planes              ; all bit planes
                jmp     short underline3        ;Jump
underline1:     xor     al,al                   ;Figure
                cmp     word ptr color,0        ; the
                je      underline2              ; color
                dec     al                      ;   mask
underline2:     stosb                           ;Underline the character
underline3:     call    _cursoron               ;Turn the cursor back on
                call    _showmouse              ;Turn the mouse pointer back on
                pop     di                      ;Restore DI
                ifdef   cpu286
                leave                           ;Restore the stack
                else
                pop     bp                      ;Restore BP
                endif
                ret                             ;Return
_underline      endp

;
; savewindow function
;
```

continued...

2 Low-level Assembly Language Functions

```
_savewindow   proc    far
row1          equ     <6[bp]>
col1          equ     <8[bp]>
row2          equ     <10[bp]>
col2          equ     <12[bp]>
buffer        equ     <14[bp]>
              ifdef   cpu286
              enter   0,0                 ;Set up the stack frame
              else
              push    bp                  ;Save BP
              mov     bp,sp               ;Point it to the stack
              endif
              push    di                  ;Save
              push    si                  ; the registers
              call    _hidemouse          ;Turn the mouse pointer off
              call    _cursoroff          ;Turn the cursor off
              mov     ax,row1             ;AX=Upper screen row
              mov     bx,col1             ;BX=Left screen column
              call    fig_vid_ptr         ;ES:DI=Video memory pointer
              push    di                  ;Save it
              push    es                  ; on the stack
              les     di,buffer           ;ES:DI=Buffer pointer
              mov     ax,row2             ;Figure
              sub     ax,row1             ; the number
              inc     ax                  ;  of rows
              mov     cx,numlines         ;CX=Number of lines per row
              mul     cx                  ;AX=Total number of lines
              mov     cx,ax               ;CX=Total number of lines
              mov     dx,col2             ;Figure
              sub     dx,col1             ; the number
              inc     dx                  ;  of columns
              cmp     egaflag,0           ;CGA?
              pop     ax                  ;AX=Video memory segment
              pop     si                  ;SI=Video memory offset
              push    ds                  ;Save DS
              mov     ds,ax               ;DS:SI=Video memory pointer
              je      savewindow3         ;Jump if CGA
savewindow1:  push    cx                  ;Save the line counter
              mov     bl,3                ;BL=Starting bit plane
savewindow2:  push    si                  ;Save the video memory offset
              mov     al,bl               ;Set the color plane's
              call    read_mask           ; read enable mask
              mov     cx,dx               ;CX=Number of columns
```

continued...

```
              rep       movsb                      ;Save the color plane's video line
                        pop       si               ;Restore the video memory offset
                        dec       bl               ;Loop for all
                        jns       savewindow2      ; color planes
                        add       si,80            ;Adjust the video memory offset
                        pop       cx               ;Restore the loop counter
                        loop      savewindow1      ;Loop for the entire window
                        jmp       short savewindow5 ;Jump
savewindow3:            shr       cx,1             ;CX = Number of lines / 2
savewindow4:            push      cx               ;Save the line counter
                        push      si               ;Save the video memory offset
                        mov       cx,dx            ;CX = Number of columns
              rep       movsb                      ;Save the video line
                        pop       si               ;Restore the video memory offset
                        push      si               ;Resave it
                        add       si,2000h         ;Point it to the next line
                        mov       cx,dx            ;CX = Number of columns
              rep       movsb                      ;Save the video line
                        pop       si               ;Restore the video memory offset
                        add       si,80            ;Adjust it for the next line
                        pop       cx               ;Restore the line counter
                        loop      savewindow4      ;Loop till done
savewindow5:            pop       ds               ;Restore DS
                        call      _cursoron        ;Turn the cursor back on
                        call      _showmouse       ;Turn the mouse pointer back on
                        pop       si               ;Restore
                        pop       di               ; the registers
                        ifdef     cpu286
                        leave                      ;Restore the stack
                        else
                        pop       bp               ;Restore BP
                        endif
                        ret
_savewindow             endp

;
;restorewindow function
;
_restorewindow          proc      far
row1                    equ       <6[bp]>
col1                    equ       <8[bp]>
row2                    equ       <10[bp]>
col2                    equ       <12[bp]>

       continued...
```

2 Low-level Assembly Language Functions

```
buffer          equ         <14[bp]>
                ifdef       cpu286
                enter       0,0                         ;Set up the stack frame
                else
                push        bp                          ;Save BP
                mov         bp,sp                       ;Point it to the stack
                endif
                push        di                          ;Save
                push        si                          ; the registers
                call        _hidemouse                  ;Turn the mouse pointer off
                call        _cursoroff                  ;Turn the cursor off
                mov         ax,row1                     ;AX = Upper screen row
                mov         bx,col1                     ;BX = Left screen column
                call        fig_vid_ptr                 ;ES:DI = Video memory pointer
                mov         ax,row2                     ;Figure
                sub         ax,row1                     ; the number
                inc         ax                          ;  of rows
                mov         cx,numlines                 ;CX = Number of lines per row
                mul         cx                          ;AX = Total number of lines
                mov         cx,ax                       ;CX = Total number of lines
                mov         dx,col2                     ;Figure
                sub         dx,col1                     ; the number
                inc         dx                          ;  of columns
                cmp         egaflag,0                   ;CGA?
                push        ds                          ;Save DS
                lds         si,buffer                   ;DS:SI = Buffer pointer
                je          short restorewindow4        ;Jump if CGA
restorewindow1: push        cx                          ;Save the line counter
                mov         bl,8                        ;BL = Starting bit plane
restorewindow2: push        di                          ;Save the video memory offset
                mov         al,bl                       ;Set the
                call        bit_planes                  ; color plane
                mov         cx,dx                       ;CX = Number of columns
restorewindow3: mov         ah,es:[di]                  ;Latch the data
                movsb                                   ;Redisplay the buffered line
                loop        restorewindow3              ;Loop for the entire line
                pop         di                          ;Restore the video memory offset
                shr         bl,1                        ;Loop until all
                jnc         restorewindow2              ; planes are done
                add         di,80                       ;Adjust the video memory offset
                pop         cx                          ;Restore the line counter
                loop        restorewindow1              ;Loop till done
                mov         al,0fh                      ;Turn on
                call        bit_planes                  ; all bit planes
                jmp         short restorewindow6        ;Jump
```

continued...

```
restorewindow4:    shr     cx,1                    ;CX = Number of lines / 2
restorewindow5:    push    cx                      ;Save the line counter
                   push    di                      ;Save the video memory offset
                   mov     cx,dx                   ;CX = Number of columns
        rep        movsb                           ;Display the video line
                   pop     di                      ;Restore the video   memory offset
                   push    di                      ;Resave it
                   add     di,2000h                ;Adjust it for the next line
                   mov     cx,dx                   ;CX = Number of columns
        rep        movsb                           ;Display the video line
                   pop     di                      ;Restore the video memory offset
                   add     di,80                   ;Adjust it for the next line
                   pop     cx                      ;Restore the lIne counter
                   loop    restorewindow5          ;Loop till done
restorewindow6:    pop     ds                      ;Restore DS
                   call    _cursoron               ;Turn the cursor back on
                   call    _showmouse              ;Turn the mouse pointer back on
                   pop     si                      ;Restore
                   pop     di                      ; the registers
                   ifdef   cpu286
                   leave                           ;Restore the stack
                   else
                   pop     bp                      ;Restore BP
                   endif
                   ret
_restorewindow     endp

;
; movewindow function
;
_movewindow        proc    far
row1               equ     <6[bp]>
col1               equ     <8[bp]>
row2               equ     <10[bp]>
col2               equ     <12[bp]>
row3               equ     <14[bp]>
col3               equ     <16[bp]>
                   ifdef   cpu286
                   enter   0,0                     ;Set up the stack frame
                   else
                   push    bp                      ;Save BP
                   mov     bp,sp                   ;Point it to the stack
                   endif
                   push    di                      ;Save
                   push    si                      ; the registers
```

continued...

2 Low-level Assembly Language Functions

```
                call    _hidemouse          ;Turn the mouse pointer off
                call    _cursoroff          ;Turn the cursor off
                mov     ax,row1             ;AX = Upper display screen row
                mov     bx,col1             ;BX = Left display screen column
                call    fig_vid_ptr         ;ES:DI = Source video pointer
                mov     si,di               ;SI = Source video offset
                mov     ax,row3             ;AX = Upper display screen row
                mov     bx,col3             ;BX = Left display screen column
                call    fig_vid_ptr         ;ES:DI = Dest video pointer
                mov     cx,row2             ;Figure
                sub     cx,row1             ; the number
                inc     cx                  ;  of rows
                mov     dx,col2             ;Figure
                sub     dx,col1             ; the number
                inc     dx                  ;  of columns
                mov     bx,80               ;BX = Number of bytes per line
                pushf                       ;Save the flags
                cld                         ;Set the direction flag for increment
                cmp     di,si               ;Jump if
                jbe     movewindow1         ; move up
                mov     ax,row2             ;AX = Lower display screen row
                inc     ax                  ;Adjust it
                mov     bx,col2             ;BX = Upper display screen column
                call    fig_vid_ptr         ;ES:DI = Source video pointer
                mov     si,di               ;SI = Source video offset
                sub     si,80               ;Back up to the end of the last line
                mov     ax,row3             ;Figure the lower
                add     ax,cx               ; display screen row
                mov     bx,col3             ;Figure the
                add     bx,dx               ; right display
                dec     bx                  ;  screen column
                call    fig_vid_ptr         ;ES:DI = Destination pointer
                sub     di,80               ;Back up to the end of the last line
                mov     bx,-80              ;BX = Number of bytes per line
                std                         ;Set the direction flag for decrement
movewindow1:    push    dx                  ;Save the number of columns
                mov     ax,cx               ;AX = Number of rows
                mov     cx,numlines         ;CX = Number of lines per row
                mul     cx                  ;AX = Total number of lines
                mov     cx,ax               ;CX = Total number of lines
                pop     dx                  ;Restore the number of columns
                cmp     egaflag,0           ;CGA?
                push    ds                  ;Save DS
                push    es                  ;Make DS:SI the
                pop     ds                  ; source pointer
```

continued...

Low-level Assembly Language Functions 2

```
                je      movewindow3         ;Jump if CGA
                push    dx                  ;Save the number of columns
                mov     dx,03ceh            ;Set
                mov     al,5                ;  the
                out     dx,al               ;  mode
                inc     dx                  ;  for
                mov     al,1                ;  32-bit
                out     dx,al               ;     operations
                pop     dx                  ;Restore the number of columns
                mov     al,0fh               ;Turn on
                call    bit_planes          ;  all bit planes
movewindow2:    push    cx                  ;Save the line counter
                push    di                  ;Save the dest pointer
                push    si                  ;Save the source pointer
                mov     cx,dx               ;CX = Number of columns
        rep     movsb                       ;Move a complete line
                pop     si                  ;Restore the source pointer
                add     si,bx               ;Adjust it
                pop     di                  ;Restore the dest pointer
                add     di,bx               ;Adjust it
                pop     cx                  ;Restore the line counter
                loop    movewindow2         ;Loop for the entire window
                mov     dx,03ceh            ;Restore
                mov     al,5                ;  the
                out     dx,al               ;  video
                inc     dx                  ;  mode
                xor     al,al               ;
                out     dx,al               ;
                jmp     short movewindow5   ;Jump
movewindow3:    shr     cx,1                ;CX = Number of lines / 2
movewindow4:    push    cx                  ;Save the line counter
                push    di                  ;Save the dest pointer
                push    si                  ;Save the source pointer
                mov     cx,dx               ;CX = Number of columns
        rep     movsb                       ;Move a complete line
                pop     si                  ;Restore the source pointer
                pop     di                  ;Restore the destination pointer
                push    di                  ;Resave the destination pointer
                push    si                  ;Resave the source pointer
                add     si,2000h            ;Adjust the source pointer
                add     di,2000h            ;Adjust the destination pointer
                mov     cx,dx               ;CX = Number of columns
```

continued...

2 Low-level Assembly Language Functions

```
                rep       movsb                     ;Move a complete line
                          pop       si              ;Restore the source pointer
                          add       si,bx           ;Adjust it
                          pop       di              ;Restore the destination pointer
                          add       di,bx           ;Adjust it
                          pop       cx              ;Loop for the
                          loop      movewindow4     ; entire window
movewindow5:    pop       ds                        ;Restore DS
                popf                                ;Restore the flags
                call      _cursoron                 ;Turn the cursor back on
                call      _showmouse                ;Turn the mouse pointer back on
                pop       si                        ;Restore
                pop       di                        ; the registers
                ifdef     cpu286
                leave                               ;Restore the stack
                else
                pop       bp                        ;Restore BP
                endif
                ret                                 ;Return
_movewindow     endp

;
; keypressed function
;
_keypressed     proc      far
                mov       ah,1                      ;Get key
                int       16h                       ; press status
                mov       ax,0                      ;AX = Key not pressed value
                jz        keypressed1               ;Jump if a key hasn't been pressed
                inc       ax                        ;AX = Key pressed value
keypressed1:    ret                                 ;Return
_keypressed     endp
;
; waitkey function
;
_waitkey        proc      far
                mov       ah,1                      ;Has a key
                int       16h                       ; been pressed?
                jz        _waitkey                  ;Loop if not
                mov       ah,0                      ;Get
                int       16h                       ; the key
                or        al,al                     ;Jump if
                jz        waitkey1                  ; extended key
                xor       ah,ah                     ;Erase scan code
                jmp       short waitkey2            ;Jump
```

continued...

Low-level Assembly Language Functions 2

```
waitkey1:       xchg    ah,al               ;AX = Scan code
                inc     ah                  ;AX = Scan code + 256
waitkey2:       ret                         ;Return
_waitkey        endp

;
; getfontvectors function
;
_getfontvectors proc    far
lfontptr        equ     <6[bp]>
ufontptr        equ     <10[bp]>
                ifdef   cpu286
                enter   0,0                 ;Set up the stack frame
                else
                push    bp                  ;Save BP
                mov     bp,sp               ;Point it to the stack
                endif
                push    ds                  ;Save DS
                mov     ah,35h              ;Get the
                mov     al,43h              ; lower font
                int     21h                 ;  table pointer
                lds     si,lfontptr         ;DS:SI = Lower font pointer address
                mov     [si],bx             ;Save the table's offset
                mov     2[si],es            ;Save the table's segment
                pop     ds                  ;Restore DS
                cmp     egaflag,0           ;Jump
                jne     getfontvectors1     ; if EGA
                push    ds                  ;Save DS
                mov     ah,35h              ;Get the
                mov     al,1fh              ; upper font
                int     21h                 ;  table pointer
                lds     si,ufontptr         ;DS:SI = Upper font pointer address
                mov     [si],bx             ;Save the table's offset
                mov     2[si],es            ;Save the table's segment
                pop     ds                  ;Restore DS
getfontvectors1: ifdef  cpu286
                leave                       ;Restore the stack
                else
                pop     bp                  ;Restore BP
                endif
                ret                         ;Return
_getfontvectors endp
```

continued...

2 Low-level Assembly Language Functions

```
;
; setfontvectors function
;
_setfontvectors proc    far
lfontptr        equ     <6[bp]>
ufontptr        equ     <10[bp]>
                ifdef   cpu286
                enter   0,0                     ;Set up the stack frame
                else
                push    bp                      ;Save BP
                mov     bp,sp                   ;Point it to the stack
                endif
                push    ds                      ;Save DS
                mov     ah,25h                  ;Set
                mov     al,43h                  ; the
                lds     dx,lfontptr             ;  lower font
                int     21h                     ;   table pointer
                pop     ds                      ;Restore DS
                cmp     egaflag,0               ;Jump
                jne     setfontvectors1         ; if EGA
                push    ds                      ;Save DS
                mov     ah,25h                  ;Get
                mov     al,1fh                  ; the
                lds     dx,ufontptr             ;  upper font
                int     21h                     ;   table pointer
                pop     ds                      ;Restore DS
setfontvectors1: ifdef  cpu286
                leave                           ;Restore the stack
                else
                pop     bp                      ;Restore BP
                endif
                ret                             ;Return
_setfontvectors endp

;
; Figure the video memory pointer routine
;
; Entry:
;       ax = row
;       bx = col
; Exit:
;       es:di = video memory pointer
;
```

continued...

Low-level Assembly Language Functions 2

```
fig_vid_ptr     proc    near
                push    ax              ;Save
                push    bx              ; the
                push    cx              ;  registers
                push    dx              ;
                dec     ax              ;Adjust the row number
                mov     cx,bytesrow     ;CX = Bytes per row
                mul     cx              ;AX = Video row offset
                add     ax,bx           ;Add in the column number
                dec     ax              ;AX = Video memory offset
                mov     di,ax           ;DI = Video memory offset
                mov     ax,displayseg   ;AX = Video memory segment
                mov     es,ax           ;ES:DI = Video memory pointer
                pop     dx              ;Restore
                pop     cx              ; the
                pop     bx              ;  registers
                pop     ax              ;
                ret                     ;Return
fig_vid_ptr     endp

;
; Figure the font table pointer routine
;
; Entry:
;               AX = Character code
;
; Exit:
;               DS:SI = Font table pointer
;
font_tab_ptr    proc    near
                push    ax              ;Save
                push    bx              ; the registers
                mov     bx,numlines     ;BX = Number of lines per row
                push    bx              ;Save it
                cmp     egaflag,0       ;EGA?
                mov     bx,0            ;Set DS to
                mov     ds,bx           ; the INT segment
                jne     font_tab_ptr1   ;Jump if EGA
                cmp     ax,128          ;Jump if the
                jb      font_tab_ptr1   ; character's 0 to 127
                mov     bx,ufont        ;BX = Upper font table offset
                lds     si,[bx]         ;DS:SI = Font table base pointer
                sub     ax,128          ;Adjust the character value
                jmp     short font_tab_ptr2 ;Jump
font_tab_ptr1:  mov     bx,lfont        ;BX = Lower font table offset
                lds     si,[bx]         ;DS:SI = Font table base pointer
```

continued...

2 Low-level Assembly Language Functions

```
font_tab_ptr2:  pop     bx                      ;Restore the number of lines per row
                mul     bx                      ;AX = Character offset
                add     si,ax                   ;Adjust the font table offset
                pop     bx                      ;Restore
                pop     ax                      ; the registers
                ret
font_tab_ptr    endp

;
; Display a character routine
;
; Entry:
;       BX = Background
;       DS:SI = Font table pointer
;       ES:SI = Video memory pointer
;
disp_char       proc    near
                push    ax                      ;Save
                push    cx                      ; the
                push    di                      ;  registers
                push    si                      ;
                mov     cx,4                    ;CX = Loop count
disp_char1:     lodsb                           ;AL = Font byte
                and     bx,bx                   ;Jump if
                jnz     disp_char2              ; black background
                not     al                      ;AL = White on black character
disp_char2:     stosb                           ;Display the character byte
                lodsb                           ;AL = Font byte
                and     bx,bx                   ;Jump if
                jnz     disp_char3              ; black background
                not     al                      ;AL = White on black character
disp_char3:     mov     es:[di+1fffh],al        ;Display the character byte
                add     di,79                   ;Adjust the video memory offset
                loop    disp_char1              ;Loop till done
                pop     si                      ;Restore
                pop     di                      ; the
                pop     cx                      ;  registers
                pop     ax                      ;
                ret                             ;Return
disp_char       endp
```

continued...

Low-level Assembly Language Functions 2

```
;
; Turn on the bit planes routine
;
;
; Entry:
;     al = bit plane mask
;
bit_planes      proc    near
                push    dx              ;Save DX
                push    ax              ;Save the bit plane mask
                mov     dx,03c4h        ;Select
                mov     al,2            ; the map
                out     dx,al           ; select register
                inc     dx              ;Point to the output port
                pop     ax              ;Restore the bit plane mask
                out     dx,al           ;Turn on the bit planes
                pop     dx              ;Restore DX
                ret                     ;Return
bit_planes      endp

;
; Set the read enable mask routine
;
; Entry:
;     al = read enable mask
;
read_mask       proc    near
                push    dx              ;Save DX
                push    ax              ;Save the read enable mask
                mov     dx,03ceh        ;Select
                mov     al,4            ; the read map
                out     dx,al           ; select register
                inc     dx              ;Point to the output port
                pop     ax              ;Restore the read enable mask
                out     dx,al           ;Set the read enable mask
                pop     dx              ;Restore DX
                ret                     ;Return
read_mask       endp

;
; Set the write enable bit mask routine
;
; Entry:
;     al = write enable bit mask
;
```

continued...

2 Low-level Assembly Language Functions

```
write_mask      proc    near
                push    dx              ;Save DX
                push    ax              ;Save the write enable bit mask
                mov     dx,03ceh        ;Select
                mov     al,8            ; the bit
                out     dx,al           ;  mask register
                inc     dx              ;Point to the output port
                pop     ax              ;Restore the write enable bit mask
                out     dx,al           ;Set the write enable bit mask
                pop     dx              ;Restore DX
                ret                     ;Return
write_mask      endp

GRAPHICS_TEXT ends

                end
```

Function Description: graphinit

The **graphinit** function initializes the GWINDOWS operating environment. This implementation is illustrated with the following pseudocode:

```
if (video mode ! = CGA 640 x 200) {
    switch (display adapter) {
        case EGA:
            set video mode to EGA 640 x 350
            return
        case CGA:
            set video mode to CGA 640 x 200
    }
}
set video mode flag for CGA
set the video memory segment address to the CGA segment
set the number of lines per character to 8
set the number of bytes per row to 320
set the underline offset
```

Function Description: egamode

The **egamode** function returns the display adapter type. This implementation is illustrated with the following pseudocode:

```
switch (display adapter) {
    case EGA:
        return TRUE
    case CGA:
        return FALSE
}
```

Function Description: resetmouse

The **resetmouse** function resets the mouse driver and determines if a mouse is attached to the computer. This implementation is illustrated with the following pseudocode:

call the mouse driver's reset routine
save the mouse driver's status in **m_flag**

Function Description: showmouse

The **showmouse** function turns on the mouse pointer. This implementation is illustrated with the following pseudocode:

```
if (mouse is attached) {
    turn on the mouse pointer
}
```

Function Description: hidemouse

The **hidemouse** function turns off the mouse pointer. This implementation is illustrated with the following pseudocode:

```
if (mouse is attached) {
    turn off the mouse pointer
}
```

Function Description: readmouse

The **readmouse** function retrieves the mouse's button status and pointer position. This implementation is illustrated with the following pseudocode:

left button = released
right button = released
mouse x-coordinate = 0
mouse y-coordinate = 0
mouse row = 0

continued...

2 Low-level Assembly Language Functions

```
mouse column = 0
if (mouse is attached) {
    get the mouse values
    save the left button status
    save the right button status
    save the x-coordinate
    save the y-coordinate
    figure and save the column position
    figure and save the row position
}
```

Function Description: cursoron

The **cursoron** function turns the cursor on. This implementation is illustrated with the following pseudocode:

```
if (cursor isn't on) {
    bump the cursor flag
    if (turn the cursor on) {
        turn off the mouse pointer
        get the current cursor position
        figure the video memory pointer
        switch (video mode) {
            case EGA:
                save the 13th and 14th character lines
                display the cursor line
                break
            case CGA:
                save the 8th character line
                display the cursor line
        }
        turn on the mouse pointer
    }
}
```

Function Description: ucursoron

The **ucursoron** function unconditionally turns the cursor on. This implementation is illustrated with the following pseudocode:

```
save the current cursor flag
set the cursor flag to force the cursor on
call cursoron to turn the cursor on
```

Function Description: cursoroff

The **cursoroff** function turns the cursor off. This implementation is illustrated with the following pseudocode:

```
if (cursor is on) {
    turn off the mouse pointer
    get the current cursor position
    figure the video memory pointer
    switch (video mode) {
        case EGA:
            restore the 13th and 14th character lines
            break
        case CGA:
            restore the 8th character line
    }
    turn on the mouse pointer
}
```

Function Description: ucursoroff

The **ucursoroff** function unconditionally turns the cursor off. This implementation is illustrated with the following pseudocode:

```
set the cursor flag to indicate the cursor is on
call cursoroff to turn the cursor off
restore the previous state of the cursor flag
```

Function Description: cursorcolor

The **cursorcolor** function sets the cursor character's color. This implementation is illustrated with the following pseudocode:

```
turn the cursor off
save the new color value
turn the cursor on
```

Function Description: displaychar

The **displaychar** function displays a character at a specified display screen position. This implementation is illustrated with the following pseudocode:

2 Low-level Assembly Language Functions

turn off the mouse pointer
turn off the cursor
figure the video memory pointer
figure the font table pointer
switch (video mode) {
    case EGA:
        turn on all of the color planes
        turn off all of the character's pixels
        turn on the background color's color planes
        display the character's background
        turn on the foreground color's color planes
        display the character's foreground
        turn on all of the color planes
        break
    case CGA:
        display the character
}
turn on the cursor
turn on the mouse pointer

Function Description: displaystring

The **displaystring** function displays a string at a specified display screen position. This implementation is illustrated with the following pseudocode:

turn off the mouse pointer
turn off the cursor
get the string pointer
while (not end of the string) {
    figure the video memory pointer
    figure the font table pointer
    switch (video mode) {
        case EGA:
            turn on all of the color planes
            turn off all of the character's pixels
            turn on the background color's color planes
            display the character's background
            turn on the foreground color's color planes
            display the character's foreground
            turn on all of the color planes
            break
        case CGA:
            display the character
    }

continued...

bump the string pointer
bump the column number
}
turn on the cursor
turn on the mouse pointer

Function Description: clearwindow

The **clearwindow** function clears a display screen window to a specified color. This implementation is illustrated with the following pseudocode:

turn off the mouse pointer
turn off the cursor
figure the video memory pointer
figure the number of horizontal lines
figure the number of columns
switch (video mode) {
    case EGA:
        do {
            turn on all of the color planes
            turn off all of the horizontal line's pixels
            turn on the color value's color planes
            turn on all of the horizontal line's pixels
            adjust the video memory pointer
            decrement the horizontal line counter
        } while (horizontal line counter != 0)
        break
    case CGA:
        horizontal line counter /= 2
        figure the color mask
        do {
            turn the bits on or off for the horizontal line
            adjust the video memory pointer for the next horizontal line
            turn the bits on or off for the horizontal line
            adjust the video memory pointer for the next even line
            decrement the horizontal line counter
        } while (horizontal line counter != 0)
}
turn on the cursor
turn on the mouse pointer

2 Low-level Assembly Language Functions

Function Description: fillwindow

The **fillwindow** function fills a display screen window with a specified character. This implementation is illustrated with the following pseudocode:

turn off the mouse pointer
turn off the cursor
figure the number of rows
figure the number of columns
figure the video memory pointer
figure the font table pointer
switch (video mode) {
    case EGA:
        set the column counter
        for (i = 0; i < number of rows; i++) {
            for (j = 0; j < number of columns; j++) {
                turn on all of the color planes
                turn off all of the character's pixels
                turn on the background color's color planes
                display the character's background
                turn on the foreground color's color planes
                display the character's foreground
            }
            adjust the video memory pointer for the next row
        }
        turn on all of the color planes
        break
    case CGA:
        for (i = 0; i < number of rows; i++) {
            for (j = 0; j < number of columns; j++) {
                display a character
            }
            adjust the video memory pointer for the next row
        }
}
turn on the cursor
turn on the mouse pointer

Function Description: underline

The **underline** function underlines the character at a specified display screen position. This implementation is illustrated with the following pseudocode:

turn off the mouse pointer
turn off the cursor
figure the video memory pointer
switch (video mode) {
    case EGA:
        turn on all of the color planes
        turn off all of the underline line's pixels
        turn on the underline color's color planes
        turn on all of the underline line's pixels
        turn on all of the color planes
        break
    case CGA:
        figure the color mask
        save it at the video memory location
}
turn on the cursor
turn on the mouse pointer

Function Description: savewindow

The **savewindow** function saves the entire contents of a display screen window in a specified buffer area. This implementation is illustrated with the following pseudocode:

turn off the mouse pointer
turn off the cursor
figure the video memory pointer
figure the number of horizontal lines
figure the number of columns
switch (video mode) {
    case EGA:
        for (i = 0; i < number of horizontal lines; i++) {
            for (bit_plane = 3; bit_plane > 0; bit_plane--) {
                for (j = 0; j < number of columns; j++) {
                      save the video memory location's value
                      bump the video memory pointer
                }
                restore the video memory pointer
            }
            adjust the video memory pointer for the next line
        }
        break

continued...

2 Low-level Assembly Language Functions

```
        case CGA:
            number of horizontal lines /= 2
            for (i = 0; i < number of horizontal lines; i++) {
                for (j = 0; j < number of columns; j++) {
                    save the video memory location's value
                    bump the video memory pointer
                }
                adjust the video memory pointer for the next odd line
                for (j = 0; j < number of columns; j++) {
                    save the video memory location's value
                    bump the video memory pointer
                }
                back up the video memory pointer for the next even line
            }
    }
    turn on the cursor
    turn on the mouse pointer
```

Function Description: restorewindow

The **restorewindow** function redisplays a previously buffered display screen window. This implementation is illustrated with the following pseudocode:

```
turn off the mouse pointer
turn off the cursor
figure the video memory pointer
figure the number of horizontal lines
figure the number of columns
switch (video mode) {
    case EGA:
        for (i = 0; i < number of horizontal lines; i++) {
            for (bit_plane = 3; bit_plane > 0; bit_plane--) {
                for (j = 0; j < number of columns; j++) {
                    restore the video memory location's value
                    bump the video memory pointer
                }
                restore the video memory pointer
            }
            adjust the video memory pointer for the next line
        }
        break
```

continued...

```
            case CGA:
                number of horizontal lines /= 2
                for (i = 0; i < number of horizontal lines; i++) {
                    for (j = 0; j < number of columns; j++) {
                        restore the video memory location's value
                        bump the video memory pointer
                    }
                    adjust the video memory pointer for the next odd line
                    for (j = 0; j < number of columns; j++) {
                        restore the video memory location's value
                        bump the video memory pointer
                    }
                    back up the video memory pointer for the next even line
                }
        }
        turn on the cursor
        turn on the mouse pointer
```

Function Description: movewindow

The **movewindow** function moves a display screen window from one location to another. This implementation is illustrated with the following pseudocode:

```
turn off the mouse pointer
turn off the cursor
figure the source's video memory pointer
figure the destination's video memory pointer
figure the number of rows
figure the number of columns
set the row adjustment value
if (windows would overlap) {
    figure the new source pointer
    figure the new destination pointer
    negate the row adjustment value
}
figure the number of horizontal lines
switch (video mode) {
    case EGA:
        set the video controller for 32-bit operations
        turn on all of the color planes
        for (i = 0; i < number of horizontal lines; i++) {
            move the complete line
        }
        restore the video controller status
        break

    continued...
```

2 Low-level Assembly Language Functions

```
        case CGA:
            number of horizontal line /= 2
            for (i = 0; i < number of horizontal lines; i++) {
                move the even line
                move the odd line
            }
    }
turn on the cursor
turn on the mouse pointer
```

Function Description: keypressed

The **keypressed** function determines whether or not a key has been pressed. This implementation is illustrated with the following pseudocode:

```
if (key has been pressed)
    return TRUE
else
    return FALSE
```

Function Description: waitkey

The **waitkey** function waits for the operator to press a key. Once a key is pressed, the key's ASCII code is returned for nonextended keys or the key's scan code +256 is returned for extended keys. The implementation is illustrated with the following pseudocode:

```
while (key not pressed) ;
get the key's value
if (extended key)
    return scan code + 256
else
    return ASCII code
```

Function Description: getfontvectors

The **getfontvectors** function retrieves the upper and lower font table pointers. This implementation is illustrated with the following pseudocode:

```
get the lower font table pointer
if (video mode = CGA) {
    get the upper font table pointer
}
return the font table pointers
```

Low-level Assembly Language Functions 2

Function Description: setfontvectors

The **setfontvectors** function sets the upper and lower font table pointers. This implementation is illustrated with the following pseudocode:

set the lower font table pointer
if (video mode = CGA) {
    set the upper font table pointer
}

Function Description: fig_vid_ptr

The **fig_vid_ptr** function is used internally by the GWINDOWS operating environment to figure video memory pointers. This implementation is illustrated with the following pseudocode:

figure the row offset
add in the column offset
return the video memory pointer

Function Description: font_tab_ptr

The **font_tab_ptr** function is used internally by the GWINDOWS operating environment to figure font table pointers. This implementation is illustrated with the following pseudocode:

get the base pointer
figure the character code offset
add the character code offset to the base pointer
return the font table pointer

Function Description: disp_char

The **disp_char** function is used internally by the GWINDOWS operating environment to display CGA characters. This implementation is illustrated with the following pseudocode:

for (i = 0; i < 4; i++) {
    get a font table byte mask
    if (black-on-white character) {
        invert the byte mask
    }

   continued...

2 Low-level Assembly Language Functions

```
    save the byte mask at the current video memory location
    get a font table byte mask
    if (black-on-white character) {
        invert the byte mask
    }
    save the byte mask in the next odd line's video memory location
}
```

Function Description: bit_planes

The **bit_planes** function is used internally by the GWINDOWS operating environment to enable or disable the EGA color planes. This implementation is illustrated with the following pseudocode:

select the map mask register
send the color plane mask to the map mask register

Function Description: read_mask

The **read_mask** function is used internally by the GWINDOWS operating environment to select the EGA read operation's color plane. This implementation is illustrated with the following pseudocode:

select the read map select register
send the color plane's value to the read map select register

Function Description: write_mask

The **write_mask** function is used internally by the GWINDOWS operating environment to set the EGA's write-enable bit mask. This implementation is illustrated with the following pseudocode:

select the bit mask register
send the write-enable bit mask to the bit mask register

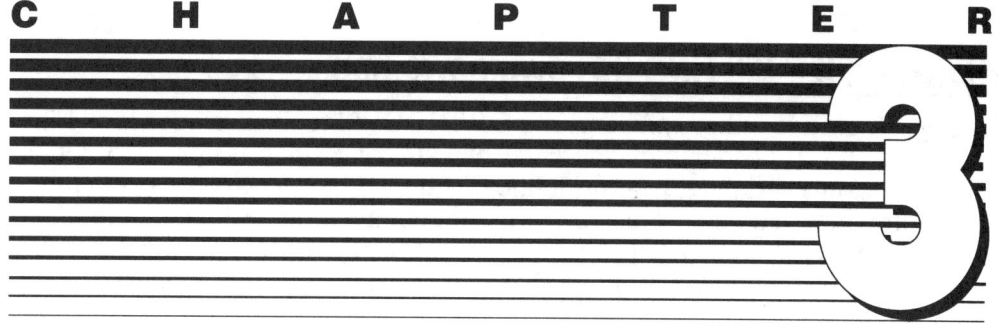

C++ INPUT/OUTPUT FUNCTION

Chapter 3 presents the low-level C++ input/output functions for initializing the GWINDOWS operating environment, positioning the cursor, and closing and opening user-defined fonts. The chapter contains the header file listing for the GWINDOWS toolbox, which defines the program's characteristics, including constants, variables and functions. It concludes with a source listing, a description for resetting the video mode and detailed function descriptions for moving the cursor.

HEADER FILE LISTING 3.1: gwindows.hpp

Listing 3.1, **gwindows.hpp**, presents the GWINDOWS toolbox header file. Like most other C++ header files, the chief purpose of **gwindows.hpp** is to define constants, global variables, macros, inline functions, class declarations, and function prototypes. To achieve correct program compilation, **gwindows.hpp** is included in all GWINDOWS programs. Additionally, **gwindows.hpp** must be included in any application program that uses the GWINDOWS toolbox.

```
/***********************************************************************
* gwindows.hpp — For the GWINDOWS Toolbox
*                         Definition File
***********************************************************************/
#ifndef GWINDOWS
#define GWINDOWS

// define NULL if not already defined */
#ifndef NULL
#ifdef LPTR
#define NULL 0L
#else
#define NULL 0
#endif
#endif

// logic constants
#define TRUE 1
#define FALSE 0

// color constants
#define BLACK 0
#define BLUE 1
#define GREEN 2
#define CYAN 3
#define RED 4
#define MAGENTA 5
#define BROWN 6
#define WHITE 7
#define DARK_GRAY 8
#define LIGHT_BLUE 9
#define LIGHT_GREEN 10
#define LIGHT_CYAN 11
#define LIGHT_RED 12
#define LIGHT_MAGENTA 13
#define YELLOW 14
#define BRIGHT_WHITE 15
```

continued...

```c
// border line constants
#define SINGLE_LINE 0
#define DOUBLE_LINE 1
#define NO_BORDER 2

// window constants
#define NO_CLEAR 0
#define CLEAR 1
#define NO_SCROLL 0
#define SCROLL 1
#define UP 0
#define DOWN 1
#define LEFT 2
#define RIGHT 3

// boolean data type
typedef int boolean;

// structure declarations
struct MENU {
    char *string;
    int hotkey;
    void (*function)(void);
    void (*help)(void);
};

struct MENU_HEAD {
    char *heading;
    int hotkey, number;
    MENU *mptr;
};

struct date {
    int month, day, year;
};

struct phone {
    int area, exchange, no;
};

struct ssn {
    int no1, no2, no3;
};

// function prototypes
void clearwindow(int, int, int, int, int);
```

continued...

3 C++ Input/Output Function

```
void cursorcolor(int);
void cursoroff(void);
void cursoron(void);
char *date_string(char *, date &);
void displaycenter(int, int, int, char *);
void displaychar(int, int, int, int);
void display_date(int, int, int, date &);
void display_dollar(int, int, int, int, double &);
void display_number(int, int, int, int, unsigned long &);
void display_phone(int, int, int, phone &);
void display_ssn(int, int, int, ssn &);
void display_string(int, int, int, int, char *);
void displaystring(int, int, int, char *);
void drawborder(int, int, int, int, int, int);
int egamode(void);
void fillwindow(int, int, int, int, int, int);
void getcurpos(int *, int *);
void getfontvectors(unsigned char **, unsigned char **);
void graphinit(void);
void hidemouse(void);
void hotstring(int, int, int, int, char *);
int input_date(int, int, int, date &);
int input_dollar(int, int, int, int, double &);
int input_number(int, int, int, int, unsigned long &);
int input_phone(int, int, int, phone &);
int input_ssn(int, int, int, ssn &);
int input_string(int, int, int, int, char *);
int keypressed(void);
void movewindow(int, int, int, int, int, int);
char *phone_string(char *, phone &);
void readmouse(void);
void resetmouse(void);
void restorewindow(int, int, int, int, char *);
void savewindow(int, int, int, int, char *);
void setcurpos(int, int);
void setfontvectors(unsigned char *, unsigned char *);
void showmouse(void);
char *ssn_string(char *, ssn &);
void ucursoroff(void);
void ucursoron(void);
void underline(int, int, int);
int waitkey(void);

// inline function declarations
#ifndef max
inline int max(int a, int b) { return a > b ? a : b; }
#endif
```

continued...

```
#ifndef min
inline int min(int a, int b) { return a < b ? a : b; }
#endif

inline int background(int color)
{
    return egamode() ? color >> 8 : !color;
}

inline void clearcolumn(int row1, int col, int row2, int color)
{
    clearwindow(row1, col, row2, col, color);
}

inline void clearrow(int row, int col1, int col2, int color)
{
    clearwindow(row, col1, row, col2, color);
}

inline int egacolor(int back, int fore)
{
    return ((back & 0xf) << 8) | (fore &0xf);
}

inline void fillcolumn(int row1, int col, int row2, int color, int chr)
{
    fillwindow(row1, col, row2, col, color, chr);
}

inline void fillrow(int row, int col1, int col2, int color, int chr)
{
    fillwindow(row, col1, row, col2, color, chr);
}
// class declarations
class environment {
    static old_video_mode;
public:
    environment();
    ~environment();
};

class font {
    boolean oflag;
    unsigned char *fontptr, *oldlptr, *olduptr;
public:
```
continued...

3 C++ Input/Output Function

```cpp
        font(unsigned char *fp);
        font(font &);
        ~font();
        void open(void);
        void close(void);
        unsigned char *getptr(void) { return fontptr; }
};

class pointer {
public:
        pointer();
        ~pointer();
        void on(void);
        void off(void);
        void read(void);
        int x(void);
        int y(void);
        int row(void);
        int col(void);
        int lbutton(void);
        int rbutton(void);
};

class window {
        int row1, col1, row2, col2, watt, bflg;
        char *buffer;
        boolean oflag, sflag;
        int orow, ocol, ostart, oend;
        int crow, ccol;
        int b_adj(int cols) { return bflg != NO_BORDER ? cols : 0; }
        int urow() { return row1 + b_adj(1); }
        int lcol() { return col1 + b_adj(1); }
        int brow() { return row2 - b_adj(1); }
        int rcol() { return col2 - b_adj(1); }
public:
        window(int r1 = 1, int c1 = 1, int r2 = 25, int c2 = 80, int w = 7,
            int b = NO_BORDER, int s = NO_SCROLL);
        window(window &);
        ~window();
        void draw(void);
        void open(void);
        void close(void);
        void setcurpos(int, int);
        int currow(void) { return crow; }
        int curcol(void) { return ccol; }
        int p_row(int row) { return urow() + row - 1; }
        int p_col(int col) { return lcol() + col - 1; }
```

continued...

```cpp
        void cls(void);
        void clreol(void);
        void scroll(int, int, boolean);
        void horizontal_bar(int, int);
        void vertical_bar(int, int);
        void print(char *);
        void println(char *);
        void printat(int, int, char *);
        void printlnat(int, int, char *);
};

class menucolors {
        int col, high;
public:
        menucolors();
        menucolors(menucolors &);
        void setcolor(int c) { col = c; }
        void sethighlight(int h) { high = h; }
        int color(void) { return egamode() ? col : 0; }
        int highlight(void) {return egamode() ? high : 1; }
};

class popup {
        int row, col1;
        boolean ESC_flag;
public:
        popup(int, int, boolean e = FALSE);
        popup(popup &);
        int get(int, MENU *);
};

class dialog {
        int row, col;
        boolean ESC_flag;
public:
        dialog(int, int, boolean e = FALSE);
        dialog(dialog &);
        int get(int, MENU *, int, ...);
};

class pulldown {
        int row, number, *tabs;
        char *hotkeys;
        MENU_HEAD *menus;
        void (*menu_help)(void);
public:
        pulldown(int, int, MENU_HEAD *, void(*m_h)(void) = NULL);
```
continued...

```
        pulldown(pulldown &);
        void display(void);
        int get(int);
};

// external variable declarations
extern mouse_x, mouse_y;
extern mouse_row, mouse_col;
extern left_button, right_button;
extern pointer mouse;
extern menucolors gmenu;

#endif
```

SOURCE LISTING 3.2: lowlevel.cpp

Listing 3.2, **lowlevel.cpp**, contains all of the low-level C++ input/output functions. These functions support diverse operations such as, initializing the GWINDOWS operating environment, positioning the cursor, and opening and closing user-defined fonts.

```
/************************************************************************
* lowlevel.cpp — For the GWINDOWS Toolbox
*          Universal Low-Level Functions
************************************************************************/
#include <dos.h>
#include <string.h>
#ifdef ZORTECH
#include <fig.h>
#endif
#include "gwindows.hpp"

static environment video;

environment::environment()
{
    #ifndef ZORTECH
    union REGS regs;
    #endif

    #ifdef ZORTECH
    fg_init_all();
    #else
    regs.h.ah = 0x0f;

    continued...
```

```cpp
        int86(0x10, &regs, &regs);
        old_video_mode = regs.h.al;
    #endif
    graphinit();
}

environment::~environment()
{
    #ifdef ZORTECH
    fg_term();
    #else
    union REGS regs;

    regs.h.ah = 0;
    regs.h.al = old_video_mode;
    int86(0x10, &regs, &regs);
    #endif
}

font::font(unsigned char *fp)
{
    oflag = FALSE;
    fontptr = fp;
}

font::font(font &arg)
{
    oflag = arg.oflag;
    fontptr = arg.fontptr;
    oldlptr = arg.oldlptr;
    olduptr = arg.olduptr;
}

font::~font()
{
    close();
}

void font::open(void)
{
    if (oflag)
        return;
    getfontvectors(&oldlptr, &olduptr);
    setfontvectors(fontptr, fontptr + 1024);
    oflag = TRUE;
}
```

continued...

3 C++ Input/Output Function

```c++
void font::close(void)
{
    if (!oflag)
        return;
    setfontvectors(oldlptr, olduptr);
    oflag = FALSE;
}

void setcurpos(int row, int col)
{
    union REGS regs;

    cursoroff();
    regs.h.ah = 2;
    regs.h.bh = 0;
    regs.h.dh = --row;
    regs.h.dl = --col;
    int86(0x10, &regs, &regs);
    cursoron();
}

void getcurpos(int *row, int *col)
{
    union REGS regs;

    regs.h.ah = 3;
    regs.h.bh = 0;
    int86(0x10, &regs, &regs);
    *row = ++regs.h.dh;
    *col = ++regs.h.dl;
}

void displaycenter(int row, int col, int color, char *string)
{
    displaystring(row, col - (strlen(string) >> 1), color, string);

}

void drawborder(int row1, int col1, int row2, int col2, int color, int type)
{
    hidemouse();
    cursoroff();
    displaychar(row1, col1, color, type ? 201 : 218);
    fillrow(row1, col1 + 1, col2 - 1, color, type ? 205 : 196);
    displaychar(row1, col2, color, type ? 187 : 191);
    fillcolumn(row1 + 1, col1, row2 - 1, color, type ? 186 : 179);
```
continued...

```
    fillcolumn(row1 + 1, col2, row2 - 1, color, type ? 186 : 179);
    displaychar(row2, col1, color, type ? 200 : 192);
    fillrow(row2, col1 + 1, col2 - 1, color, type ? 205 : 196);
    displaychar(row2, col2, color, type ? 188 : 217);
    cursoron();
    showmouse();
}
```

Constructor Description: environment::environment

The **environment::environment** constructor initializes GWINDOWS operating environment. This implementation is illustrated with the following pseudocode:

set the video mode
initialize the operating environment

Destructor Description: environment ::~environment

When an environment object goes out of scope, the **environment:: ~ environment** destructor resets the video mode to its former value. This implementation is illustrated with the following pseudocode:

restore the former video mode

Constructor Description: font::font

The **font::font** constructor sets a font object's font table pointer and flags the font as closed. This implementation is illustrated with the following pseudocode:

flag the font as closed
set the font table pointer

Destructor Description: font::~font

The **font:: ~ font** destructor closes the font when the font object goes out of scope. This implementation is illustrated with the following pseudocode:

close the font

Function Description: font::open

The **font::open** function opens a font object's font. This implementation is illustrated with the following pseudocode:

3 C++ Input/Output Function

```
if (font isn't already opened) {
    save the current font table pointers
    set the font table pointers to point to the object's font table
    flag the font as opened
}
```

Function Description: font::close

The **font::close** function closes a previously opened font. This implementation is illustrated with the following pseudocode:

```
if (font is open) {
    restore the former font table pointers
    flag the font as closed
}
```

Function Description: setcurpos

The **setcurpos** function sets the display screen's cursor position. This implementation is illustrated with the following pseudocode:

decrement the row
decrement the column
use the ROM BIOS to position the cursor

Function Description: getcurpos

The **getcurpos** function retrieves the cursor's row position and column position. This implementation is illustrated with the following pseudocode:

use the ROM BIOS to get the cursor values
bump the row position
bump the column position
return the cursor values

Function Description: displaycenter

The **displaycenter** function centers a string on a specified display screen position. This implementation is illustrated with the following pseudocode:

*use the **displaystring** function to display the string at the*
 position defined by (column - (length of the string / 2))

Function Description: drawborder

Drawborder function draws a border around a display screen window. This implementation is illustrated with the following pseudocode:

turn off the mouse pointer
turn off the cursor
display the upper left corner
for (i = 0; i < number of interior columns; i++) {
    display a horizontal line character
}
display the upper right corner
for (i = 0; i < number of interior rows; i++) {
    display the left side character
    display the right side character
}
display the lower left corner
for (i = 0; i < number of interior columns; i++) {
    display a horizontal line character
}
turn on the cursor
turn on the mouse pointer

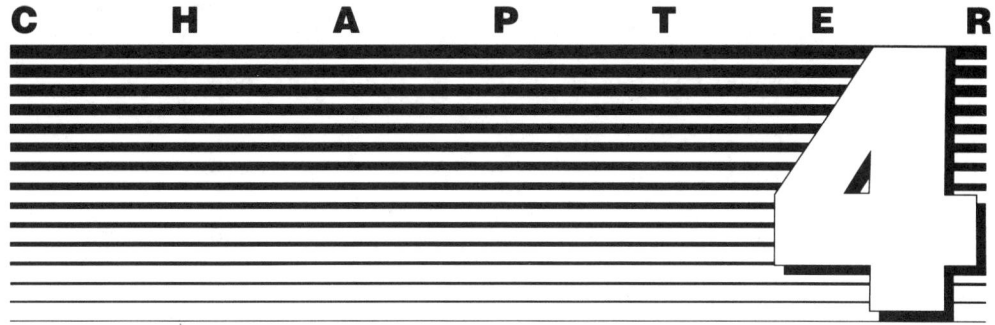

POINTING DEVICES

By using the GWINDOWS toolbox, a mouse's many desirable traits can be implemented. This chapter presents the C++ functions for incorporating a Microsoft-compatible mouse into the GWINDOWS operating environment. The chapter also examines the Microsoft mouse driver functions to provide supporting knowledge for implementing the GWINDOWS toolbox mouse functions.

4 Pointing Devices

Function Name	Function Code
Reset the Mouse Driver	00H
Turn on the Mouse Pointer	01H
Turn off the Mouse Pointer	02H
Get Button Status and Ptr Pos	03H
Set Pointer Position	04H
Get Button Press Status	05H
Get Button Release Status	06H
Set Horizontal Limits	07H
Set Vertical Limits	08H
Set Graphic Shape	09H
Set Text Pointer Type	0AH
Get Motion Count	0BH
Set User-Defined Event Handler	0CH
Turn on Light Pen Emulation	0DH
Turn off Light Pen Emulation	0EH
Set Mickey:Pixels Ratios	0FH
Set Exclusion Area	10H
Set Double Speed Threshold	13H
Swap User-Defined Event Handlers	14H
Get Mouse Status Buffer Size	15H
Save Mouse Driver Status	16H
Restore Mouse Driver Status	17H
Set Alt Event Handler	18H
Get Alt Event Handler's Address	19H
Set Sensitivity	1AH
Get Sensitivity	1BH
Set Interrupt Rate	1CH
Set Pointer Display Page	1DH
Get Pointer Display Page	1EH
Disable Mouse Driver	1FH
Enable Mouse Driver	20H
Reset Mouse Driver	21H
Set Language	22H
Get Language Code	23H
Get Mouse Information	24H

Figure 4.1 Microsoft mouse driver functions.

MICROSOFT MOUSE DRIVER FUNCTIONS

The Microsoft mouse driver presents a variety of mouse functions that can meet the most demanding needs of a graphical user interface. Like the ROM BIOS video functions, the Microsoft mouse driver functions are called by an **INT** call. Instead of a call to the ROM BIOS video functions' INT 10H, the Microsoft mouse driver functions are utilized by issuing a call to INT 33H. Figure 4.1 outlines the Microsoft mouse driver functions. Furthermore, Appendix C provides a complete description of all Microsoft mouse driver functions. Although the list of mouse functions in Figure 4.1 may seem formidable, most application programs employ only a small fraction of available mouse functions. Thus, effectively incorporating a mouse into an application program's graphical user interface is surprisingly easy.

SOURCE LISTING 4.1: pointer.cpp

The low-level mouse functions in **graphics.asm** provide all that is necessary to incorporate a mouse into the GWINDOWS operating environment. Listing 4.1, **pointer.cpp**, provides the C++ functions for an entire class of pointer objects. Because these pointer functions allow access to the mouse as an abstract data object, the higher level GWINDOWS functions can be customized to fit a particular application program's requirements. For example, the GWINDOWS toolbox could be customized easily for a joystick by simply making a few minor changes to the pointer object's code. This ability to customize the GWINDOWS toolbox is a direct result of the C++ programming language's support for object-oriented programming. In contrast, changing the pointing device in a C implementation of the GWINDOWS toolbox would require a major rewrite of the complete toolbox. Fortunately, the power of object-oriented programming will allow a major change in the GWINDOWS operating environment without a corresponding need to rewrite the entire toolbox.

```
/************************************************************************
* pointer.cpp — For the GWINDOWS Toolbox
*          Text Pointer Routines
************************************************************************/
#include "gwindows.hpp"

pointer::pointer()
{
    resetmouse();
}
```

continued...

4 Pointing Devices

```cpp
pointer::~pointer()
{
    hidemouse();
}

void pointer::on(void)
{
    showmouse();
}

void pointer::off(void)
{
    hidemouse();
}

void pointer::read(void)
{
    readmouse();
}

int pointer::x(void)
{
    return mouse_x;
}

int pointer::y(void)
{
    return mouse_y;
}

int pointer::row(void)
{
    return mouse_row;
}

int pointer::col(void)
{
    return mouse_col;
}

int pointer::lbutton(void)
{
    return left_button;
}
```

continued...

```
int pointer::rbutton(void)
{
    return right_button;
}

pointer mouse;
```

Constructor Description: pointer::pointer

The **pointer::pointer** constructor resets the pointer object's driver. This implementation is illustrated with the following pseudocode:

reset the mouse driver

Destructor Description: pointer::~pointer

The **pointer::~pointer** destructor turns off the pointer object's display screen pointer. This implementation is illustrated with the following pseudocode:

turn off the mouse pointer

Function Description: pointer::on

The **pointer::on** function turns on the pointer object's display screen pointer. This implementation is illustrated with the following pseudocode:

turn on the mouse pointer

Function Description: pointer::off

The **pointer::off** function turns off the pointer object's display screen pointer. This implementation is illustrated with the following pseudocode:

turn off the mouse pointer

Function Description: pointer::read

The **pointer::read** function reads the pointer object's button status and display screen position. This implementation is illustrated with the following pseudocode:

retrieve the mouse's button status and pointer position

Function Description: pointer::x

The **pointer::x** function returns the pointer object's x-coordinate. This implementation is illustrated with the following pseudocode:

return the mouse's x-coordinate

Function Description: pointer::y

The **pointer::y** function returns the pointer object's y-coordinate. This implementation is illustrated with the following pseudocode:

return the mouse's y-coordinate

Function Description: pointer::row

The **pointer::row** function returns the pointer object's row position. This implementation is illustrated with the following pseudocode:

return the mouse's row position

Function Description: pointer::col

The **pointer::col** function returns the pointer object's column position. This implementation is illustrated with the following pseudocode:

return the mouse's column position

Function Description: pointer::lbutton

The **pointer::lbutton** function returns the pointer object's left button status. This implementation is illustrated with the following pseudocode:

return the mouse's left button status

Function Description: pointer::rbutton

The **pointer::rbutton** function returns the pointer object's right button status. This implementation is illustrated with the following pseudocode:

return the mouse's right button status

Object Description: mouse

The **mouse** object is a predefined pointer object. By employing **mouse** in an application program, the application programer can easily incorporate the mouse into the application program by simply accessing the mouse as an abstract data object.

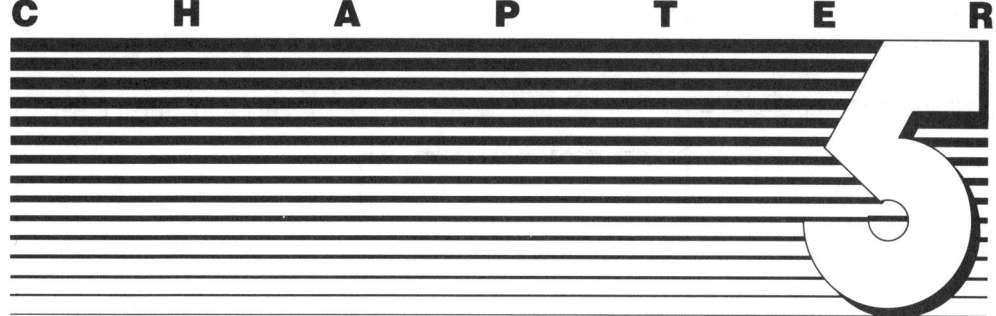

DYNAMIC WINDOW FUNCTIONS

This chapter presents the C++ functions for implementing a class of dynamic display screen window objects. These dynamic display screen window functions perform diverse operations such as opening windows, closing windows, drawing windows, moving windows, displaying horizontal and vertical scroll bars, scrolling windows, clearing windows, and displaying window strings. A display screen window's components and the C++ dynamic memory management operators and functions are discussed before introducing the source code for dynamic window functions.

5 Dynamic Window Functions

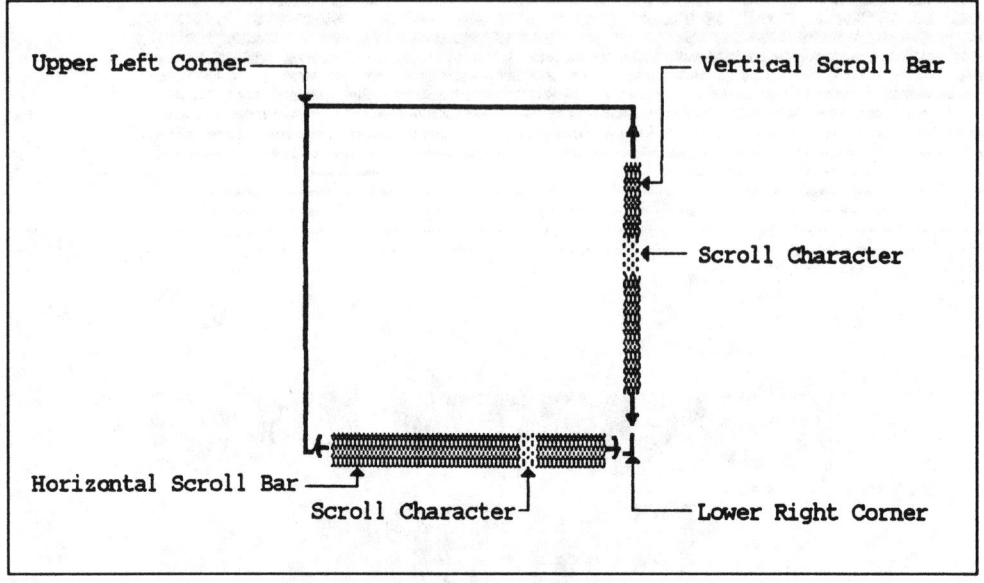

Figure 5.1 A text window.

DISPLAY SCREEN WINDOW

Figure 5.1 illustrates the many components used to construct a dynamic display screen window. Because many of these components are optional features, a dynamic display screen window may require only a few key components to generate the desired appearance on the display screen. The following are more detailed explanations of these components:

> **Upper Left and Lower Right Coordinates:** Upper left and lower right coordinates are used to define a display screen window's size and position. A display screen window can be as small as a single text character or as large as the whole screen.
>
> **Border:** The GWINDOWS toolbox supports both single- and double-lined window borders. Borders are an optional display screen window component.
>
> **Horizontal Scroll Bar:** A horizontal scroll bar is used by the display screen window to indicate the cursor's current line position. Because a display screen window may not be wide enough to display an entire line, a horizontal scroll bar provides a very useful visual aid for indicating the displayed portion's relation to the whole line. Horizontal scroll bars are an optional display screen window component.

Vertical Scroll Bar: A vertical scroll bar is used by the display screen window to indicate the cursor's current file position. Because a display screen window may not be tall enough to display an entire file, a vertical scroll bar provides a useful visual aid for indicating the displayed portion's relation to the whole file. Vertical scroll bars are an optional display screen window component.

C++ DYNAMIC MEMORY MANAGEMENT OPERATORS AND FUNCTIONS

The GWINDOWS toolbox must save the current window's portion of the display screen before displaying a window. If the current contents of the display screen window are not saved, the GWINDOWS toolbox would not be able to restore properly a closed window's portion of the display screen. Because the GWINDOWS operating environment doesn't know in advance the number and size of an application program's windows, the GWINDOWS toolbox makes extensive use of the C++ dynamic memory management operators and functions to obtain and to release display screen window buffer space.

The C++ programming language provides two dynamic memory management operators, **new** and **delete**. The **new** operator is used to dynamically allocate a memory block. The following program demonstrates using the **new** operator to allocate space for a 100-element array of type **int**:

```
//
// new operator demo program
//
#include <stdio.h>
#include <stdlib.h>

int *intarray;

main()
{
    // Allocate space for a 100 element integer array
    intarray = new int[100];
    if (intarray == NULL)
        printf("Not enough memorytoallocatetherequested array\n");
    else
        printf("A 100 element integer array has been allocated space\n");
    exit(0);
}
```

5 Dynamic Window Functions

The preceding example illustrates that **new** returns a **NULL** pointer if it is unable to allocate an adequate amount of memory space; therefore, allocation errors can be trapped easily by performing a **NULL** pointer check.

The **delete** operator releases a previously allocated memory block. The following program in demonstrates using the **delete** operator to deallocate a 25-element array of type **float**:

```
//
// delete operator demo program
//
#include <stdio.h>
#include <stdlib.h>

float *fltarray;

main()
{
    // Allocate space for a 25 element float array
    fltarray = new float[25];
    if (fltarray == NULL) {
        printf("Memory allocation failed\n");
        exit(1);
    }

    // Release the array's allocated memory space
    delete fltarray;
    exit(0);
}
```

Besides the two dynamic memory management operators, the C++ programming language provides four dynamic memory management library functions: **malloc**, **calloc**, **realloc**, and **free**. The **malloc** function is used to dynamically allocate a memory block. The following program demonstrates using **malloc** to allocate space for a 100-element array of type **int**:

```
//
// malloc function demo program
//
#include <stdio.h>
#include <stdlib.h>

int *intarray;
```

continued...

```
main()
{
    // Allocate space for a 100 element integer array
    intarray = (int *)malloc(100 * sizeof(int));
    if (intarray == NULL)
        printf("Not enough memory to allocate the requestedarray\n");
    else
        printf("A 100 element integer array has been allocated space\n");
    exit(0);
}
```

The **malloc** function returns a **NULL** pointer to indicate a memory space allocation error, which is similar to the **new** operator.

The **calloc** function allocates a memory block for an array of *n* elements, each with a length of *size* bytes. Each of the array elements is initialized with a value of zero. The following program demonstrates the **calloc** function by allocating memory space for a 50-element array of type **double**:

```
//
// calloc function demo program
//
#include <stdio.h>
#include <stdlib.h>

double *dblarray;

main()
{
    // Allocate memory space for a 50 element double array
    dblarray = (double *)calloc(50, sizeof(double));
    if (dblarray == NULL)
        printf("Insufficient memory space\n");
    else
        printf("Allocation was successfully completed\n");
    exit(0);
}
```

Similar to the **new** operator and the **malloc** function, the **calloc** function returns a **NULL** pointer to indicate a memory space allocation error.

The **realloc** function changes the size of a previously allocated memory block. Additionally, most compilers automatically call the **malloc** function if a **NULL** pointer is passed to the **realloc** function. The following example demonstrates using the **realloc** function to change a previously allocated array's size:

5 Dynamic Window Functions

```c
//
// realloc function demo program
//
#include <stdio.h>
#include <stdlib.h>

int *intarray;

main()
{
    // Allocate memory space for a 50 element integer array
    intarray = (int *)malloc(50 * sizeof(int));
    if (intarray == NULL) {
        printf("Initial memory allocation failed\n");
        exit(0);
    }

    // Reallocate the array's memory space
    intarray = (int *)realloc(intarray, 100 * sizeof(int));
    if (intarray == NULL)
        printf("The reallocation attempt failed\n");
    else
        printf("The reallocation was successful\n");
    exit(0);
}
```

Similar to the **new** operator and the **malloc** and **calloc** functions, the **realloc** function returns a **NULL** pointer to indicate a memory allocation error.

Similar to the **delete** operator, the **free** function also releases a previously allocated memory block. The program in the following example demonstrates using the **free** function to deallocate a 25-element array of type **float**:

```c
//
// free function demo program
//
#include <stdio.h>
#include <stdlib.h>

float *fltarray;
```

continued...

```
main()
{
    // Allocate space for a 25 element float array
    fltarray = (float *)malloc(25 * sizeof(float));
    if (fltarray = = NULL) {
        printf("Memory allocation failed\n");
        exit(1);
    }

    // Release the array's allocated memory space
    free(fltarray);
    exit(0);
}
```

Availability of dynamic memory management operators and functions of C++ programing language allows the GWINDOWS toolbox to dynamically open and close display screen windows. Before displaying a window, GWINDOWS allocates a memory block large enough to hold the current contents of the display screen window. Redisplaying the window's former contents is followed by releasing the display screen window's dynamically allocated memory block.

SOURCE LISTING 5.1: windows.cpp

Listing 5.1, **windows.cpp**, presents the functions for a class of dynamic display screen window objects. These functions include:

- Opening and closing display-screen windows
- Drawing display screen windows
- Displaying horizontal and vertical scroll bars
- Scrolling display screen windows
- Clearing display screen windows
- Displaying window strings

```
/***********************************************************************
* windows.cpp — For the GWINDOWS Toolbox
*                   Dynamic Windows Routines
***********************************************************************/
#include <string.h>
#include <dos.h>
#include <stdio.h>
#include <stdlib.h>
#include "gwindows.hpp"
```

continued...

5 Dynamic Window Functions

```cpp
window::window(int r1, int c1, int r2, int c2, int w, int b, int s)
{
    row1 = r1;
    col1 = c1;
    row2 = r2;
    col2 = c2;
    watt = w;
    bflg = b;
    sflag = s;
    oflag = FALSE;
}

window::window(window &arg)
{
    row1 = arg.row1;
    col1 = arg.col1;
    row2 = arg.row2;
    col2 = arg.col2;
    watt = arg.watt;
    bflg = arg.bflg;
    sflag = arg.sflag;
    buffer = arg.buffer;
    oflag = arg.oflag;
    orow = arg.orow;
    ocol = arg.ocol;
    ostart = arg.ostart;
    oend = arg.oend;
    crow = arg.crow;
    ccol = arg.ccol;
}

window::~window()
{
    if (oflag)
        close();
}

void window::draw(void)
{
    clearwindow(row1, col1, row2, col2, background(watt));
    if (bflg != NO_BORDER)
        drawborder(row1, col1, row2, col2, watt, bflg);
}
```

continued...

Dynamic Window Functions 5

```
void window::open(void)
{
    buffer = farmalloc((long)(col2-col1 + 1)*(egamode()? 56 : 8)*
        (row2 - row1 + 1));
    if (buffer == NULL) {
        printf("Not enough memory to open window\n");
        exit(1);
    }
    savewindow(row1, col1, row2, col2, buffer);
    draw();
    oflag = TRUE;
    getcurpos(&orow, &ocol);
    setcurpos(1, 1);
    cursoroff();
}

void window::close(void)
{
    if (oflag) {
        restorewindow(row1, col1, row2, col2, buffer);
        farfree(buffer);
        oflag = FALSE;
        ::setcurpos(orow, ocol);
        cursoron();
    }
}

void window::setcurpos(int row, int col)
{
    if (oflag) {
        crow = row;
        ccol = col;
        ::setcurpos(p_row(crow), p_col(ccol));
    }
}

void window::cls(void)
{
    if (oflag) {
        clearwindow(urow(), lcol(), brow(), rcol(),
            background(watt));
        setcurpos(1, 1);
    }
}
```

continued...

5 Dynamic Window Functions

```cpp
void window::clreol(void)
{
    if (oflag)
        clearwindow(p_row(crow),p_col(ccol), p_row(crow), rcol(),
            background(watt));
}

void window::scroll(int num, int dir, boolean clear)
{
    switch (dir) {
        case UP:
            movewindow(urow() + num, lcol(), brow(), rcol(), urow(), lcol());
            break;
        case DOWN:
            movewindow(urow(), lcol(),brow()-num,rcol(),urow()+num, lcol());
            break;
        case LEFT:
            movewindow(urow(), lcol() + num, brow(), rcol(), urow(), lcol());
            break;
        default:
            movewindow(urow(), lcol(), brow(), rcol()- num, urow(), lcol() + num);
    }
    if (clear) {
        switch (dir) {
            case UP:
                clearwindow(brow() - num + 1, lcol(), brow(), rcol(),
                    background(watt));
                break;
            case DOWN:
                clearwindow(urow(), lcol(), urow() + num - 1, rcol(),
                    background(watt));
                break;
            case LEFT:
                clearwindow(urow(), rcol() - num + 1, brow(), rcol(),
                    background(watt));
                break;
            default:
                clearwindow(urow(), lcol(), brow(), lcol() + num - 1,
                    background(watt));
        }
    }
}
```

continued...

Dynamic Window Functions 5

```
void window::print(char *string)
{
    int i, off;
    char *line = new char[rcol() - lcol() + 2];

    if (oflag) {
        if (sflag) {
            off = 0;
            while (off < strlen(string)) {
                i = 0;
                while(i +off< strlen(string)&& p_col(ccol + i) < = rcol())
                    line[i++] = string[i + off];
                line[i] = 0;
                off += i;
                displaystring(p_row(crow), p_col(ccol), watt, line);
                ccol += strlen(line);
                if (p_col(ccol) rcol()) {
                    ccol = 1;
                    crow++;
                    if (p_row(crow) brow()) {
                        scroll(1, UP, CLEAR);
                        crow--;
                    }
                }
                setcurpos(crow, ccol);
            }
        }
        else {
            i = 0;
            while (i < strlen(string) && p_col(ccol + i) < = rcol())
                line[i++] = string[i];
            line[i] = 0;
            displaystring(p_row(crow), p_col(ccol), watt, line);
            ccol += strlen(line);
            if (p_col(ccol) > rcol()) {
                ccol = 1;
                crow++;
                if (p_row(crow) > brow())
                    crow--;
            }
            setcurpos(crow, ccol);
        }
    }
    delete line;
}
```

continued...

5 Dynamic Window Functions

```
void window::println(char *string)
{
    if (oflag) {
        print(string);
        ccol = 1;
        crow++;
        if (p_row(crow) > brow()) {
            if (sflag)
                scroll(1, UP, CLEAR);
            crow--;
        }
        setcurpos(crow, ccol);
    }
}

void window::printat(int row, int col, char *string)
{
    if (oflag) {
        setcurpos(row, col);
        print(string);
    }
}

void window::printlnat(int row, int col, char *string)
{
    if (oflag) {
        setcurpos(row, col);
        println(string);
    }
}

void window::horizontal_bar(int current, int total)
{
    if (!total) {
        current = 0;
        total = 1;
    }
    displaychar(row2, col1 + 1, watt, 27);
    fillrow(row2, col1 + 2, col2 - 2, watt, 177);
    displaychar(row2, col2 - 1, watt, 26);
    displaychar(row2, (int)((long)(col2 - col1 - 4) * current / total + col1
        + 2), watt, 176);
}
```

continued...

```
void window::vertical_bar(int current, int total)
{
    if (!total) {
        current = 0;
        total = 1;
    }
    displaychar(row1 + 1, col2, watt, 24);
    fillcolumn(row1 + 2, col2, row2 - 2, watt, 177);
    displaychar(row2 - 1, col2, watt, 25);
    displaychar((int)((long)(row2 - row1 - 4) * current / total + row1 + 2),
        col2, watt, 176);
}
```

Constructor Description: window::window

The **window::window** constructor saves the dynamic display screen window object's upper left coordinates, lower right coordinates, color, border type, and scroll type. Additionally, the **window::window** constructor flags the dynamic display screen window as closed. This implementation is illustrated with the following pseudocode:

save the display screen window's upper left coordinates
save the display screen window's lower right coordinates
save the display screen window's color
save the display screen window's border type
save the display screen window's scroll type
flag the display screen window as closed

Destructor Description: window::~window

When a dynamic display screen window object goes out of scope, the **window::~window** destructor closes its corresponding display screen window. This implementation is illustrated with the following pseudocode:

if (display screen window is open) {
    close the display screen window
}

Function Description: window::draw

The **window::draw** function draws a window onto the display screen. This implementation is illustrated with the following pseudocode:

5 Dynamic Window Functions

clear the window's portion of the display screen
if (border is requested) {
   draw the requested border
}

Function Description: window::open

The **window::open** function dynamically opens a display screen window. This implementation is illustrated with the following pseudocode:

allocate memory for the display screen window's contents
if (memory allocation failed) {
   abort the program
}
save the display screen window's contents
draw the display screen window
flag the window as opened
save the cursor values
move the cursor to the display screen window's upper left corner
turn off the cursor

Function Description: window::close

The **window::close** function closes a previously opened display screen window. This implementation is illustrated with the following pseudocode:

if (display screen window is open) {
   redisplay the window's former contents
   free the display screen window's memory allocation
   flag the window as closed
   restore the old cursor position
   turn on the cursor
}

Function Description: window::setcurpos

The **window::setcurpos** function sets the display screen window's cursor position. This implementation is illustrated with the following pseudocode:

if (display screen window is open) {
   save the cursor's new row position
   save the cursor's new column position
   move the cursor to its actual physical display screen position
}

Dynamic Window Functions 5

Function Description: window::cls

The **window::cls** function clears a display screen window. This implementation is illustrated with the following pseudocode:

```
if (display screen window is open) {
    clear the display screen window's interior contents
    home the display screen window's cursor
}
```

Function Description: window::clreol

Starting at the current cursor column, the **window::clreol** function clears to the end of the current cursor line. This implementation is illustrated with the following pseudocode:

```
if (display screen window is open) {
    clear the remainder of the current cursor line
}
```

Function Description: window::scroll

The **window::scroll** function scrolls the contents of a display screen window up, down, left, or right. This implementation is illustrated with the following pseudocode:

```
switch (scroll direction) {
    case up:
        scroll the display screen window up by the specified number
            of lines
    case down:
        scroll the display screen window down by the specified
            number of lines
    case left:
        scroll the display screen window left by the specified
            number of lines
    case right:
        scroll the display screen window right by the specified
            number of lines
}
if (clear the scrolled lines is requested) {
    switch (scroll direction) {
        case up:
            clear the specified number of scroll lines at the display
                screen window's bottom
```

continued...

5 Dynamic Window Functions

>   *case down:*
>   *clear the specified number of scroll lines at the display*
>   *screen window's top*
>   *case left:*
>   *clear the specified number of scroll columns at the*
>   *display screen window's right*
>   *case right:*
>   *clear the specified number of scroll columns at the*
>   *display screen window's left*
>   }
> }

Function Description: window::print

The **window::print** function displays a string at the display screen window's current cursor position. This implementation is illustrated with the following pseudocode:

```
if (display screen window is open) {
    if (scrollable display screen window) {
        offset = 0
            while (character's remain in the string) {
                counter = 0
                while (character's remain in the string && right border
                    hasn't been reached) {
                    move a character into the display string
                }
                flag the end of the display string
                adjust the offset
                display the display string
                adjust the cursor column
                if (right border has been reached) {
                    reset the cursor column
                    adjust the cursor row
                    if (bottom border has been reached) {
                        scroll the window up one line
                        adjust the cursor row
                    }
                }
                move the cursor to the end of the string + 1
            }
    }
```

continued...

```
        else {
            counter = 0
            while (characters remain in the string && the right border
                hasn't been reached) {
                move a character into the display string
            }
            flag the end of the display string
            display the display string
            adjust the cursor column
            if (right border has been reached) {
                reset the cursor column
                adjust the cursor row
                if (bottom border has been reached) {
                    adjust the cursor row
                }
            }
            set the new cursor position
        }
}
```

Function Description: window::println

The **window::println** function displays a string at the current cursor position and moves the cursor to the start of the next line. This implementation is illustrated with the following pseudocode:

```
if (display screen window is open) {
    display the string
    reset the cursor column
    adjust the cursor row
    if (bottom border has been reached) {
        if (scrollable window) {
            scroll the window's contents up one line
        }
    }
    set the new cursor position
}
```

Function Description: window::printat

The **window::printat** function displays a string at a specified display screen window position. This implementation is illustrated with the following pseudocode:

5 Dynamic Window Functions

```
if (display screen window is open) {
    set the cursor position
    display the string
}
```

Function Description: window::printlnat

The **window::printlnat** function displays a string at a specified display screen window position and moves the cursor to the start of the next line. This implementation is illustrated with the following pseudocode:

```
if (display screen window is open) {
    set the cursor position
    display the string
}
```

Function Description: window::horizontal_bar

The **window::horizontal_bar** function displays a horizontal scroll bar at the bottom of a display screen window. This implementation is illustrated with the following pseudocode:

trap any possible divide-by-zero errors
display a left arrow at the beginning of the scroll bar
display the scroll bar's body
display a right arrow at the end of the scroll bar
display the scroll character

Function Description: window::vertical_bar

The **window::vertical_bar** function displays a vertical scroll bar on the right side of a display screen window. This implementation is illustrated with the following pseudocode:

trap any possible divide-by-zero errors
display an up arrow at the scroll bar's top
display the scroll bar's body
display a down arrow at the scroll bar's bottom
display the scroll character

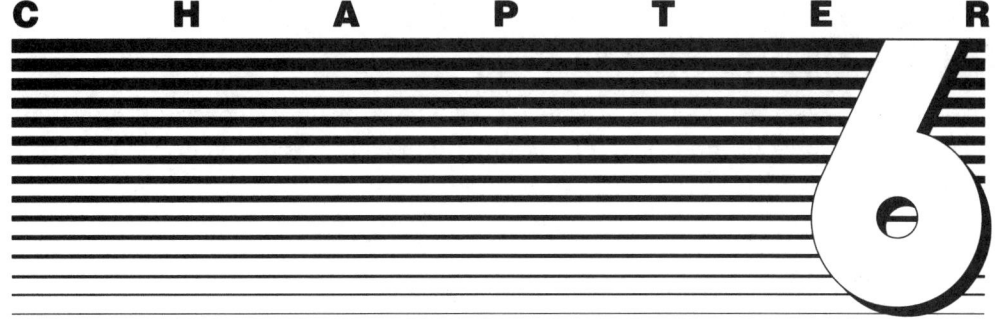

MENU FUNCTIONS

This chapter presents the GWINDOWS toolbox menu functions that implement three extremely useful menu objects: pop-up menu objects, dialog box menu objects, and pull-down menu objects. Although other menu types exist, the three supported by the GWINDOWS menu objects are the most popular menu types found in state-of-the-art application programs. These menus not only increase operator efficiency but also provide a much shorter learning curve for operators who are unfamiliar with an application program.

6 Menu Functions

SOURCE LISTING 6.1: menus.cpp

Listing 6.1, **menus.cpp**, defines a class of color objects which control the display screen appearance of the GWINDOWS menu objects. Additionally, **menus.cpp** defines a function for displaying menu-item hotstrings.

```
/************************************************************************
* menus.cpp — For the GWINDOWS Toolbox
*               General Purpose Menu Functions
************************************************************************/
#include "gwindows.hpp"

menucolors::menucolors()
{
    col = egacolor(CYAN, BLACK);
    high = egacolor(RED, WHITE);
}

menucolors::menucolors(menucolors &arg)
{
    col = arg.col;
    high = arg.high;
}

void hotstring(int row, int col, int hotkey, int color, char *string)
{
    displaystring(row, col, color, string);
    underline(row, col + hotkey, color);
}

menucolors gmenu;
```

Function Description: hotstring

The **hotstring** function displays a menu-item hotstring at a specified display screen position. This implementation is illustrated with the following pseudo-code:

display the string at the specified position
underline the hotkey character

Menu Functions 6

POP-UP MENUS

Figure 6.1 illustrates a pop-up menu's components. Essentially, a pop-up menu is a display screen window that lists a variety of possible menu selections. The following are more complete descriptions of a pop-up menu's components:

Menu Items: A pop-up menu is composed of one or more menu items.

Highlighted Menu Item: As Figure 6.1 illustrates, one of the menu's items will be highlighted. By pressing either the **UP ARROW** or **DOWN ARROW** key, the highlighting can be moved from one menu item to the next. The highlighted menu item can be selected by pressing the **ENTER** key. If available, help can be accessed by pressing the **F1** key.

Hotkeys: Each of the pop-up menu items has an associated hotkey. As Figure 6.1 shows, a menu item's hotkey character (i.e., **S** for Save, **L** for Load, and **E** for Exit) is displayed as an underlined character. A pop-up menu item can be selected simply by pressing its corresponding hotkey.

Figure 6.1 A pop-up menu.

SOURCE LISTING 6.2: popup.cpp

Listing 6.2, **popup.cpp,** presents the functions for a class of pop-up menu objects.

```
/************************************************************************
 * popup.cpp — For the GWINDOWS Toolbox
 *              Pop-up Menu Functions
 ************************************************************************/
#include <stdlib.h>
#include <string.h>
#include <ctype.h>
#include "gwindows.hpp"
```
   continued...

6 Menu Functions

```
popup::popup(int r, int c, boolean e)
{
    row = r;
    col1 = c;
    ESC_flag = e;
}

popup::popup(popup &arg)
{
    row = arg.row;
    col1 = arg.col1;
    ESC_flag = arg.ESC_flag;
}

int popup::get(int number, MENU *menu)
{
    int i, col2, key, mlen = 0, select, mrow, mcol;
    window w1;

    for (i = 0; i < number; i++)
        mlen = max(mlen, strlen(menu[i].string));
    mlen += 4;
    col2 = col1 + mlen - 1;
    w1 = window(row, col1, row + number + 1, col2, gmenu.color(),
        SINGLE_LINE);
    w1.open();
    for (i = 0; i < number; i++)
        hotstring(row + i + 1, col1 + 2, menu[i].hotkey, gmenu.color(),
            menu[i].string);
    select = 0;
    while (TRUE) {
        clearrow(row + 1 + select, col1 + 1, col2 - 1,
            background(gmenu.highlight()));
        hotstring(row + 1 + select, col1 + 2, menu[select].hotkey,
            gmenu.highlight(), menu[select].string);
        while (TRUE) {
            do {
                mouse.read();
            } while (!keypressed() && !mouse.lbutton()) ;
            if (mouse.lbutton()) {
                do {
                    mouse.read();
                } while (mouse.lbutton()) ;
```

continued...

Menu Functions 6

```
            if (mouse.row() > row && mouse.row() < row + number + 1 &&
                mouse.col() > col1 && mouse.col() < col2) {
                key = menu[mouse.row() - row - 1].string[
                    menu[mouse.row() - row - 1].hotkey];
                break;
            }
            else {
                if (ESC_flag && (mouse.row() < row ||
                    mouse.row() > row + number + 1 ||
                    mouse.col() < col1 || mouse.col() > col2)) {
                    key = 27;
                    break;
                }
            }
            continue;
        }
        key = waitkey();
        switch (key) {
            case 13:
                key = menu[select].string[menu[select].hotkey];
                break;
            case 27:
                if (!ESC_flag)
                    continue;
                break;
            case 315:
                if (menu[select].help != NULL)
                    (*menu[select].help)();
                continue;
        }
        break;
    }
    clearrow(row + 1 + select, col1 + 1, col2 - 1,
        background(gmenu.color()));
    hotstring(row + 1 + select, col1 + 2, menu[select].hotkey,
        gmenu.color(), menu[select].string);
    switch (key) {
        case 27:
            return(27);
        case 328:
            select = (--select + number) % number;
            continue;
        case 336:
            select = ++select % number;
            continue;
```

continued...

6 Menu Functions

```
                default:
                    if (key > 31 && key < 128) {
                        for (i = 0; i < number; i + +) {
                            if (toupper(key) = = toupper(menu[i].string[menu
                                [i].hotkey])) {
                                if (menu[i].function ! = NULL) {
                                    w1.close();
                                    (*menu[i].function)();
                                    return(0);
                                }
                            }
                        }
                    }
                }
            }
        }
    }
}
```

Function Description: popup::get

The **popup::get** function executes pop-up menus. This implementation is illustrated with the following pseudocode:

figure the menu's width
figure the menu's right column
open a display screen window for the menu
for (i = 0; i < number of menu items; i + +) {
    display a menu item
}
highlighted menu item = first menu item
while (TRUE) {
    display the highlighted menu item
    while (TRUE) {
        do {
            read the mouse values
        } while (key not pressed && left mouse button not pressed)
        if (left mouse button pressed) {
            do {
                read the mouse values
            } while (left mouse button not released)
            if (mouse pointer is within the pop-up menu) {
                key = pointed to menu item's hotkey character
                break
            }

    continued...

Menu Functions 6

```
        else {
            if (ESC flag && mouse is outside the pop-up menu) {
                key = ESC
                break
            }
        }
        continue
    }
    get a key
    switch (key) {
        case ENTER:
            key = highlighted menu item's hotkey
            break
        case ESC:
            if (!ESC flag) {
                continue
            }
            break
        case F1:
            if (highlighted menu item's help function != NULL) {
                call the function
            }
            continue
    }
    break
}
restore the highlighted menu item's appearance
switch (key) {
    case ESC:
        return 27
    case UP ARROW:
        move the highlighting up to the previous menu item
        continue
    case DOWN ARROW:
        move the highlighting down to the next menu item
        continue
    default:
        if (key is a printable character) {
            for (i = 0; i < number of menu items; i++) {
                if (key = menu item[i]'s hotkey) {
                    if (menu item[i]'s function != NULL) {
                        erase the menu by closing its window
                        call the function
```

continued...

```
                        return 0
                      }
                    }
                  }
                }
              }
            }
```

DIALOG BOX MENUS

Figure 6.2 illustrates a dialog box menu's components. Basically, a dialog box menu is a display screen window that displays a statement or that asks a question, or both. In response, the operator must choose from a relatively short list of menu items. The following are more complete descriptions of a dialog box menu's components:

Titles: A dialog box menu always has one or more titles. These titles are used to either display a statement or ask a question, or both.

Menu Items: In addition to the titles, a dialog box menu always will have one or more menu items.

Highlighted Menu Item: As Figure 6.2 illustrates, one of the dialog box menu's items will be highlighted. The highlighting can be moved from one menu item to the next by pressing either the **LEFT ARROW** or **RIGHT ARROW** key. The highlighted menu item can be selected by pressing the **ENTER** key. If available, help can be accessed by pressing the **F1** key.

Hotkeys: Each of the dialog box menu items has an associated hotkey. As Figure 6.2 shows, a menu item's hotkey character (i.e., **Y** for Yes, **N** for No, and **C** for Cancel) is displayed as an underlined character. A dialog box menu item is selected by simply pressing the corresponding hotkey.

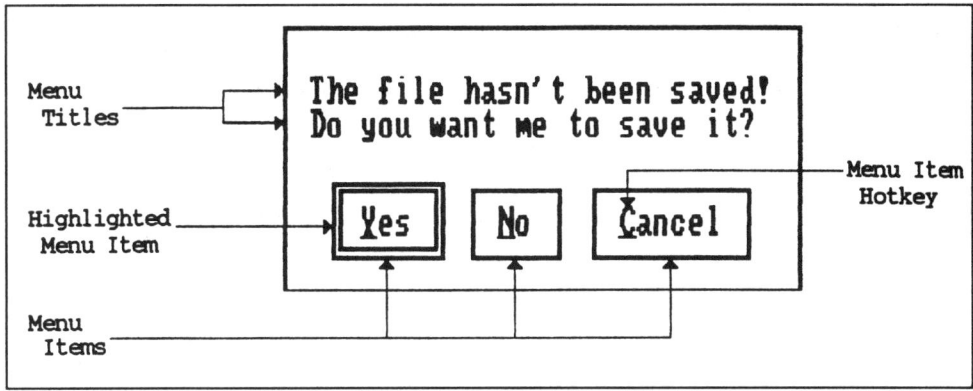

Figure 6.2 A dialog box menu.

SOURCE LISTING 6.3: dialog.cpp

Listing 6.3, **dialog.cpp**, presents the functions for a class of dialog box menu objects.

```
/************************************************************************
* dialog.cpp — For the GWINDOWS Toolbox
*                       Dialog Box Menu Functions
************************************************************************/
#include <stdlib.h>
#include <string.h>
#include <stdarg.h>
#include <ctype.h>
#include "gwindows.hpp"

dialog::dialog(int r, int c, boolean e)
{
    row = r;
    col = c;
    ESC_flag = e;
}

dialog::dialog(dialog &arg)
{
    row = arg.row;
    col = arg.col;
    ESC_flag = arg.ESC_flag;
}
```

continued...

6 Menu Functions

```
int dialog::get(int nmenus, MENU *menu, int ntitles, ...)
{
    int i, j, key, row1, col1, row2, col2, mlen = 0, chlen, select, *tabs;
    char **titles;
    window w;
    va_list arg_marker;

    titles = new char *[ntitles];
    tabs = new int[nmenus];
    va_start(arg_marker, ntitles);
    for (i = 0; i < ntitles; i++) {
        titles[i] = va_arg(arg_marker, char *);
        mlen = max(mlen, strlen(titles[i]));
    }
    chlen = nmenus - 1;
    for (i = 0; i < nmenus; i++)
        chlen += strlen(menu[i].string) + 4;
    mlen = max(mlen, chlen);
    row1 = row - (ntitles + 7) / 2;
    row2 = row1 + ntitles + 6;
    col1 = col - (mlen + 4) / 2;
    col2 = col1 + mlen + 3;
    w = window(row1, col1, row2, col2, gmenu.color(), SINGLE_LINE);
    w.open();
    for (i = 0; i < ntitles; i++)
        displaycenter(row1 + i + 2, col, gmenu.color(),
            (char *)titles[i]);
    j = col - chlen / 2;
    for (i = 0; i < nmenus; i++) {
        tabs[i] = j;
        if (!i)
            drawborder(row2 - 3, j, row2 - 1,
                j + strlen(menu[i].string) + 3,
                gmenu.color(), DOUBLE_LINE);
        else
            drawborder(row2 - 3, j, row2 - 1,
                j + strlen(menu[i].string) + 3,
                gmenu.color(), SINGLE_LINE);
        hotstring(row2 - 2, j + 2, menu[i].hotkey, gmenu.color(),
            (char *)menu[i].string);
        j += strlen(menu[i].string) + 5;
    }
```

continued...

Menu Functions 6

```
select = 0;
while (TRUE) {
    while (TRUE) {
        do {
            mouse.read();
        } while (!keypressed() && !mouse.lbutton()) ;
        if (mouse.lbutton()) {
            do {
                mouse.read();
            } while (mouse.lbutton());
            if (mouse.row() >= row2-3 && mouse.row() <= row2 - 1 &&
                mouse.col() >= col1 && mouse.col() <= col2 {
                for (i = 0; I < nmenus; i++) {
                    if (mouse.col() >= tabs[i] && mouse.col() <=
                        tabs[i] + strlen(menu[i].string) + 3)
                            break;
                }
                if (i < nmenus) {
                    key = menu[i].string[menu[i].hotkey];
                    break;
                }
                continue;
            }
            else {
                if (ESC_flag &&(mouse.row() < row1 ||mouse.row() > row2
                    || mouse.col() < col1 || mouse.col() > col2)) {
                    key = 27;
                    break;
                }
            }
        }
        else {
            key = waitkey();
            switch (key) {
                case 13:
                    key = menu[select].string[menu[select].hotkey];
                    break;
                case 27:
                    if (!ESC_flag)
                        continue;
                    break;
                case 315:
                    if (menu[select].help != NULL)
                        (*menu[select].help)();
                    continue;
            }
```

continued...

6 Menu Functions

```
                break;
            }
        }
        switch (key) {
            case 27:
                return(27);
            case 331:
                if (nmenus != 1) {
                    drawborder(row2 - 3, tabs[select], row2 - 1,
                        tabs[select] + strlen(menu[select].string) + 3,
                        gmenu.color(), SINGLE_LINE);
                    select = (--select + nmenus) % nmenus;
                    drawborder(row2 - 3, tabs[select], row2 - 1,
                        tabs[select] + strlen(menu[select].string) + 3,
                        gmenu.color(), DOUBLE_LINE);
                }
                continue;
            case 333:
                if (nmenus != 1) {
                    drawborder(row2 - 3, tabs[select], row2 - 1,
                        tabs[select] + strlen(menu[select].string) + 3,
                        gmenu.color(), SINGLE_LINE);
                    select = ++select % nmenus;
                    drawborder(row2 - 3, tabs[select], row2 - 1,
                        tabs[select] + strlen(menu[select].string) + 3,
                        gmenu.color(), DOUBLE_LINE);
                }
                continue;
            default:
                if (key > 31 && key < 128) {
                    for (i = 0; i < nmenus; i++) {
                        if (toupper(key) == toupper(menu[i].string[
                            menu[i].hotkey])) {
                            w.close();
                            delete titles;
                            delete tabs;
                            if (menu[i].function != NULL) {
                                (*menu[i].function)();
                                return(0);
                            }
                            return(toupper(key));
                        }
                    }
                }
            }
        }
    }
}
```

Function Description: dialog::get

The **dialog::get** function executes dialog box menus. This implementation is illustrated with the following pseudocode:

```
allocate memory for an array of title string pointers
allocate memory for an array of menu item tab positions
for (i = 0; i < number of titles; i++) {
    save a title pointer
}
figure the menu's width
figure the menu's top row
figure the menu's bottom row
figure the menu's right column
open up a window for the menu
for (i = 0; i < number of titles; i++) {
    display a title
}
for (i = 0; i < number of menu items; i++) {
    save the menu item's tab position
    if (first menu item) {
        draw a highlight box
    }
    else {
        draw a regular box
    }
    display the menu item
    figure the next tab position
}
highlighted menu item = first menu item
while (TRUE) {
    while (TRUE) {
        do {
            read the mouse values
        } while (key not pressed && left mouse button not pressed)
        if (left mouse button pressed) {
            do {
                read the mouse values
            } while (left mouse button not released)
            if (mouse pointer is inside the menu) {
                for (i = 0; i < number of menu items; i++) {
                    if (mouse pointer is within the menu item's box) {
                        break
                    }
                }
```

continued...

6 Menu Functions

```
                if (mouse pointer was within a menu item's box) {
                    key = pointed to menu item's hotkey character
                    break
                }
                continue
            }
            else {
                if (ESC flag && mouse pointer is outside the menu) {
                    key = ESC
                    break
                }
            }
        }
        else {
            get a key
            switch (key) {
                case ENTER:
                    key = highlighted menu item's hotkey character
                    break
                case ESC:
                    if (ESC flag) {
                        continue
                    }
                    break
                case F1:
                    if (highlighted menu item's help function != NULL) {
                        call the function
                    }
                    continue
            }
            break
        }
    }
    switch (key) {
        case ESC:
            return 27
        case LEFT ARROW:
            move the highlighting left to the previous menu item
            continue
        case RIGHT ARROW:
            move the highlighting right to the next menu item
            continue
```

continued...

Menu Functions 6

```
                default:
                    if (key is a printable character) {
                        for (i = 0; i < number of menu items; i++) {
                            if (key = menu item[i]'s hotkey) {
                                erase the menu by closing its window
                                deallocate the array of title pointers
                                deallocate the array of tab positions
                                if (menu item[i]'s function != NULL) {
                                    call the function
                                    return 0
                                }
                                return the menu item[i]'s hotkey character
                            }
                        }
                    }
                }
            }
        }
    }
}
```

PULL-DOWN MENUS

Pull-down menus are considered the best choice of menu systems among today's programmers and operators. All pull-down menu systems are composed of two basic components: the pull-down menu bar and the associated pull-down menus.

Figure 6.3 illustrates a pull-down menu bar's headings. When a heading is opened, a box similar to that of a pop-up menu appears. Figure 6.4 illustrates a typical pull-down menu. The following paragraphs further describe pull-down menus.

Pull-down Menu Bar Headings: A pull-down menu bar is made up of one or more pull-down menu headings. Essentially, a pull-down menu heading categorizes the corresponding pull-down menu items.

Each menu bar heading has an associated hotkey. As Figure 6.3 shows, a pull-down menu heading's hotkey character (i.e., **F** for File, **A** for Accounts, **T** for Transactions, and **P** for Print) is displayed as an underlined character.

6 Menu Functions

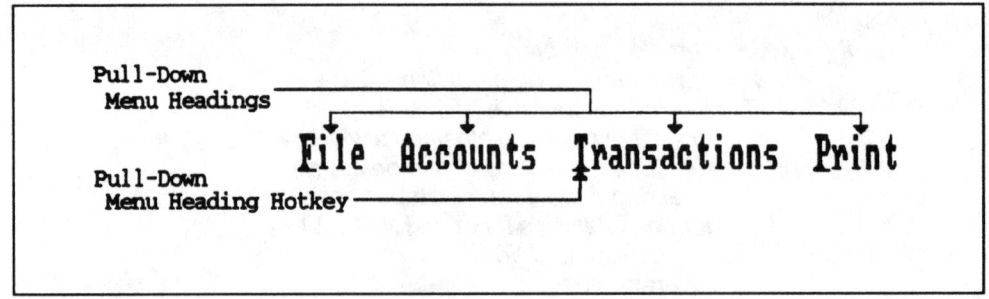

Figure 6.3   A pull-down menu bar.

Menu Items: A pull-down menu is composed of one or more menu items.

Each of the pull-down menu items also has an associated hotkey. As Figure 6.4 shows, a pull-down menu item's hotkey character (i.e., **S** for Save, **R** for Read, and **E** for Exit) is displayed as an underlined character. A menu item can be selected by simply pressing the corresponding hotkey.

Highlighted Menu Item: In Figure 6.4, one of the pull-down menu's items is highlighted. By pressing either the **UP ARROW** or **DOWN ARROW** key, the highlighting can be moved from one menu item to the next. The highlighted menu item can be selected by pressing the **ENTER** key. If available, help can be requested by pressing the **F1** key.

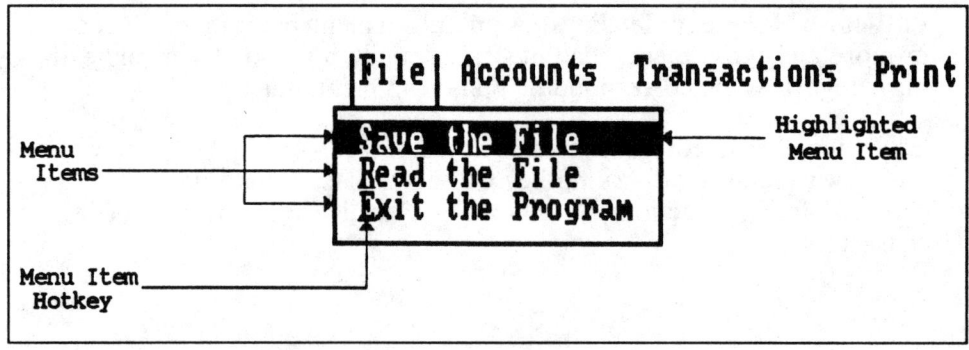

Figure 6.4   A pull-down menu.

SOURCE LISTING 6.4: pulldown.cpp

Listing 6.4, **pulldown.cpp,** presents the functions for a class of pull-down menu objects

```cpp
/************************************************************************
 * pulldown.cpp — For the GWINDOWS Toolbox
 *                          Pull-down Menu Routine
 *
 ************************************************************************/
#include <stdio.h>
#include <stdlib.h>
#include <string.h>
#include <ctype.h>
#include "gwindows.hpp"

pulldown::pulldown(int r, int n, MENU_HEAD *m, void(*m_h)(void))
{
    row = r;
    number = n;
    menus = m;
    menu_help = m_h;
    tabs = NULL;
    hotkeys = NULL;
}

pulldown::pulldown(pulldown &arg)
{
    row = arg.row;
    number = arg.number;
    menus = arg.menus;
    menu_help = arg.menu_help;
    tabs = arg.tabs;
    hotkeys = arg.hotkeys;
}

void pulldown::display(void)
{
    int i, col, crow, ccol;

    getcurpos(&crow, &ccol);
    cursoroff();
    if (tabs != NULL)
        delete tabs;
    tabs = new int[number];
    if (hotkeys != NULL)
        delete hotkeys;
```

continued...

6 Menu Functions

```
        hotkeys = new char[number + 1];
        clearrow(row, 1, 80, background(gmenu.color()));
        col = 3;
        for (i = 0; i < number; i++) {
            tabs[i] = col;
            hotkeys[i] = toupper(menus[i].heading[menus[i].hotkey]);
            hotstring(row, col, menus[i].hotkey, gmenu.color(),
                (char *)menus[i].heading);
            col += strlen(menus[i].heading) + 2;
        }
        hotkeys[number] = '0';
        setcurpos(crow, ccol);
        cursoron();
}

int pulldown::get(int ikey)
{
        int i, key, col, menu, rcol, select, crow, ccol;
        char *match;
        MENU *mptr;
        window w1;
        static char alts[27] = "QWERTYUIOPASDFGHJKLZXCVBNM";

        getcurpos(&crow, &ccol);
        if (!ikey) {
            while (TRUE) {
                do {
                    mouse.read();
                } while (!keypressed() && !mouse.lbutton()) ;
                if (mouse.lbutton()) {
                    do {
                        mouse.read();
                    } while (mouse.lbutton()) ;
                    if (mouse.row() != row)
                        continue;
                    for (i = 0; i < number; i++) {
                        if (mouse.col() >= tabs[i] &&
                            mouse.col() < tabs[i] + strlen(menus[i].heading)) {
                                key = i + 512;
                                break;
                        }
                    }
                    if (i < number)
                        break;
                }
```
continued...

Menu Functions 6

```
                else {
                    key = waitkey();
                    break;
                }
            }
        }
        else
            key = ikey;
        if (menu_help != NULL && key == 315) {
            cursoroff();
            (*menu_help)();
            setcurpos(crow, ccol);
            cursoron();
            return(0);
        }
        if (key >= 272 && key <= 281
            menu = alts[key - 272];
        else {
            if (key >= 286 && key <= 294)
                menu = alts[key - 276];
            else {
                if (key >= 300 && key <= 306)
                    menu = alts[key - 281];
                else {
                    if (key < 512)
                        return(key);
                }
            }
        }
        if (key >= 512)
            menu = key - 512;
        else {
            if (!(match = strchr(hotkeys, menu)))
                return(key);
            else
                menu = match - hotkeys;
        }
        cursoroff();
        while (TRUE) {
            mptr = menus[menu].mptr;
            if (menus[menu].number == 1) {
                if (mptr[0].function != NULL)
                    (mptr[0].function)();
                setcurpos(crow, ccol);
                cursoron();
                return(0);
```
    continued...

6 Menu Functions

```
    }
    mptr = menus[menu].mptr;
    col = tabs[menu];
    rcol = strlen(menus[menu].heading);
    for (i = 0; i < menus[menu].number; i++)
        rcol = max(rcol, strlen(mptr[i].string));
    rcol += col + 1;
    w1 = window(row + 1, col - 2, row + 2 + menus[menu].number,
        rcol, gmenu.color(), SINGLE_LINE);
    w1.open();
    displaychar(row, col - 1, gmenu.color(), 0xb3);
    displaychar(row, col + strlen(menus[menu].heading), gmenu.color(),
        0xb3);
    displaychar(row + 1, col - 1, gmenu.color(), 0xc1);
    displaychar(row + 1, col + strlen(menus[menu].heading), gmenu.color(),
        0xc1);
    for (i = 0; i < menus[menu].number; i++)
        hotstring(row + 2 + i, col, mptr[i].hotkey, gmenu.color(),
            mptr[i].string);
    select = 0;
    while (TRUE) {
        clearrow(row + 2 + select, col - 1, rcol - 1,
            background(gmenu.highlight()));
        hotstring(row + 2 + select, col, mptr[select].hotkey,
            gmenu.highlight(), mptr[select].string);
        while (TRUE) {
            do {
                mouse.read();
            } while (!keypressed() && !mouse.lbutton()) ;
            if (mouse.lbutton()) {
                do {
                    mouse.read();
                } while (mouse.lbutton()) ;
                if (mouse.row() == row) {
                    for (i = 0; i < number; i++) {
                        if (mouse.col() >= tabs[i] &&
                            mouse.col() <= tabs[i] + strlen(
                                menus[i].heading)) {
                                key = i + 512;
                                break;
                        }
                    }
                    if (i != number)
                        break;
                }
```

continued...

Menu Functions 6

```
            else {
                if (mouse.row() > row + 1 && mouse.row() < row + 2 +
                    menus[menu].number && mouse.col() > col - 2 &&
                    mouse.col() < rcol) {
                        key = mptr[mouse.row() - row - 2].string[
                            mptr[mouse.row() - row - 2].hotkey];
                        break;
                }
                if (mouse.row() < row + 1 || mouse.row() > row + 2 +
                    menus[menu].number || mouse.col() > col - 2 ||
                    mouse.col() < rcol) {
                        key = 27;
                        break;
                }
            }
        }
        else {
            key = waitkey();
            switch (key) {
                case 13:
                    key = mptr[select].string[mptr[select].hotkey];
                    break;
                case 315:
                    if (mptr[select].help != NULL)
                        (*mptr[select].help)();
                    continue;
            }
            break;
        }
    }
    clearrow(row + 2 + select, col - 1, rcol - 1,
        background(gmenu.color()));
    hotstring(row + 2 + select, col, mptr[select].hotkey,
        gmenu.color(), mptr[select].string);
    if (key > = 512) {
        w1.close();
        displaychar(row, col - 1, gmenu.color(), ' ');
        displaychar(row, col + strlen(menus[menu].heading),
            gmenu.color(), ' ');
        menu = key - 512;
        break;
    }
```

continued...

6 Menu Functions

```c
      else {
        switch (key) {
          case 27:
            w1.close();
            displaychar(row, col - 1, gmenu.color(), ' ');
            displaychar(row,col+strlen(menus[menu].heading),
                gmenu.color(), ' ');
            setcurpos(crow, ccol);
            cursoron();
            return(0);
          case 328:
            select = (--select + menus[menu].number) %
                menus[menu].number;
            continue;
          case 331:
            w1.close();
            displaychar(row, col - 1, gmenu.color(), ' ');
            displaychar(row,col+strlen(menus[menu].heading),
                gmenu.color(), ' ');
            do {
              menu = (--menu + number) % number;
            } while (menus[menu].number = = 1);
            break;
          case 333:
            w1.close();
            displaychar(row, col - 1, gmenu.color(), ' ');
            displaychar(row,col+strlen(menus[menu].heading),
                gmenu.color(), ' ');
            do {
              menu = + +menu % number;
            } while (menus[menu].number = = 1);
            break;
          case 336:
            select = + +select % menus[menu].number;
            continue;
          default:
            if (key > 31 && key < 128) {
              for (i = 0; i < menus[menu].number; i+ +) {
                if(toupper(key) = =toupper(mptr[i].string[
                    mptr[i].hotkey])) {
                  w1.close();
                  displaychar(row,col-1,gmenu.color(), ' ');
                  displaychar(row, col +
                      strlen(menus[menu].heading),
                      gmenu.color(), ' ');
```

continued...

```
                            if (mptr[i].function != NULL)
                                (*mptr[i].function)();
                            setcurpos(crow, ccol);
                            cursoron();
                            return(0);
                        }
                    }
                }
                continue;
            }
        }
        break;
    }
}
```

Function Description: pulldown::display

The **pulldown::display** function, displays pull-down menu bars. This implementation is illustrated with the following pseudocode:

```
save the cursor values
turn off the cursor
if (array of tab positions has already been allocated) {
    deallocate the array of tab positions
}
allocate memory for an array of tab positions
if (string of hotkeys has already been allocated) {
    deallocate the string of hotkeys
}
allocate memory for a string of hotkeys
clear the menu bar's row
for (i = 0; i < number of headings; i++) {
    save the heading's tab position
    save the heading's hotkey character
    display the heading
    figure the next tab position
}
flag the end of the string of hotkeys
restore the cursor position
turn on the cursor
```

Function Description: pulldown::get

The **pulldown::get** function executes a pull-down menu system. This implementation is illustrated with the following pseudocode:

6 Menu Functions

```
save the cursor values
if (an initial key wasn't pressed) {
    while (TRUE) {
        do {
            read the mouse values
        } while (key not pressed && left mouse button not pressed)
        if (left mouse button pressed) {
            do {
                read the mouse values
            } while (left mouse button not released)
            if (mouse pointer isn't in the menu bar row) {
                continue
            }
            for (i = 0; i < number of headings; i++) {
                if (mouse pointer is pointing to menu heading[i]) {
                    key = i + 512
                    break
                }
            }
            if (menu heading was selected) {
                break
            }
        }
        else {
            get a key
            break
        }
    }
}
else {
    key = initial key
}
if (overall help function != NULL and key = F1) {
    turn off the cursor
    call the help function
    restore the cursor position
    turn on the cursor
    return 0
}
if (key isn't an ALT key && mouse wasn't used) {
    return the key
}
if (heading was selected with the mouse) {
    menu = mouse menu
}
        continued...
```

```
    else {
        if (key isn't a heading hotkey) {
            return the key
        }
        else {
            menu = hotkey menu
        }
    }
}
turn off the cursor
while (TRUE) {
    if (number of menu items = 1) {
        if (menu item[0]'s function != NULL) {
            call the function
        }
        restore the cursor position
        turn on the cursor
        return 0
    }
    figure the menu's width
    open a window for the menu
    draw the menu's frame
    for (i = 0; i < number of menu items; i++) {
        display a menu item
    }
    highlighted menu item = first menu item
    while (TRUE) {
        highlight the highlighted menu item
        while (TRUE) {
            do {
                read the mouse values
            } while (key not pressed && left mouse button not pressed)
            if (left mouse button pressed) {
                do {
                    read mouse values
                } while (left mouse button not released)
                if (mouse pointer is in the menu bar row) {
                    for (i = 0; i < number of headings; i++) {
                        if (mouse pointer is pointing to menu heading[i]) {
                            key = i + 512
                            break
                        }
                    }
                    if (menu heading was selected) {
                        break
                    }
                }
            }
    continued...
```

6 Menu Functions

```
            else {
                if (mouse pointer is inside the menu) {
                    key = pointed to menu item's hotkey character
                    break
                }
                if (mouse pointer is outside the menu) {
                    key = ESC
                    break
                }
            }
        }
        else {
            get a key
            switch (key) {
                case ENTER:
                    key = highlighted menu item's hotkey character
                    break
                case F1:
                    if(highlighted menu item's help function != NULL){
                        call the function
                        continue
                    }
            }
            break
        }
    }
    restore the highlighted menu item
    if (a new menu was selected by the mouse) {
        menu = mouse menu
        erase the pull-down menu
        break
    }
    else {
        switch (key) {
            case ESC:
                erase the pulldown menu
                restore the cursor position
                turn on the cursor
                return 0
            case UP ARROW:
                move the highlighting up to the previous menu item
                continue
            case LEFT ARROW:
                erase the pull-down menu
                heading hotkey = previous heading's hotkey
                break
```
continued...

```
                case RIGHT ARROW:
                    erase the pull-down menu
                    heading hotkey = next heading's hotkey
                    break
                case DOWN ARROW:
                    move the highlighting down to the next menu item
                    continue
                default:
                    if (key is a printable character) {
                        for (i = 0; i < number of menu items; i++) {
                            if (key = menu item[i]'s hotkey) {
                                erase the pull-down menu
                                if (menu item[i]'s function != NULL) {
                                    call the function
                                }
                                restore the cursor position
                                turn on the cursor
                                return 0
                            }
                        }
                    }
                    continue
                }
            }
            break
        }
    }
```

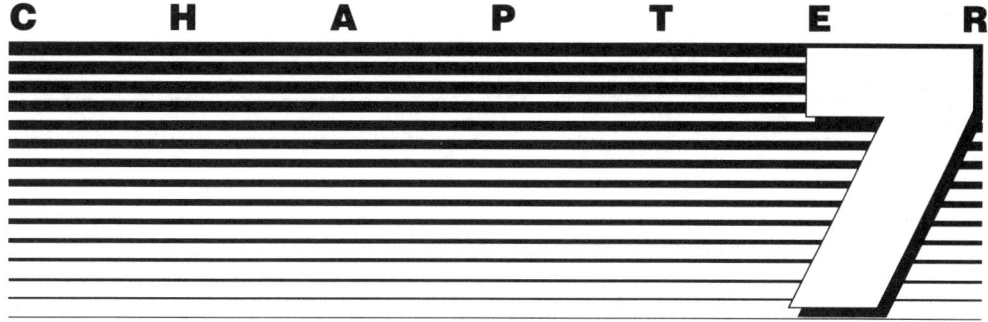

GWINDOWS DATA ENTRY FUNCTIONS

This chapter presents data entry functions for displaying and retrieving a variety of data types including: dates, dollar values, numeric values, telephone numbers, Social Security numbers, and strings.

To fulfill the data entry requirements of today's modern graphical user interface, the GWINDOWS toolbox provides six basic formatted input functions including: dates, dollar values, numeric data, telephone numbers, Social Security numbers, and generic string data. By using these formatted input functions as basic building blocks, application programmers can quickly build complex data entry screens. Besides data entry functions, the GWINDOWS toolbox provides corresponding data display functions for displaying data fields on the display screen.

7 GWINDOWS Data Entry Functions

SOURCE LISTING 7.1: idate.cpp

Listing 7.1, **idate.cpp,** presents functions for displaying dates, retrieving dates, and building date strings.

```
/************************************************************************
* idate.cpp  — For the GWINDOWS Toolbox
*                     Formatted Date Functions
************************************************************************/
#include <stdio.h>
#include <stdlib.h>
#include "gwindows.hpp"

char *date_string(char *string, date &date)
{
    sprintf(string, "%02d/%02d/%02d", date.month % 100, date.day % 100,
        date.year % 100);
    return(string);
}

static int date_func(boolean flag, int row, int col, int color, date &date)
{
    int cpos = 0, key;
    char field[9];

    date_string(field, date);
    while (TRUE) {
        displaystring(row, col, color, field);
        if (!flag)
            return(0);
        setcurpos(row, col + cpos);
        cursorcolor(color & 0xff);
        ucursoron();
        key = waitkey();
        ucursoroff();
        switch (key) {
            case 47:
                continue;
            case 327:
                cpos = 0;
                continue;
            case 8:
            case 331:
                switch (cpos) {
                    case 1:
```
continued...

```
                case 4:
                case 7:
                    cpos--;
                    break;
                case 3:
                case 6:
                    cpos -= 2;
            }
            continue;
        case 333:
            switch (cpos) {
                case 0:
                case 3:
                case 6:
                    cpos++;
                    break;
                case 1:
                case 4:
                    cpos += 2;
            }
            continue;
        case 335:
            cpos = 7;
            continue;
        default:
            if (key >= 48 && key <= 57) {
                field[cpos] = key;
                switch (cpos) {
                    case 0:
                    case 3:
                    case 6:
                        cpos++;
                        break;
                    case 1:
                    case 4:
                        cpos += 2;
                }
                continue;
            }
            date.month = atoi(field);
            date.day = atoi(field + 3);
            date.year = atoi(field + 6);
            return(key);
        }
    }
}
```

continued...

7 GWINDOWS Data Entry Functions

```
void display_date(int row, int col, int color, date &date)
{
    date_func(FALSE, row, col, color, date);
}

int input_date(int row, int col, int color, date &date)
{
    return(date_func(TRUE, row, col, color, date));
}
```

Function Description: date_string

The **date_string** function builds date strings. This implementation is illustrated with the following pseudocode:

build the date string
return a pointer to the string

Function Description: date_func

The **date_func** function is used internally by the **display_date** and **input_date** functions to display and to retrieve dates. This implementation is illustrated with the following pseudocode:

field = date string
while (TRUE) {
    display field
    *if (called by **display_date**) {*
        return 0
    }
    move the cursor to the current character position
    set the cursor color
    turn on the cursor
    get a key
    turn off the cursor
    switch (key) {
        case /:
            continue
        *case **HOME**:*
            current character position = 0
            continue
        *case **BACKSPACE**:*

continued...

```
        case LEFT ARROW:
            switch (current character position) {
                case 1:
                case 4:
                case 7:
                    current character position--
                    break
                case 3:
                case 6:
                    current character position -= 2
            }
            continue
        case RIGHT ARROW:
            switch (current character position) {
                case 0:
                case 3:
                case 6:
                    current character position++
                    break
                case 1:
                case 4:
                    current character position += 2
            }
            continue
        case END:
            current character position = 7
            continue
        default:
            if (key is numeric) {
                field[current character position] = key
                switch (current character position) {
                    case 0:
                    case 3:
                    case 6:
                        current character position++
                        break
                    case 1:
                    case 4:
                        current character position += 2
                }
                continue
            }
    }
    save the date's month
    save the date's day
    save the date's year
    return the key
}
}
```

7 GWINDOWS Data Entry Functions

Function Description: display_date

The **display_date** function displays dates. This implementation is illustrated with the following pseudocode:

display the date

Function Description: input_date

The **input_date** function retrieves dates. This implementation is illustrated with the following pseudocode:

retrieve the date
return the last key pressed

SOURCE LISTING 7.2: idollar.cpp

Listing 7.2, **idollar.cpp**, presents the functions for displaying and for retrieving dollar values.

```
/*************************************************************************
* idollar.cpp - For the GWINDOWS Toolbox
*               Formatted Dollar Functions
*************************************************************************/
#include <stdio.h>
#include <stdlib.h>
#include <string.h>
#include "gwindows.hpp"

static int dollar_func(boolean flag, int row, int col, int length, int color,
    double &value)
{
    int i, d_cnt = 2, key;
    boolean d_flag = TRUE, s_flag = FALSE;
    char field[81];

    if (value > -.01 && value < .01)
        value = 0;
    if (value < 0)
        s_flag = TRUE;
    sprintf(field, "%*.2f", length, value);
    if (field[length - 1] == '0' && field[length - 2] == '0')
        d_flag = FALSE;

    continued...
```

GWINDOWS Data Entry Functions 7

```
while (TRUE) {
    sprintf(field, "%*.2f", length, value);
    if (value = = 0 && s_flag)
        field[length - 5] = '-';
    else {
        if (strlen(field) > length) {
            for (i = 0; i < length; i++)
                field[i] = '*';
            field[length] = 0;
        }
    }
    displaystring(row, col, color, field);
    if (!flag)
        return(0);
    if (d_flag)
        if (d_cnt)
            setcurpos(row, col + length - 1);
        else
            setcurpos(row, col + length - 2);
    else
        setcurpos(row, col + length - 4);
    cursorcolor(color & 0xff);
    ucursoron();
    key = waitkey();
    ucursoroff();
    switch (key) {
        case 8:
            if (d_flag) {
                switch (d_cnt) {
                    case 0:
                        d_flag = FALSE;
                        break;
                    default:
                        field[length + d_cnt - 3] = '0';
                        value = atof(field);
                        d_cnt--;
                }
            }
            else {
                field[length - 4] = '0';
                value = atof(field);
                value /= 10;
                sprintf(field, "%*.2f", length, value);
                value = atof(field);
            }
```

continued...

153

7 GWINDOWS Data Entry Functions

```
                if (!value)
                    s_flag = FALSE;
                continue;
            case 46:
                if (!d_flag) {
                    d_flag = TRUE;
                    d_cnt = 0;
                }
                continue;
            case 45:
                value = -value;
                s_flag = !s_flag;
                continue;
            case 327:
                value = 0;
                d_flag = s_flag = FALSE;
                continue;
            default:
                if (key > = 48 && key < = 57) {
                    if (d_flag) {
                        switch (d_cnt) {
                            case 0:
                                field[length - 2] = key;
                                value = atof(field);
                                d_cnt + +;
                                break;
                            case 1:
                                field[length - 1] = key;
                                value = atof(field);
                                d_cnt + +;
                        }
                    }
                    else {
                        if (field[1] = = ' ' || field[1] = = '-') {
                            strncpy(field, field + 1, length - 4);
                            field[length - 4] = key;
                            value = atof(field);
                        }
                    }
                    if (value > = 0 && s_flag)
                        value = -value;
                }
                else
                    return(key);
        }
    }
}
    continued...
```

154

```
void display_dollar(int row, int col, int length, int color, double &value)
{
    dollar_func(FALSE, row, col, length, color, value);
}

int input_dollar(int row, int col, int length, int color, double &value)
{
    return(dollar_func(TRUE, row, col, length, color, value));
}
```

Function Description: dollar_func

The **dollar_func** function is used internally by the **display_dollar** and **input_dollar** functions respectively to display and retrieve dollar values. This implementation is illustrated with the following pseudocode:

```
if (dollar value > -.01 && dollar value < .01) {
    dollar value = 0
}
if (dollar value is negative) {
    sign flag = TRUE
}
field = dollar value string
if (last two characters = "00") {
    decimal flag = FALSE
}
while (TRUE) {
    field = dollar value string
    if (dollar value = 0 && dollar value is negative) {
        field = "-0.00"
    }
    else {
        if (field is too long) {
            set field to all "*"
        }
    }
    display the dollar value
    if (called by display_dollar) {
        return 0
    }
    position the cursor
    set the cursor color
    turn on the cursor
    get a key
    turn off the cursor
    switch (key) {
      continued...
```

7 GWINDOWS Data Entry Functions

```
case BACKSPACE:
    if (decimal flag) {
        switch (decimal count) {
            case 0:
                decimal flag = FALSE
                break
            default:
                last decimal character = '0'
                decimal value = atof(field)
                decimal count--
        }
    }
    else {
        one's place digit = '0'
        dollar value = atof(field) /10
        round the value
    }
    if (dollar value = 0) {
        sign flag = FALSE
    }
    continue
case .:
    if (!decimal flag) {
        decimal flag = TRUE
        decimal count = 0
    }
    continue
case HOME:
    dollar value = 0
    decimal flag = FALSE
    sign flag = FALSE
    continue
default:
    if (key is numeric) {
        if (decimal flag) {
            switch (decimal count) {
                case 0:
                    save the tenth's place digit
                    dollar value = atof(field)
                    decimal count + +
                    break
                case 1:
                    save the hundredth's place digit
                    dollar value = atof(field)
                    decimal count + +
            }
        }
continued...
```

```
        else {
            if (data entry field isn't full) {
                save the key as the new one's place digit
                dollar value = atof(field)
            }
        }
        if (dollar value is positive & sign flag = FALSE) {
            dollar value = -dollar value
        }
        else {
            return the key
        }
      }
    }
}
```

Function Description: display_dollar

The **display_dollar** function displays dollar values. This implementation is illustrated with the following pseudocode:

display the dollar value

Function Description: input_dollar

The **input_dollar** function retrieves dollar values. This implementation is illustrated with the following pseudocode:

retrieve the dollar value
return the last key pressed

SOURCE LISTING 7.3: inumber.cpp

Listing 7.3, **inumber.cpp**, presents the functions for displaying and for retrieving numeric values.

```
/***********************************************************************
* inumber.cpp - For the GWINDOWS Toolbox
*                   Formatted Number Functions
***********************************************************************/
#include <stdio.h>
#include <stdlib.h>
#include <string.h>
#include "gwindows.hpp"
```

continued...

7 GWINDOWS Data Entry Functions

```c
static int number_func(boolean flag, int row, int col, int length, int color,
    unsigned long &value)
{
    int i, key;
    char field[81];

    while (TRUE) {
        if (value) {
            sprintf(field, "%*lu", length, value);
            if (strlen(field) > length) {
                for (i = 0; i < length; i++)
                    field[i] = '*';
                field[length] = '\0';
            }
        }
        else
            sprintf(field, "%*s", length, "");
        displaystring(row, col, color, field);
        if (!flag)
            return(0);
        setcurpos(row, col + length - 1);
        cursorcolor(color & 0xff);
        ucursoron();
        key = waitkey();
        ucursoroff();
        switch (key) {
            case 8:
                field[length - 1] = '0';
                value = atol(field) / 10;
                continue;
            case 327:
                value = 0;
                continue;
            default:
                if (key >= 48 && key <= 57) {
                    if (field[0] == ' ')
                        value = value * 10 + (key - 48);
                    continue;
                }
                return(key);
        }
    }
}

void display_number(int row, int col, int length, int color,
    unsigned long &value)
{
```

continued...

```
    number_func(FALSE, row, col, length, color, value);
}

int input_number(int row, int col, int length, int color,
    unsigned long &value)
{
    return(number_func(TRUE, row, col, length, color, value));
}
```

Function Description: number_func

The **number_func** function is used internally by the **display_number** and **input_number** functions respectively to display and retrieve numeric values. This implementation is illustrated with the following pseudocode:

```
while (TRUE) {
    if (numeric value != 0) {
        field = numeric value string
        if (field is too long) {
            set the field to all '*'
        }
    }
    else {
        field = all spaces
    }
    display the numeric value string
    if (called by display_number) {
        return 0
    }
    move the cursor to the last character position
    set the cursor color
    turn on the cursor
    get a key
    turn off the cursor
    switch (key) {
        case BACKSPACE:
            set the one's place digit to '0'
            numeric value = atol(field) / 10
            continue
        case HOME:
            numeric value = 0
            continue
        default:
            if (key is numeric) {
                if (data entry field isn't full) {
                    numeric value = numeric value * 10 + (key - '0')
```

continued...

7 GWINDOWS Data Entry Functions

```
            }
                continue
        }
            return the key
    }
}
```

Function Description: display_number

The **display_number** function displays numeric values. This implementation is illustrated with the following pseudocode:

display the numeric value

Function Description: input_number

The **input_number** function retrieves numeric values. This implementation is illustrated with the following pseudocode:

retrieve the numeric value
return the last key pressed

SOURCE LISTING 7.4: iphone.cpp

Listing 7.4, **iphone.cpp**, presents functions to display phone numbers and to retrieve phone numbers, as well as building phone number strings.

```
/************************************************************************
* iphone.cpp - For the GWINDOWS Toolbox
*                  Formatted Phone Number Functions
************************************************************************/
#include <stdio.h>
#include <stdlib.h>
#include <string.h>
#include "gwindows.hpp"

char *phone_string(char *string, phone &pn)
{
    sprintf(string, "(%03d) %03d-%04d", pn.area % 1000, pn.exchange % 1000,
        pn.no % 10000);
    return(string);
}
```

continued...

GWINDOWS Data Entry Functions 7

```
static int phone_func(boolean flag, int row, int col, int color, phone &pn)
{
    int cpos = 1, key;
    char field[15];

    phone_string(field, pn);
    while (TRUE) {
        displaystring(row, col, color, field);
        if (!flag)
            return(0);
        setcurpos(row, col + cpos);
        cursorcolor(color & 0xff);
        ucursoron();
        key = waitkey();
        ucursoroff();
        switch (key) {
            case 327:
                cpos = 1;
                continue;
            case 8:
            case 331:
                switch (cpos) {
                    case 2:
                    case 3:
                    case 7:
                    case 8:
                    case 11:
                    case 12:
                    case 13:
                        cpos--;
                        continue;
                    case 6:
                        cpos = 3;
                        continue;
                    case 10:
                        cpos = 8;
                };
                continue;
            case 333:
                switch (cpos) {
                    case 1:
                    case 2:
                    case 6:
                    case 7:
                    case 10:
                    case 11:
```
continued...

7 GWINDOWS Data Entry Functions

```
                    case 12:
                        cpos++;
                        continue;
                    case 3:
                        cpos = 6;
                        continue;
                    case 8:
                        cpos = 10;
                }
                continue;
            case 335:
                cpos = 13;
                continue;
            default:
                if (key >= 48 && key <= 57) {
                    field[cpos] = key;
                    switch (cpos) {
                        case 1:
                        case 2:
                        case 6:
                        case 7:
                        case 10:
                        case 11:
                        case 12:
                            cpos++;
                            continue;
                        case 3:
                            cpos = 6;
                            continue;
                        case 8:
                            cpos = 10;
                    }
                    continue;
                }
                pn.area = atoi(field + 1);
                pn.exchange = atoi(field + 6);
                pn.no = atoi(field + 10);
                return(key);
        }
    }
}

void display_phone(int row, int col, int color, phone &pn)
{
    phone_func(FALSE, row, col, color, pn);
}
```

continued...

```
int input_phone(int row, int col, int color, phone &pn)
{
    return(phone_func(TRUE, row, col, color, pn));
}
```

Function Description: phone_string

The **phone_string** function builds phone number strings. This implementation is illustrated with the following pseudocode:

build the phone number string
return a pointer to the string

Function Description: phone_func

The **phone_func** function is used internally by the **display_phone** and **input_phone** functions respectively to display and retrieve phone numbers. This implementation is illustrated with the following pseudocode:

field = phone number string
while (TRUE) {
    display field
    *if (called by **display_phone**) {*
        return 0
    }
    move the cursor to the current character position
    set the cursor color
    turn on the cursor
    get a key
    turn off the cursor
    switch (key) {
        *case **HOME**:*
            current character position = 1
            continue
        *case **BACKSPACE**:*
        *case **LEFT ARROW**:*
            switch (current character position) {
                case 2:
                case 3:
                case 7:
                case 8:
                case 11:
                case 12:
                case 13:
                      current character position--
                      continue

continued...

7 GWINDOWS Data Entry Functions

```
            case 6:
                current character position = 3
                continue
            case 10:
                current character position = 8
        }
        continue
    case RIGHT ARROW:
        switch (current character position) {
            case 1:
            case 2:
            case 6:
            case 7:
            case 10:
            case 11:
            case 12:
                current character position++
                continue
            case 3:
                current character position = 6
                continue
            case 8:
                current character position = 10
        }
        continue
    case END:
        current character position = 13
        continue
    default:
        if (key is numeric) {
            field[current character position] = key
            switch (current character position) {
                case 1:
                case 2:
                case 6:
                case 7:
                case 10:
                case 11:
                case 12:
                    current character position++
                    continue
                case 3:
                    current character position = 6
                    continue
                case 8:
                    current character position = 10
```

continued...

                }
                    continue
            }
            save the phone number's area code
            save the phone number's exchange
            save the phone number's number
            return the key
        }
}

Function Description: display_phone

The **display_phone** function displays phone numbers. This implementation is illustrated with the following pseudocode:

display the phone number

Function Description: input_phone

The **input_phone** function retrieves phone numbers. This implementation is illustrated with the following pseudocode:

retrieve the phone number
return the last key pressed

SOURCE LISTING 7.5: issn.cpp

Listing 7.5, **issn.cpp**, presents the routines for displaying and for retrieving Social Security numbers, as well as building Social Security number strings.

```
/************************************************************************
 * issn.cpp - For the GWINDOWS Toolbox
 *              Formatted Social Security Number Functions
 ************************************************************************/
#include <stdio.h>
#include <stdlib.h>
#include <string.h>
#include "gwindows.hpp"

char *ssn_string(char *string, ssn &ssn)
{
    sprintf(string,"%03d-%02d-%04d",ssn.no1%1000,ssn.no2%100,
        ssn.no3 % 10000);
    return(string);
}
```
    continued...

7 GWINDOWS Data Entry Functions

```
static int ssn_func(boolean flag, int row, int col, int color, ssn &ssn)
{
    int cpos = 0, key;
    char field[12];

    ssn_string(field, ssn);
    while (TRUE) {
        displaystring(row, col, color, field);
        if (!flag)
            return(0);
        setcurpos(row, col + cpos);
        cursorcolor(color & 0xff);
        ucursoron();
        key = waitkey();
        ucursoroff();
        switch (key) {
            case 45:
                continue;
            case 327:
                cpos = 0;
                continue;
            case 8:
            case 331:
                switch (cpos) {
                    case 1:
                    case 2:
                    case 5:
                    case 8:
                    case 9:
                    case 10:
                        cpos--;
                        continue;
                    case 4:
                    case 7:
                        cpos -= 2;
                }
                continue;
            case 333:
                switch (cpos) {
                    case 0:
                    case 1:
                    case 4:
                    case 7:
                    case 8:
                    case 9:
                        cpos++;
                        continue;
```

continued...

```
                    case 2:
                    case 5:
                        cpos + = 2;
                }
                continue;
            case 335:
                cpos = 10;
                continue;
            default:
                if (key > = 48 && key < = 57) {
                    field[cpos] = key;
                    switch (cpos) {
                        case 0:
                        case 1:
                        case 4:
                        case 7:
                        case 8:
                        case 9:
                            cpos + +;
                            continue;
                        case 2:
                        case 5:
                            cpos + = 2;
                    }
                    continue;
                }
                ssn.no1 = atoi(field);
                ssn.no2 = atoi(field + 4);
                ssn.no3 = atoi(field + 7);
                return(key);
        }
    }
}

void display_ssn(int row, int col, int color, ssn &ssn)
{
    ssn_func(FALSE, row, col, color, ssn);
}

int input_ssn(int row, int col, int color, ssn &ssn)
{
    return(ssn_func(TRUE, row, col, color, ssn));
}
```

7 GWINDOWS Data Entry Functions

Function Description: ssn_string

The **ssn_string** function builds Social Security number strings. This implementation is illustrated with the following pseudocode:

build the Social Security number string
return a pointer to the string

Function Description: ssn_func

The **ssn_func** function is used internally by the **display_ssn** and **input_ssn** functions to display and to retrieve Social Security numbers. This implementation is illustrated with the following pseudocode:

field = Social Security number string
while (TRUE) {
    display field
    *if (called by **display_ssn**) {*
        return 0
    }
    move the cursor to the current character position
    set the cursor color
    turn on the cursor
    get a key
    turn off the cursor
    switch (key) {
        case -:
            continue
        *case **HOME**:*
            current character position = 0
            continue
        *case **BACKSPACE**:*
        *case **LEFT ARROW**:*
            switch (current character position) {
                case 1:
                case 2:
                case 5:
                case 8:
                case 9:
                case 10:
                      current character position--
                    continue
                case 4:
                case 7:
                    current character position -= 2
            }
            continue

continued...

GWINDOWS Data Entry Functions 7

```
            case RIGHT ARROW:
                switch (current character position) {
                    case 0:
                    case 1:
                    case 4:
                    case 7:
                    case 8:
                    case 9:
                        current character position + +
                        continue
                    case 2:
                    case 5:
                        current character position + = 2
                }
                continue
            case END:
                current character position = 10
                continue
            default:
                if (key is numeric) {
                    field[current character position] = key
                    switch (current character position) {
                        case 0:
                        case 1:
                        case 4:
                        case 7:
                        case 8:
                        case 9:
                            current character position + +
                            continue
                        case 2:
                        case 5:
                            current character position + = 2
                    }
                    continue
                }
                save the Social Security number's first three digits
                save the Social Security number's middle two digits
                save the Social Security number's last four digits
                return the key
        }
    }
```

7 GWINDOWS Data Entry Functions

Function Description: display_ssn

The **display_ssn** function displays Social Security numbers. This implementation is illustrated with the following pseudocode:

display the Social Security number

Function Description: input_ssn

The **input_ssn** function retrieves Social Security numbers. This implementation is illustrated with the following pseudocode:

retrieve the Social Security number
return the last key pressed

SOURCE LISTING 7.6: istring.cpp

Listing 7.6, **istring.cpp**, presents functions for displaying and for retrieving strings.

```
/************************************************************************
* istring.cpp - For the GWINDOWS Toolbox
*                    Formatted String Input Routines
************************************************************************/
#include <stdio.h>
#include <stdlib.h>
#include <string.h>
#include "gwindows.hpp"

static int string_func(boolean flag, int row, int col, int length, int color,
    char *string)
{
    int i, key;
    char field[81];

    if (strlen(string) > length)
        string[length] = '\0';
    while (TRUE) {
        sprintf(field, "%-*s", length, string);
        displaystring(row, col, color, field);
        if (!flag)
            return(0);

    continued...
```

```
            setcurpos(row, col + strlen(string) - (strlen(string) = = length));
            cursorcolor(color & 0xff);
            ucursoron();
            key = waitkey();
            ucursoroff();
            switch (key) {
                case 8:
                    if (strlen(string))
                        string[strlen(string) - 1] = '\0';
                    continue;
                case 327:
                    string[0] = '\0';
                    continue;
                default:
                    if (key > 31 && key < 128) {
                        if (strlen(string) ! = length) {
                            string[strlen(string) + 1] = '\0';
                            string[strlen(string)] = key;
                        }
                        continue;
                    }
                    return(key);
            }
        }
}
void display_string(int row, int col, int length, int color, char *string)
{
    string_func(FALSE, row, col, length, color, string);
}

int input_string(int row, int col, int length, int color, char *string)
{
    return(string_func(TRUE, row, col, length, color, string));
}
```

Function Description: string_func

The **string_func** function is used internally by the **display_string** and **input_string** functions respectively to display and retrieve strings. This implementation is illustrated with the following pseudocode:

7 GWINDOWS Data Entry Functions

```
if (string length > length of data entry field) {
    truncate the string
}
while (TRUE) {
    field = formatted string
    display field
    if (called by display_string) {
        return 0
    }
    move the cursor to the end of the string
    set the cursor color
    turn on the cursor
    get a key
    turn off the cursor
    switch (key) {
        case BACKSPACE:
            erase the last character
            continue
        case HOME:
            string = ""
            continue
        default:
            if (key is a printable character) {
                if (data entry field isn't full) {
                    field[length(string)] = key
                }
                continue
            }
            return the key
    }
}
```

Function Description: display_string

The **display_string** function displays strings. This implementation is illustrated with the following pseudocode:

display the string

Function Description: input_string

The **input_string** function retrieves strings. This implementation is illustrated with the following pseudocode:

retrieve the string
return the last key pressed

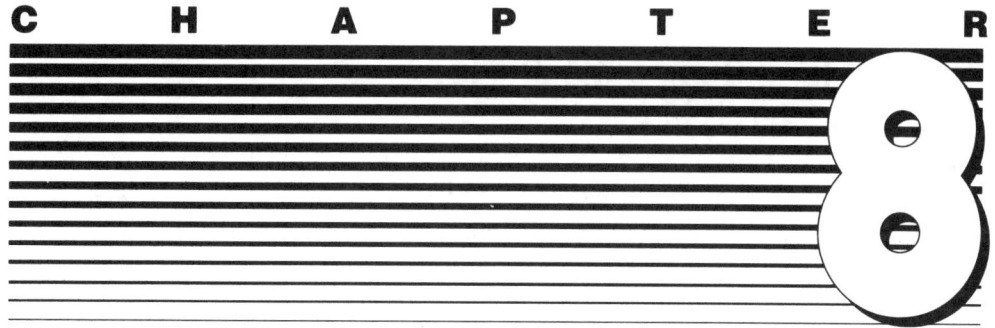

FONTEDIT

This chapter presents a sample GWINDOWS application program called FONTEDIT. Essentially, FONTEDIT is a program for creating GWINDOWS font tables. A GWINDOWS application programmer can create a new font table by simply editing a graphical representation of each character in the font table. A font table can be incorporated into a GWINDOWS application program by first instructing FONTEDIT to generate a C++ source code file for GWINDOWS font table. The resulting C++ source code file then can be compiled and linked with the desired GWINDOWS application program.

8 FONTEDIT

SOURCE LISTING 8.1: fontedit.cpp

Listing 8.1, **fontedit.cpp**, is a computer-assisted software engineering (CASE) tool for creating GWINDOWS font tables. This demonstration program illustrates many of the functions that are found in GWINDOWS toolbox including:

- pull-down menus for program navigation
- extensive use of dynamic display screen windows for screen displays
- dialog box menus for operator prompts
- formatted data routines to display and retrieve data values
- extensive use of the display screen pointer object for editing the font table characters.

Additionally, **fontedit.cpp** extensively uses the C++ programming language's object-oriented programming techniques to successfully implement the application program with the GWINDOWS graphical user interface.

```
/************************************************************************
* fontedit.cpp - For the GWINDOWS Toolbox
*                    Font Editor Program
************************************************************************/
#include <stdio.h>
#include <stdlib.h>
#include <dos.h>
#include <io.h>
#include <fg.h>
#include "gwindows.hpp"
class editfont : public font {
    int fontchar, fontflag;
public:
    editfont(unsigned char *fp) : (fp) { fontflag = FALSE; }
    ~editfont() { };
    void copycharacter(void);
    void csfont(void);
    void display(void);
    void erase(void);
    void erasecharacter(void);
    void fillcharacter(void);
    int getflag(void) { return fontflag; }
    void set(unsigned char *fp);
    void setchar(int);
    void setflag(int flag) { fontflag = flag; }
    void drawgridbox(int, int, int);
    void toggle(int, int);
};
```
continued...

FONTEDIT 8

```c
void new_func(void);
void cs_func(void);
void lf_func(void);
void sf_func(void);
void ga_func(void);
void ep_func(void);
void ec_func(void);
void fc_func(void);
void cc_func(void);
void copysysfont(unsigned char *);
void displayerror(char *);

static MENU file[6] = {
    {"New", 0, new_func, NULL},
    {"Copy System Font", 0, cs_func, NULL},
    {"Load Font File...", 0, lf_func, NULL},
    {"Save Font File...", 0, sf_func, NULL},
    {"Generate ASCII File...", 0, ga_func, NULL},
    {"Exit the Program", 0, ep_func, NULL} };

static MENU character[3] = {
    {"Erase the Character", 0, ec_func, NULL},
    {"Fill in the Character", 0, fc_func, NULL},
    {"Copy System Character", 0, cc_func, NULL} };

static MENU_HEAD heads[2] = {
    {"File", 0, 6, file},
    {"Character", 0, 3, character} };

static unsigned char fontbuffer[3584];
unsigned char *systemfont;
int genatt = egamode() ? egacolor(BLUE, WHITE) : WHITE;
editfont efont(fontbuffer);
static char filename[13];

main()
{
    int i, row, col;
    pulldown menu(1, 2, heads);

    systemfont = new unsigned char[3584];
    if (systemfont = = NULL) {
        printf("Not enough memory for system font buffer\n");
        exit(1);
    }
```

continued...

8 FONTEDIT

```
        copysysfont(systemfont);
        clearwindow(1, 1, 25, 80, background(genatt));
        mouse.on();
        menu.display();
        efont.display();
        clearrow(25, 1, 80, background(gmenu.color()));
        while (TRUE) {
            if (keypressed()) {
                menu.get(0);
                continue;
            }
            mouse.read();
            if (!mouse.lbutton())
                continue;
            if (mouse.row() == 1) {
                menu.get(0);
                continue;
            }
            do {
                mouse.read();
            } while (mouse.lbutton());
            if (mouse.row() > 3 && mouse.row() < 20 && mouse.col() > 61 &&
                    mouse.col() < 78) {
                efont.setchar((mouse.row()- 4) * 16 + mouse.col()- 62);
                continue;
            }
            if (mouse.x() > 7 && mouse.x() < 136 && mouse.y() > (egamode()? 27
                    : 15) && mouse.y() < (egamode() ? 252 : 143)) {
                efont.toggle((mouse.y() - (egamode() ? 28 : 16)) / 16,
                    (mouse.x() - 8) / 16);
                efont.setflag(TRUE);
            }
        }
    }
}

void editfont::csfont(void)
{
    static char *title1 =
        "Copying the system font will destroy the current font!!";
    static char *title2 = "Are you sure?";
    static MENU menu[2] = {
        {"Yes", 0, NULL, NULL},
        {"No", 0, NULL, NULL} };
```

continued...

```
        if (fontflag && dialog(13, 40, TRUE).get(2, menu, 2, title1, title2)
            != 'Y')
            return;
        memcpy(getptr(), systemfont, egamode() ? 3584 : 2048);
        display();
        fontflag = TRUE;
}

void editfont::erase(void)
{
    int i;
    unsigned char *fontptr = getptr();

    static char *title1 = "Font file will be destroyed!!";
    static char *title2 = "Are you sure?";
    static MENU menu[2] = {
        {"Yes", 0, NULL, NULL},
        {"No", 0, NULL, NULL} };

    if (fontflag && dialog(13, 40, TRUE).get(2, menu, 2, title1, title2)
        != 'Y')
        return;
    for (i = 0; i < 3584; fontptr[i++] = 0) ;
    display();
    fontflag = FALSE;
    ::filename[0] = 0;
    clearrow(25, 1, 80, background(gmenu.color()));
}

void editfont::erasecharacter(void)
{
    int i;
    unsigned char *fontptr = getptr();

    fontptr += fontchar * (egamode() ? 14 : 8);
    for (i = 0; i < (egamode() ? 14 : 8); fontptr[i++] = 0) ;
    setchar(fontchar);
    fontflag = TRUE;
}

void editfont::fillcharacter(void)
{
    int i;
    unsigned char *fontptr = getptr();
```

continued...

8 FONTEDIT

```
        fontptr + = fontchar * (egamode() ? 14 : 8);
        for (i = 0; i < (egamode() ? 14 : 8); fontptr[i + + ] = 0xff) ;
        setchar(fontchar);
        fontflag = TRUE;
}

void editfont::copycharacter(void)
{
        int i;
        unsigned char *fontptr = getptr();

        memcpy(fontptr + fontchar*(egamode()?14:8),systemfont + fontchar*
            (egamode() ? 14 : 8), egamode() ? 14 : 8);
        setchar(fontchar);
        fontflag = TRUE;
}

void editfont::display(void)
{
        int i, j;

        for (i = 0; i < 16; i + +) {
            displaychar(4 + i, 60, genatt, i < 10 ? i + '0' : i - 10 +'A');
            displaychar(3, i + 62, genatt, i <10 ? i + '0' : i - 10 +'A');
            displaychar(4 + i, 79, genatt, i < 10 ? i + '0' : i - 10 +'A');
            displaychar(20, i + 62, genatt, i < 10 ? i + '0' : i - 10 + 'A');
        }
        mouse.off();
        open();
        for (i = 0; i < 16; i + +) {
            for (j = 0; j < 16; j + +)
                displaychar(4 + i, 62 + j, genatt, i * 16 + j);
        }
        close();
        mouse.on();
        setchar(0);
}

void editfont::setchar(int chr)
{
        int i, j, lines = egamode() ? 14 : 8;
        char line[81];
        unsigned char cmask, *fontptr = getptr();
```

continued...

FONTEDIT 8

```
    mouse.off();
    sprintf(line, "Font Character Code: %02X", chr);
    displaystring(3, 19, genatt, line);
    displaystring(4, 19, genatt, "System Character: ");
    displaychar(4, 41, genatt, chr);
    displaystring(5, 19, genatt, "Font Character:");
    open();
    displaychar(5, 41, genatt, chr);
    displaychar(4 + fontchar / 16, 62 + fontchar % 16, genatt, fontchar);
    close();
    fontchar = chr;
    fontptr + = chr * lines;
    for (i = 0; i < lines; i + +) {
        cmask = 0x80;
        for (j = 0; j < 8; j + +) {
            drawgridbox(i, j, (*fontptr & cmask) ! = 0);
            cmask > > = 1;
        }
        fontptr + +;
    }
    mouse.on();
}

void editfont::toggle(int row, int col)
{
    int i;
    unsigned char cmask, *fontptr = getptr();

    fontptr + = fontchar * (egamode() ? 14 : 8) + row;
    cmask = 0x80;
    for (i = 0; i < col; i + +)
        cmask > > = 1;
    *fontptr ^ = cmask;
    mouse.off();
    open();
    displaychar(5, 41, genatt, fontchar);
    displaychar(4 + fontchar / 16, 62 + fontchar % 16, genatt, fontchar);
    close();
    drawgridbox(row, col, (*fontptr & cmask) ! = 0);
    mouse.on();
}

void editfont::drawgridbox(int row, int col, int flag)
{
    fg_box_t box;
    int x, y;
```
continued...

8 FONTEDIT

```
    mouse.off();
    box[FG_X1] = col * 16 + 8;
    box[FG_X2] = box[FG_X1] + 16;
    box[FG_Y2] = (egamode() ? 321 : 183) - row * 16;
    box[FG_Y1] = box[FG_Y2] - 16;
    fg_drawbox(FG_WHITE, FG_MODE_SET, ~0, FG_LINE_SOLID,
        box, fg_displaybox);
    box[FG_X1]++;
    box[FG_X2]--;
    box[FG_Y1]++;
    box[FG_Y2]--;
    fg_fillbox(egamode() ? FG_BLUE : FG_BLACK, FG_MODE_SET, ~0, box);
    fg_drawarc(FG_WHITE, FG_MODE_SET, ~0, box[FG_X1] + 7,
        box[FG_Y2] - 7, 7, 0, 3600, fg_displaybox);
    if (flag) {
        y = box[FG_Y2] - 7;
        while (fg_readdot(box[FG_X1] + 7, y) != FG_WHITE) y++;
        y--;
        do {
            x = box[FG_X1] + 7;
            while (fg_readdot(x, y) != FG_WHITE)
                fg_drawdot(FG_WHITE, FG_MODE_SET, ~0, x--, y);
            x = box[FG_X1] + 8;
            while (fg_readdot(x, y) != FG_WHITE)
                fg_drawdot(FG_WHITE, FG_MODE_SET, ~0, x++, y);
        } while (fg_readdot(box[FG_X1] + 7, --y) != FG_WHITE) ;
    }
    mouse.on();
}

void new_func(void)
{
    efont.erase();
}

void lf_func(void)
{
    window w1(11, 28, 15, 52, gmenu.color(), DOUBLE_LINE);
    FILE *fileptr;
    char *title1 = "Existing font file will be destroyed!";
    char *title2 = "Load font file?";
    static MENU menu[2] = {
        {"Yes", 0, NULL, NULL},
        {"No", 0, NULL, NULL} };
```

continued...

```
    if (efont.getflag()) {
        if (dialog(13,40,TRUE).get(2,menu, 2,title1, title2)! = 'Y')
            return;
    }
    filename[0] = 0;
    clearrow(25, 1, 80, background(gmenu.color()));
    w1.open();
    displaystring(13, 30, gmenu.color(), "File Name:");
    drawborder(12, 41, 14, 50, gmenu.color(), SINGLE_LINE);
    while (TRUE) {
        switch (input_string(13, 42, 8, gmenu.color(), filename)){
            case 13:
                if (filename[0])
                    break;
                else
                    continue;
            case 27:
                return;
            default:
                continue;
        }
        break;
    }
    w1.close();
    sprintf(filename, "%s.fon", filename);
    displaycenter(25, 40, gmenu.color(), filename);
    if (filesize(filename) = = -1) {
        efont.setflag(FALSE);
        efont.erase();
        return;
    }
    if ((fileptr = fopen(filename, "r+b")) = = NULL) {
        displayerror("Couldn't Open File!");
        efont.setflag(FALSE);
        efont.erase();
        return;
    }
    if (fread(efont.getptr(), sizeof(unsigned char),
        (egamode() ? 3584 : 2048), fileptr) != (egamode() ? 3584 : 2048)) {
            displayerror("Disk Read Error!");
            efont.setflag(FALSE);
            efont.erase();
            fclose(fileptr);
            return;
    }
```

continued...

8 FONTEDIT

```
        efont.display();
        fclose(fileptr);
}

void sf_func(void)
{
        window w1(11, 28, 15, 52, gmenu.color(), DOUBLE_LINE);
        FILE *fileptr;
        char *title1 = "File Already Exists!";
        char *title2 = "Overwrite It?";
        static MENU menu[2] = {
            {"Yes", 0, NULL, NULL},
            {"No", 0, NULL, NULL} };

        if (filename[0] == 0) {
            w1.open();
            displaystring(13, 30, gmenu.color(), "File Name:");
            drawborder(12, 41, 14, 50, gmenu.color(), SINGLE_LINE);
            while (TRUE) {
                switch (input_string(13, 42, 8,gmenu.color(),filename)){
                    case 13:
                        if (filename[0])
                            break;
                        else
                            continue;
                    case 27:
                        return;
                    default:
                        continue;
                }
                break;
            }
            w1.close();
            clearrow(25, 1, 80, background(gmenu.color()));
            sprintf(filename, "%s.fon", filename);
            displaycenter(25, 40, gmenu.color(), filename);
            if (filesize(filename) != -1 &&
                dialog(13, 40, TRUE).get(2, menu, 2, title1, title2) != 'Y') {
                filename[0] = 0;
                clearrow(25, 1, 80, background(gmenu.color()));
                return;
            }
        }
        if ((fileptr = fopen(filename, "w+b")) == NULL) {
            displayerror("Couldn't Open File!");
            return;
```

continued...

```
    }
    if (fwrite(efont.getptr(), sizeof(unsigned char),
        (egamode() ? 3584 : 2048), fileptr) != (egamode() ? 3584 : 2048))
            displayerror("Disk Write Error!");
    fclose(fileptr);
    efont.setflag(FALSE);
}

void ga_func(void)
{
    int i, j;
    window w1(11, 28, 15, 52, gmenu.color(), DOUBLE_LINE);
    FILE *fileptr;
    unsigned char *fontptr = efont.getptr();
    char fname[13], fontname[9];
    char *title1 = "File Already Exists!";
    char *title2 = "Overwrite It?";
    static MENU menu[2] = {
        {"Yes", 0, NULL, NULL},
        {"No", 0, NULL, NULL} };

    if (filename[0] == 0) {
        w1.open();
        displaystring(13, 30, gmenu.color(), "File Name:");
        drawborder(12, 41, 14, 50, gmenu.color(), SINGLE_LINE);
        while (TRUE) {
            switch (input_string(13, 42, 8, gmenu.color(), filename)) {
                case 13:
                    if (filename[0])
                        break;
                    else
                        continue;
                case 27:
                    return;
                default:
                    continue;
            }
            break;
        }
        w1.close();
        sprintf(fontname, "%s", filename);
        sprintf(fname, "%s.cpp", filename);
        clearrow(25, 1, 80, background(gmenu.color()));
        sprintf(filename, "%s.fon", filename);
        displaycenter(25, 40, gmenu.color(), filename);
    }
```

continued...

8 FONTEDIT

```
    else {
        for (i = 0; i < 8 && filename[i] != '.'; i++)
                fontname[i] = filename[i];
        fontname[i] = 0;
        sprintf(fname, "%s.cpp", fontname);
    }
    if (filesize(fname) != -1 &&
        dialog(13, 40, TRUE).get(2, menu, 2, title1, title2) != 'Y')
        return;
    if ((fileptr = fopen(fname, "w+")) == NULL) {
        displayerror("Couldn't Open File!");
        return;
    }
    if (fprintf(fileptr, "// GWINDOWS Font File\n") < 0) {
        displayerror("Disk Write Error!");
        fclose(fileptr);
        return;
    }
    if (fprintf(fileptr, "#include \"gwindows.hpp\"\n\n") < 0) {
        displayerror("Disk Write Error!");
        fclose(fileptr);
        return;
    }
    if (fprintf(fileptr, "static unsigned char fontptr[] = {\n") < 0) {
        displayerror("Disk Write Error!");
        fclose(fileptr);
        return;
    }
    for (i = 0; i < 256; i++) {
        if (fprintf(fileptr, "\t") < 0) {
            displayerror("Disk Write Error!");
            fclose(fileptr);
            return;
        }
        for (j = 0; j < (egamode() ? 14 : 8); j++) {
            if (fprintf(fileptr, "%d,", fontptr[i *
                (egamode() ? 14 : 8) + j]) < 0) {
                displayerror("Disk Write Error!");
                fclose(fileptr);
                return;
            }
        }
        if (fprintf(fileptr, "\n") < 0) {
            displayerror("Disk Write Error!");
            fclose(fileptr);
            return;
```

continued...

```c
        }
    }
    if (fprintf(fileptr, "};\n\n") < 0) {
        displayerror("Disk Write Error!");
        fclose(fileptr);
        return;
    }
    if (fprintf(fileptr, "font %s(fontptr);\n", fontname) < 0)
        displayerror("Disk Write Error!");
    fclose(fileptr);
}
void cs_func(void)
{
    efont.csfont();
}
void ep_func(void)
{
    char *title1 = "File Hasn't Been Saved!";
    char *title2 = "Save It?";
    static MENU menu[2] = {
        {"Yes", 0, NULL, NULL},
        {"No", 0, NULL, NULL} };

    if (efont.getflag()) {
        switch (dialog(13,40,TRUE).get(2,menu,2,title1,title2)){
            case 'Y':
                sf_func();
                break;
            case 'N':
                break;
            default:
                return;
        }
    }
    exit(0);
}

void ec_func(void)
{
    efont.erasecharacter();
}

void fc_func(void)
{
    efont.fillcharacter();
}
```

continued...

8 FONTEDIT

```
void cc_func(void)
{
    efont.copycharacter();
}

void copysysfont(unsigned char *fontptr)
{
    int i;
    unsigned char *slfontptr, *sufontptr;

    getfontvectors(&slfontptr, &sufontptr);
    if (egamode())
        memcpy(fontptr, slfontptr, 3584);
    else {
        memcpy(fontptr, slfontptr, 1024);
        memcpy(fontptr + 1024, sufontptr, 1024);
    }
}

void displayerror(char *string)
{
    static MENU menu[1] = {"OK", 0, NULL, NULL};

    dialog(13, 40, FALSE).get(1, menu, 1, string);
}
```

Function Description: main

As with all C++ programs, the **main** function is the main program loop. This implementation is illustrated with the following pseudocode:

```
allocate memory for the system font buffer
if (memory allocation error occurred) {
    abort the program
}
copy the system font into the buffer
clear the display screen
turn on the mouse pointer
display the pull-down menu bar
display the current font
clear the bottom display screen row
while (TRUE) {
    if (key is being pressed) {
        do the pull-down menu routine
        continue
    }
```
continued...

```
    read the mouse values
    if (left mouse button isn't being pressed) {
        continue
    }
    if (menu bar was clicked) {
        do the pull-down menu routine
        continue
    }
    do {
        read the mouse values
    } while (left button is being pressed)
    if (font table character was clicked) {
        set the character as the current edit font character
        continue
    }
    if (an edit font character dot was clicked) {
        toggle the character's font table bit
    }
}
```

Function Description: editfont::csfont

The **editfont::csfont** function copies the system font buffer's contents to the edit font buffer. This implementation is illustrated with the following pseudocode:

```
if (font has been edited && operator doesn't want to destroy
    the edit buffer's contents) {
    return
}
copy the system font buffer's contents to the edit font buffer
display the edit font buffer's new contents
```

Function Description: editfont::erase

The **editfont::erase** function clears the edit font buffer. This implementation is illustrated with the following pseudocode:

```
if (font has been edited && operator doesn't want to destroy
    the edit buffer's contents) {
    return
}
erase the edit font buffer's contents
filename = ""
clear the bottom display screen row
```

8 FONTEDIT

Function Description: editfont::erasecharacter

The **editfont::erasecharacter** function erases a character's contents in the edit font buffer. This implementation is illustrated with the following pseudocode:

figure the edit font buffer pointer
for (i = 0; i < number of lines per character; i+ +) {
    edit font buffer byte = 0
}
redisplay the character

Function Description: editfont::fillcharacter

The **editfont::fillcharacter** function fills a character's contents in the edit font buffer. This implementation is illustrated with the following pseudocode:

figure the edit font buffer pointer
for (i = 0; i < number of lines per character; i+ +) {
    edit font buffer byte = 0xff
}
redisplay the character

Function Description: editfont::copycharacter

The **editfont::copycharacter** function copies the character contents of a system font buffer to the edit font buffer. This implementation is illustrated with the following pseudocode:

copy the character's contents from the system font buffer to
    the edit font buffer
redisplay the character

Function Description: editfont::display

The **editfont::display** function displays the contents of the edit font buffer. This implementation is illustrated with the following pseudocode:

display the font table
set the current font table character to 0x00

Function Description: editfont::setchar

The **editfont::setchar** function displays a graphical representation of the current font table character. This implementation is illustrated with the following pseudocode:

turn off the mouse pointer
display the character's code
display the character's system font representation
display the character's edit font representation
for (i = 0; i < 8; i++) {
    for (j = 0; j < 8; j++) {
        display the font character's graphical dot representation
    }
}
turn on the mouse pointer

Function Description: editfont::toggle

The **editfont::toggle** function toggles a character dot on or off. This implementation is illustrated with the following pseudocode:

figure the edit font buffer pointer
figure the character dot's bit mask
toggle the character dot's bit
turn off the mouse pointer
display the character's edit font representation
display the character dot's new graphical representation
turn on the mouse pointer

Function Description: editfont::drawgridbox

The **editfont::drawgridbox** function draws a character dot's graphical representation. This implementation is illustrated with the following pseudocode:

turn off the mouse pointer
draw a box around the character dot
clear the character dot's box
draw a circle inside of the character dot's box
if (character dot is on) {
    fill in the interior of the character dot's circle
}
turn on the mouse pointer

Function Description: new_func

The **new_func** function erases the edit buffer's contents. This implementation is illustrated with the following pseudocode:

erase the edit font buffer's contents

8 FONTEDIT

Function Description: lf_func

The **lf_func** function replaces the edit buffer's contents with a binary disk file. This implementation is illustrated with the following pseudocode:

```
if (font has been edited && operator doesn't want to destroy
        the edit buffer's contents) {
    return
}
filename = ""
clear the bottom line of the display screen
get the filename
display the filename on the bottom line of the display screen
if (file doesn't exist) {
    erase the edit buffer's contents
    return
}
open the font file
load the font file
display the edit buffer's new contents
close the font file
```

Function Description: sf_func

The **sf_func** function saves the edit buffer's contents as a binary disk file. This implementation is illustrated with the following pseudocode:

```
if (font table doesn't have a name) {
    get the filename
}
open the font file
save the font file
close the font file
```

Function Description: ga_func

The **ga_func** function generates a C++ source code file for the edit buffer's contents. This implementation is illustrated with the following pseudocode:

```
if (font table doesn't have a name) {
    get the filename
}
open the source code file
write the source code file
close the source code file
```

Function Description: cs_func

The **cs_func** function copies the contents of the system font buffer to the edit buffer. This implementation is illustrated with the following pseudocode:

copy the system font buffer's contents to the edit font buffer

Function Description: ep_func

The **ep_func** function terminates program execution. This implementation is illustrated with the following pseudocode:

if (font has been edited && operator doesn't want to destroy
*   the edit buffer's contents) {*
*   return*
}
exit the program

Function Description: ec_func

The **ec_func** function erases a character's contents in the edit font buffer. This implementation is illustrated with the following pseudocode:

erase the character's contents

Function Description: fc_func

The **fc_func** function fills a character's contents in the edit font buffer. This implementation is illustrated with the following pseudocode:

fill the character's contents

Function Description: cc_func

The **cc_func** function copies a character's contents from the system font buffer to the edit font buffer. This implementation is illustrated with the following pseudocode:

copy the system font character's contents into the edit font buffer

Function Description: copysysfont

The **copysysfont** function copies the system font tables into the FONTEDIT system font buffer. This implementation is illustrated with the following pseudocode:

8 FONTEDIT

get the system font table pointers
copy the system font tables into the FONTEDIT system font buffer

Function Description: displayerror

The **displayerror** function displays an error message. This implementation is illustrated with the following pseudocode:

display the error message in an "OK" dialog box

SOURCE LISTING 8.2: sanscga.cpp

Listing 8.2, **sanscga.cpp,** is a sample sans serif CGA font that was generated with the FONTEDIT program.

```
// GWINDOWS Font File
#include "gwindows.hpp"

static unsigned char fontptr[] = {
    0,0,0,0,0,0,0,0,
    126,129,165,129,189,153,129,126,
    126,255,219,255,195,231,255,126,
    108,254,254,254,124,56,16,0,
    16,56,124,254,124,56,16,0,
    56,124,56,254,254,214,16,56,
    16,16,56,124,254,124,16,56,
    0,0,24,60,60,24,0,0,
    255,255,231,195,195,231,255,255,
    0,60,102,66,66,102,60,0,
    255,195,153,189,189,153,195,255,
    15,7,15,125,204,204,204,120,
    60,102,102,102,60,24,126,24,
    63,51,63,48,48,112,240,224,
    127,99,127,99,99,103,230,192,
    24,219,60,231,231,60,219,24,
    128,224,248,254,248,224,128,0,
    2,14,62,254,62,14,2,0,
    24,60,126,24,24,126,60,24,
    102,102,102,102,102,0,102,0,
    127,219,219,123,27,27,27,0,
    62,99,56,108,108,56,204,120,
    0,0,0,0,126,126,126,0,
    24,60,126,24,126,60,24,255,
    24,60,126,24,24,24,24,0,
    24,24,24,24,126,60,24,0,
```

continued...

FONTEDIT 8

0,24,12,254,12,24,0,0,
0,48,96,254,96,48,0,0,
0,0,192,192,192,254,0,0,
0,36,102,255,102,36,0,0,
0,24,60,126,255,255,0,0,
0,255,255,126,60,24,0,0,
0,0,0,0,0,0,0,0,
48,120,120,48,48,0,48,0,
108,108,108,0,0,0,0,0,
108,108,254,108,254,108,108,0,
48,124,192,120,12,248,48,0,
0,198,204,24,48,102,198,0,
56,108,56,118,220,204,118,0,
96,96,192,0,0,0,0,0,
24,48,96,96,96,48,24,0,
96,48,24,24,24,48,96,0,
0,102,60,255,60,102,0,0,
0,48,48,252,48,48,0,0,
0,0,0,0,0,48,48,96,
0,0,0,252,0,0,0,0,
0,0,0,0,0,48,48,0,
6,12,24,48,96,192,128,0,
124,198,198,198,198,198,124,0,
48,112,48,48,48,48,48,0,
120,204,12,56,96,192,252,0,
120,204,12,56,12,204,120,0,
28,60,108,204,254,12,12,0,
252,192,248,12,12,204,120,0,
56,96,192,248,204,204,120,0,
252,12,12,24,48,48,48,0,
120,204,204,120,204,204,120,0,
120,204,204,124,12,24,112,0,
0,48,48,0,0,48,48,0,
0,48,48,0,0,48,48,96,
24,48,96,192,96,48,24,0,
0,0,252,0,0,252,0,0,
96,48,24,12,24,48,96,0,
120,204,12,24,48,0,48,0,
124,198,222,222,222,192,120,0,
48,120,204,204,252,204,204,0,
124,102,102,124,102,102,124,0,
60,102,192,192,192,102,60,0,
120,108,102,102,102,108,120,0,
126,96,96,124,96,96,126,0,
126,96,96,124,96,96,96,0,
60,102,192,192,206,102,60,0,
204,204,204,252,204,204,204,0,
continued...

8 FONTEDIT

48,48,48,48,48,48,48,0,
12,12,12,12,204,204,120,0,
102,102,108,120,108,102,102,0,
96,96,96,96,96,96,126,0,
198,238,254,254,214,198,198,0,
198,230,246,222,206,198,198,0,
56,108,198,198,198,108,56,0,
124,102,102,124,96,96,96,0,
120,204,204,204,220,120,12,0,
124,102,102,124,108,102,102,0,
120,204,96,48,24,204,120,0,
252,48,48,48,48,48,48,0,
204,204,204,204,204,204,252,0,
204,204,204,204,204,120,48,0,
198,198,198,214,254,238,198,0,
198,198,108,56,56,108,198,0,
204,204,204,120,48,48,48,0,
254,6,12,24,48,96,254,0,
120,96,96,96,96,96,120,0,
192,96,48,24,12,6,2,0,
120,24,24,24,24,24,120,0,
16,56,108,198,0,0,0,0,
0,0,0,0,0,0,0,255,
48,48,24,0,0,0,0,0,
0,0,120,12,124,204,118,0,
96,96,96,124,102,102,124,0,
0,0,120,204,192,204,120,0,
12,12,12,124,204,204,124,0,
0,0,120,204,252,192,120,0,
56,108,96,240,96,96,96,0,
0,0,124,204,204,124,12,120,
96,96,108,118,102,102,102,0,
48,0,48,48,48,48,48,0,
12,0,12,12,12,204,204,120,
96,96,102,108,120,108,102,0,
112,48,48,48,48,48,48,0,
0,0,204,254,254,214,198,0,
0,0,248,204,204,204,204,0,
0,0,120,204,204,204,120,0,
0,0,124,102,102,124,96,96,
0,0,124,204,204,124,12,12,
0,0,92,118,102,96,96,0,
0,0,124,192,120,12,248,0,
48,48,124,48,48,52,24,0,
0,0,204,204,204,204,116,0,
0,0,204,204,204,120,48,0,
0,0,198,214,254,254,108,0,

continued...

FONTEDIT 8

0,0,198,108,56,108,198,0,
0,0,204,204,204,124,12,248,
0,0,252,24,48,96,252,0,
28,48,48,224,48,48,28,0,
24,24,24,0,24,24,24,0,
224,48,48,28,48,48,224,0,
118,220,0,0,0,0,0,0,
0,16,56,108,198,198,254,0,
120,204,192,204,120,24,12,120,
0,204,0,204,204,204,126,0,
28,0,120,204,252,192,120,0,
126,195,60,6,62,102,63,0,
204,0,120,12,124,204,126,0,
224,0,120,12,124,204,126,0,
48,48,120,12,124,204,126,0,
0,0,120,192,192,120,12,56,
126,195,60,102,126,96,60,0,
204,0,120,204,252,192,120,0,
224,0,120,204,252,192,120,0,
204,0,112,48,48,48,120,0,
124,198,56,24,24,24,60,0,
224,0,112,48,48,48,120,0,
198,56,108,198,254,198,198,0,
48,48,0,120,204,252,204,0,
28,0,252,96,120,96,252,0,
0,0,127,12,127,204,127,0,
62,108,204,254,204,204,206,0,
120,204,0,120,204,204,120,0,
0,204,0,120,204,204,120,0,
0,224,0,120,204,204,120,0,
120,204,0,204,204,204,126,0,
0,224,0,204,204,204,126,0,
0,204,0,204,204,124,12,248,
195,24,60,102,102,60,24,0,
204,0,204,204,204,204,120,0,
24,24,126,192,192,126,24,24,
56,108,100,240,96,230,252,0,
204,204,120,252,48,252,48,48,
248,204,204,250,198,207,198,199,
14,27,24,60,24,24,216,112,
28,0,120,12,124,204,126,0,
56,0,112,48,48,48,120,0,
0,28,0,120,204,204,120,0,
0,28,0,204,204,204,126,0,
0,248,0,248,204,204,204,0,
252,0,204,236,252,220,204,0,
60,108,108,62,0,126,0,0,

continued...

8 FONTEDIT

56,108,108,56,0,124,0,0,
48,0,48,96,192,204,120,0,
0,0,0,252,192,192,0,0,
0,0,0,252,12,12,0,0,
195,198,204,222,51,102,204,15,
195,198,204,219,55,111,207,3,
24,24,0,24,24,24,24,0,
0,51,102,204,102,51,0,0,
0,204,102,51,102,204,0,0,
34,136,34,136,34,136,34,136,
85,170,85,170,85,170,85,170,
219,119,219,238,219,119,219,238,
24,24,24,24,24,24,24,24,
24,24,24,24,248,24,24,24,
24,24,248,24,248,24,24,24,
54,54,54,54,246,54,54,54,
0,0,0,0,254,54,54,54,
0,0,248,24,248,24,24,24,
54,54,246,6,246,54,54,54,
54,54,54,54,54,54,54,54,
0,0,254,6,246,54,54,54,
54,54,246,6,254,0,0,0,
54,54,54,54,254,0,0,0,
24,24,248,24,248,0,0,0,
0,0,0,0,248,24,24,24,
24,24,24,24,31,0,0,0,
24,24,24,24,255,0,0,0,
0,0,0,0,255,24,24,24,
24,24,24,24,31,24,24,24,
0,0,0,0,255,0,0,0,
24,24,24,24,255,24,24,24,
24,24,31,24,31,24,24,24,
54,54,54,54,55,54,54,54,
54,54,55,48,63,0,0,0,
0,0,63,48,55,54,54,54,
54,54,247,0,255,0,0,0,
0,0,255,0,247,54,54,54,
54,54,55,48,55,54,54,54,
0,0,255,0,255,0,0,0,
54,54,247,0,247,54,54,54,
24,24,255,0,255,0,0,0,
54,54,54,54,255,0,0,0,
0,0,255,0,255,24,24,24,
0,0,0,0,255,54,54,54,
54,54,54,54,63,0,0,0,
24,24,31,24,31,0,0,0,
0,0,31,24,31,24,24,24,
  continued...

FONTEDIT 8

```
    0,0,0,0,63,54,54,54,
    54,54,54,54,255,54,54,54,
    24,24,255,24,255,24,24,24,
    24,24,24,24,248,0,0,0,
    0,0,0,0,31,24,24,24,
    255,255,255,255,255,255,255,255,
    0,0,0,0,255,255,255,255,
    240,240,240,240,240,240,240,240,
    15,15,15,15,15,15,15,15,
    255,255,255,255,0,0,0,0,
    0,0,118,220,200,220,118,0,
    0,120,204,248,204,248,192,192,
    0,252,204,192,192,192,192,0,
    0,254,108,108,108,108,108,0,
    252,204,96,48,96,204,252,0,
    0,0,126,216,216,216,112,0,
    0,102,102,102,102,124,96,192,
    0,118,220,24,24,24,24,0,
    252,48,120,204,204,120,48,252,
    56,108,198,254,198,108,56,0,
    56,108,198,198,108,108,238,0,
    28,48,24,124,204,204,120,0,
    0,0,126,219,219,126,0,0,
    6,12,126,219,219,126,96,192,
    56,96,192,248,192,96,56,0,
    120,204,204,204,204,204,204,0,
    0,252,0,252,0,252,0,0,
    48,48,252,48,48,0,252,0,
    96,48,24,48,96,0,252,0,
    24,48,96,48,24,0,252,0,
    14,27,27,24,24,24,24,24,
    24,24,24,24,24,216,216,112,
    48,48,0,252,0,48,48,0,
    0,118,220,0,118,220,0,0,
    56,108,108,56,0,0,0,0,
    0,0,0,24,24,0,0,0,
    0,0,0,0,24,0,0,0,
    15,12,12,12,236,108,60,28,
    120,108,108,108,108,0,0,0,
    112,24,48,96,120,0,0,0,
    0,0,60,60,60,60,0,0,
    0,0,0,0,0,0,0,0,
};

font sanscga(fontptr);
```

8 FONTEDIT

SOURCE LISTING 8.3: sansega.cpp

Listing 8.3, **sansega.cpp**, is a sample sans serif EGA font that was generated with the FONTEDIT program.

```cpp
// GWINDOWS Font File
#include "gwindows.hpp"

static unsigned char fontptr[] = {
    0,0,0,0,0,0,0,0,0,0,0,0,0,0,
    0,0,126,129,165,129,129,189,153,129,126,0,0,0,
    0,0,126,255,219,255,255,195,231,255,126,0,0,0,
    0,0,0,108,254,254,254,254,124,56,16,0,0,0,
    0,0,0,16,56,124,254,124,56,16,0,0,0,0,
    0,0,24,60,60,231,231,231,24,24,60,0,0,0,
    0,0,24,60,126,255,255,126,24,24,60,0,0,0,
    0,0,0,0,0,24,60,60,24,0,0,0,0,0,
    255,255,255,255,255,231,195,195,231,255,255,255,255,255,
    0,0,0,0,60,102,66,66,102,60,0,0,0,0,
    255,255,255,255,195,153,189,189,153,195,255,255,255,255,
    0,0,30,14,26,50,120,204,204,204,120,0,0,0,
    0,0,60,102,102,102,60,24,126,24,24,0,0,0,
    0,0,63,51,63,48,48,48,112,240,224,0,0,0,
    0,0,127,99,127,99,99,99,103,231,230,192,0,0,
    0,0,24,24,219,60,231,60,219,24,24,0,0,0,
    0,0,128,192,224,248,254,248,224,192,128,0,0,0,
    0,0,2,6,14,62,254,62,14,6,2,0,0,0,
    0,0,24,60,126,24,24,24,126,60,24,0,0,0,
    0,0,102,102,102,102,102,102,0,102,102,0,0,0,
    0,0,127,219,219,219,123,27,27,27,27,0,0,0,
    0,124,198,96,56,108,198,198,108,56,12,198,124,0,
    0,0,0,0,0,0,0,0,254,254,254,0,0,0,
    0,0,24,60,126,24,24,24,126,60,24,126,0,0,
    0,0,24,60,126,24,24,24,24,24,24,0,0,0,
    0,0,24,24,24,24,24,24,126,60,24,0,0,0,
    0,0,0,0,24,12,254,12,24,0,0,0,0,0,
    0,0,0,0,48,96,254,96,48,0,0,0,0,0,
    0,0,0,0,0,192,192,192,254,0,0,0,0,0,
    0,0,0,0,40,108,254,108,40,0,0,0,0,0,
    0,0,0,16,56,56,124,124,254,254,0,0,0,0,
    0,0,0,254,254,124,124,56,56,16,0,0,0,0,
    0,0,0,0,0,0,0,0,0,0,0,0,0,0,
    0,0,24,60,60,60,24,24,0,24,24,0,0,0,
    0,102,102,102,36,0,0,0,0,0,0,0,0,0,
```

continued...

FONTEDIT 8

```
0,0,108,108,254,108,108,108,254,108,108,0,0,0,
24,24,124,198,194,192,124,6,134,198,124,24,24,0,
0,0,0,0,194,198,12,24,48,102,198,0,0,0,
0,0,56,108,108,56,118,220,204,204,118,0,0,0,
0,48,48,48,96,0,0,0,0,0,0,0,0,0,
0,0,12,24,48,48,48,48,48,24,12,0,0,0,
0,0,48,24,12,12,12,12,12,24,48,0,0,0,
0,0,0,0,102,60,255,60,102,0,0,0,0,0,
0,0,0,0,24,24,126,24,24,0,0,0,0,0,
0,0,0,0,0,0,0,0,24,24,24,48,0,0,
0,0,0,0,0,0,254,0,0,0,0,0,0,0,
0,0,0,0,0,0,0,0,0,24,24,0,0,0,
0,0,2,6,12,24,48,96,192,128,0,0,0,0,
0,0,124,198,198,198,198,198,198,198,124,0,0,0,
0,0,24,24,120,24,24,24,24,24,24,0,0,0,
0,0,124,198,6,12,24,48,96,192,254,0,0,0,
0,0,124,198,6,6,60,6,6,198,124,0,0,0,
0,0,12,28,60,108,204,254,12,12,12,0,0,0,
0,0,254,192,192,192,252,6,6,198,124,0,0,0,
0,0,56,96,192,192,252,198,198,198,124,0,0,0,
0,0,254,6,6,12,24,48,48,48,48,0,0,0,
0,0,124,198,198,198,124,198,198,198,124,0,0,0,
0,0,124,198,198,198,126,6,6,12,120,0,0,0,
0,0,0,24,24,0,0,0,24,24,0,0,0,0,
0,0,0,24,24,0,0,0,24,24,48,0,0,0,
0,0,6,12,24,48,96,48,24,12,6,0,0,0,
0,0,0,0,0,126,0,0,126,0,0,0,0,0,
0,0,96,48,24,12,6,12,24,48,96,0,0,0,
0,0,124,198,198,12,24,24,0,24,24,0,0,0,
0,0,124,198,198,222,222,222,220,192,124,0,0,0,
0,0,16,56,108,198,198,254,198,198,198,0,0,0,
0,0,124,102,102,102,124,102,102,102,124,0,0,0,
0,0,60,102,194,192,192,192,194,102,60,0,0,0,
0,0,120,108,102,102,102,102,102,108,120,0,0,0,
0,0,126,96,96,96,124,96,96,96,126,0,0,0,
0,0,126,96,96,96,124,96,96,96,96,0,0,0,
0,0,60,102,194,192,192,222,198,102,60,0,0,0,
0,0,198,198,198,198,254,198,198,198,198,0,0,0,
0,0,24,24,24,24,24,24,24,24,24,0,0,0,
0,0,12,12,12,12,12,12,204,204,120,0,0,0,
0,0,102,102,108,108,120,108,108,102,102,0,0,0,
0,0,96,96,96,96,96,96,96,96,126,0,0,0,
0,0,198,238,254,254,214,198,198,198,198,0,0,0,
0,0,198,230,246,254,222,206,198,198,198,0,0,0,
0,0,56,108,198,198,198,198,198,108,56,0,0,0,
0,0,124,102,102,102,124,96,96,96,96,0,0,0,
0,0,124,198,198,198,198,214,222,124,12,6,0,0,
```

continued...

8 FONTEDIT

```
0,0,124,102,102,102,124,108,102,102,102,0,0,0,
0,0,124,198,198,96,56,12,198,198,124,0,0,0,
0,0,126,126,24,24,24,24,24,24,24,0,0,0,
0,0,198,198,198,198,198,198,198,198,124,0,0,0,
0,0,198,198,198,198,198,198,108,56,16,0,0,0,
0,0,198,198,198,198,214,214,254,124,108,0,0,0,
0,0,198,198,108,56,56,56,108,198,198,0,0,0,
0,0,102,102,102,102,60,24,24,24,24,0,0,0,
0,0,254,6,12,24,48,96,192,192,254,0,0,0,
0,0,60,48,48,48,48,48,48,48,60,0,0,0,
0,0,128,192,224,112,56,28,14,6,2,0,0,0,
0,0,60,12,12,12,12,12,12,12,60,0,0,0,
16,56,108,198,0,0,0,0,0,0,0,0,0,0,
0,0,0,0,0,0,0,0,0,0,0,0,255,0,
48,48,24,0,0,0,0,0,0,0,0,0,0,0,
0,0,0,0,0,120,12,124,204,204,118,0,0,0,
0,0,96,96,96,120,108,102,102,102,124,0,0,0,
0,0,0,0,0,124,198,192,192,198,124,0,0,0,
0,0,12,12,12,60,108,204,204,204,116,0,0,0,
0,0,0,0,0,124,198,254,192,198,124,0,0,0,
0,0,56,108,100,96,240,96,96,96,96,0,0,0,
0,0,0,0,0,116,204,204,204,124,12,204,120,0,
0,0,96,96,96,108,118,102,102,102,102,0,0,0,
0,0,24,24,0,24,24,24,24,24,0,0,0,
0,0,6,6,0,6,6,6,6,6,102,102,60,0,
0,0,96,96,96,102,108,120,108,102,102,0,0,0,
0,0,56,24,24,24,24,24,24,24,0,0,0,
0,0,0,0,0,236,254,214,214,214,198,0,0,0,
0,0,0,0,0,220,102,102,102,102,102,0,0,0,
0,0,0,0,0,124,198,198,198,198,124,0,0,0,
0,0,0,0,0,92,102,102,102,124,96,96,96,0,
0,0,0,0,0,116,204,204,204,124,12,12,12,0,
0,0,0,0,0,92,118,102,96,96,96,0,0,0,
0,0,0,0,0,124,198,112,28,198,124,0,0,0,
0,0,48,48,48,252,48,48,48,54,28,0,0,0,
0,0,0,0,0,204,204,204,204,204,116,0,0,0,
0,0,0,0,0,102,102,102,102,60,24,0,0,0,
0,0,0,0,0,198,198,214,214,254,108,0,0,0,
0,0,0,0,0,198,108,56,56,108,198,0,0,0,
0,0,0,0,0,198,198,198,198,126,6,12,248,0,
0,0,0,0,0,254,12,24,48,96,254,0,0,0,
0,0,14,24,24,24,112,24,24,24,14,0,0,0,
0,0,24,24,24,24,0,24,24,24,24,0,0,0,
0,0,112,24,24,24,14,24,24,24,112,0,0,0,
0,0,118,220,0,0,0,0,0,0,0,0,0,0,
0,0,0,0,16,56,108,198,198,254,0,0,0,0,
0,0,60,102,194,192,192,194,102,60,12,6,124,0,
```

continued...

FONTEDIT 8

```
0,0,204,204,0,204,204,204,204,204,118,0,0,0,
0,12,24,48,0,124,198,254,192,198,124,0,0,0,
0,16,56,108,0,120,12,124,204,204,118,0,0,0,
0,0,204,204,0,120,12,124,204,204,118,0,0,0,
0,96,48,24,0,120,12,124,204,204,118,0,0,0,
0,56,108,56,0,120,12,124,204,204,118,0,0,0,
0,0,0,0,60,102,96,102,60,12,6,60,0,0,
0,16,56,108,0,124,198,254,192,198,124,0,0,0,
0,0,204,204,0,124,198,254,192,198,124,0,0,0,
0,96,48,24,0,124,198,254,192,198,124,0,0,0,
0,0,102,102,0,56,24,24,24,24,60,0,0,0,
0,24,60,102,0,56,24,24,24,24,60,0,0,0,
0,96,48,24,0,56,24,24,24,24,60,0,0,0,
0,198,198,16,56,108,198,198,254,198,198,0,0,0,
56,108,56,0,56,108,198,198,254,198,198,0,0,0,
24,48,96,0,254,102,96,124,96,102,254,0,0,0,
0,0,0,0,204,118,54,126,216,216,110,0,0,0,
0,0,62,108,204,204,254,204,204,204,206,0,0,0,
0,16,56,108,0,124,198,198,198,198,124,0,0,0,
0,0,198,198,0,124,198,198,198,198,124,0,0,0,
0,96,48,24,0,124,198,198,198,198,124,0,0,0,
0,48,120,204,0,204,204,204,204,204,118,0,0,0,
0,96,48,24,0,204,204,204,204,204,118,0,0,0,
0,0,198,198,0,198,198,198,198,126,6,12,120,0,
0,198,198,56,108,198,198,198,198,108,56,0,0,0,
0,198,198,0,198,198,198,198,198,198,124,0,0,0,
0,24,24,60,102,96,96,102,60,24,24,0,0,0,
0,56,108,100,96,240,96,96,96,230,252,0,0,0,
0,0,102,102,60,24,126,24,126,24,24,0,0,0,
0,248,204,204,248,196,204,222,204,204,198,0,0,0,
0,14,27,24,24,24,126,24,24,24,24,216,112,0,
0,24,48,96,0,120,12,124,204,204,118,0,0,0,
0,12,24,48,0,56,24,24,24,24,60,0,0,0,
0,24,48,96,0,124,198,198,198,198,124,0,0,0,
0,24,48,96,0,204,204,204,204,204,118,0,0,0,
0,0,118,220,0,220,102,102,102,102,102,0,0,0,
118,220,0,198,230,246,254,222,206,198,198,0,0,0,
0,60,108,108,62,0,126,0,0,0,0,0,0,0,
0,56,108,108,56,0,124,0,0,0,0,0,0,0,
0,0,48,48,0,48,48,96,198,198,124,0,0,0,
0,0,0,0,0,0,254,192,192,192,0,0,0,0,
0,0,0,0,0,0,254,6,6,6,0,0,0,0,
0,192,192,198,204,216,48,96,220,134,12,24,62,0,
0,192,192,198,204,216,48,102,206,158,62,6,6,0,
0,0,24,24,0,24,24,60,60,60,24,0,0,0,
0,0,0,0,54,108,216,108,54,0,0,0,0,0,
0,0,0,0,216,108,54,108,216,0,0,0,0,0,
```

continued...

8 FONTEDIT

17,68,17,68,17,68,17,68,17,68,17,68,17,68,
85,170,85,170,85,170,85,170,85,170,85,170,85,170,
221,119,221,119,221,119,221,119,221,119,221,119,221,119,
24,24,24,24,24,24,24,24,24,24,24,24,24,24,
24,24,24,24,24,24,24,248,24,24,24,24,24,24,
24,24,24,24,24,248,24,248,24,24,24,24,24,24,
54,54,54,54,54,54,54,246,54,54,54,54,54,54,
0,0,0,0,0,0,0,254,54,54,54,54,54,54,
0,0,0,0,0,248,24,248,24,24,24,24,24,24,
54,54,54,54,54,246,6,246,54,54,54,54,54,54,
54,54,54,54,54,54,54,54,54,54,54,54,54,54,
0,0,0,0,0,254,6,246,54,54,54,54,54,54,
54,54,54,54,54,246,6,254,0,0,0,0,0,0,
54,54,54,54,54,54,54,254,0,0,0,0,0,0,
24,24,24,24,24,248,24,248,0,0,0,0,0,0,
0,0,0,0,0,0,0,248,24,24,24,24,24,24,
24,24,24,24,24,24,24,31,0,0,0,0,0,0,
24,24,24,24,24,24,24,255,0,0,0,0,0,0,
0,0,0,0,0,0,0,255,24,24,24,24,24,24,
24,24,24,24,24,24,24,31,24,24,24,24,24,24,
0,0,0,0,0,0,0,255,0,0,0,0,0,0,
24,24,24,24,24,24,24,255,24,24,24,24,24,24,
24,24,24,24,24,31,24,31,24,24,24,24,24,24,
54,54,54,54,54,54,54,55,54,54,54,54,54,54,
54,54,54,54,54,55,48,63,0,0,0,0,0,0,
0,0,0,0,0,0,63,48,55,54,54,54,54,54,54,
54,54,54,54,54,247,0,255,0,0,0,0,0,0,
0,0,0,0,0,255,0,247,54,54,54,54,54,54,
54,54,54,54,54,55,48,55,54,54,54,54,54,54,
0,0,0,0,0,255,0,255,0,0,0,0,0,0,
54,54,54,54,54,247,0,247,54,54,54,54,54,54,
24,24,24,24,24,255,0,255,0,0,0,0,0,0,
54,54,54,54,54,54,54,255,0,0,0,0,0,0,
0,0,0,0,0,255,0,255,24,24,24,24,24,24,
0,0,0,0,0,0,0,255,54,54,54,54,54,54,
54,54,54,54,54,54,54,63,0,0,0,0,0,0,
24,24,24,24,24,31,24,31,0,0,0,0,0,0,
0,0,0,0,0,0,31,24,31,24,24,24,24,24,
0,0,0,0,0,0,0,63,54,54,54,54,54,54,
54,54,54,54,54,54,54,255,54,54,54,54,54,54,
24,24,24,24,24,255,24,255,24,24,24,24,24,24,
24,24,24,24,24,24,24,248,0,0,0,0,0,0,
0,0,0,0,0,0,0,31,24,24,24,24,24,24,
255,255,255,255,255,255,255,255,255,255,255,255,255,255,
0,0,0,0,0,0,0,255,255,255,255,255,255,255,
240,240,240,240,240,240,240,240,240,240,240,240,240,240,
15,15,15,15,15,15,15,15,15,15,15,15,15,15,

continued...

FONTEDIT 8

```
    255,255,255,255,255,255,255,0,0,0,0,0,0,0,
    0,0,0,0,0,118,220,216,216,220,118,0,0,0,
    0,0,0,0,124,198,252,198,198,252,192,192,64,0,
    0,0,254,198,198,192,192,192,192,192,192,0,0,0,
    0,0,0,0,254,108,108,108,108,108,108,0,0,0,
    0,0,254,198,96,48,24,48,96,198,254,0,0,0,
    0,0,0,0,0,126,216,216,216,216,112,0,0,0,
    0,0,0,0,102,102,102,102,124,96,96,192,0,0,
    0,0,0,0,118,220,24,24,24,24,24,0,0,0,
    0,0,126,24,60,102,102,102,60,24,126,0,0,0,
    0,0,56,108,198,198,254,198,198,108,56,0,0,0,
    0,0,56,108,198,198,198,108,108,108,238,0,0,0,
    0,0,30,48,24,12,62,102,102,102,60,0,0,0,
    0,0,0,0,0,126,219,219,126,0,0,0,0,0,
    0,0,3,6,126,219,219,243,126,96,192,0,0,0,
    0,0,28,48,96,96,124,96,96,48,28,0,0,0,
    0,0,0,124,198,198,198,198,198,198,198,0,0,0,
    0,0,0,254,0,0,254,0,0,254,0,0,0,0,
    0,0,0,24,24,126,24,24,0,0,255,0,0,0,
    0,0,48,24,12,6,12,24,48,0,126,0,0,0,
    0,0,12,24,48,96,48,24,12,0,126,0,0,0,
    0,0,14,27,27,24,24,24,24,24,24,24,24,
    24,24,24,24,24,24,24,24,216,216,112,0,0,0,
    0,0,0,24,24,0,126,0,24,24,0,0,0,0,
    0,0,0,0,118,220,0,118,220,0,0,0,0,0,
    0,56,108,108,56,0,0,0,0,0,0,0,0,0,
    0,0,0,0,0,0,24,24,0,0,0,0,0,0,
    0,0,0,0,0,0,0,24,0,0,0,0,0,0,
    0,15,12,12,12,12,12,236,108,60,28,0,0,0,
    0,216,108,108,108,108,108,0,0,0,0,0,0,0,
    0,112,216,48,96,200,248,0,0,0,0,0,0,0,
    0,0,0,0,124,124,124,124,124,124,0,0,0,0,
    0,0,0,0,0,0,0,0,0,0,0,0,0,0,
};

font sansega(fontptr);
```

THE REFERENCE GUIDE

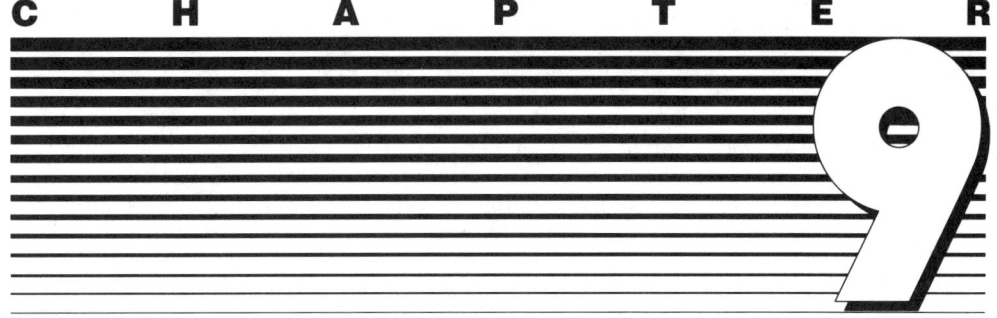

GWINDOWS REFERENCE GUIDE

The GWINDOWS toolbox defines global variables in the **gwindows.hpp** header file. These global variables are used by the application programmer to change default settings for the GWINDOWS operating environment. As a result, the GWINDOWS operating environment is easily customized to meet the needs of application programs. Additionally, the **gwindows.hpp** header file defines global variables for a variety of mouse operations.

gmenu

Defined As: menucolors gmenu;

Description: The **gmenu** variable is a globally defined **menucolors** object that application programs can access to determine current color settings for GWINDOWS menu objects (**dialog**, **popup**, and **pulldown**). Also, **gmenu** objects can be used to redefine the colors of GWINDOWS menu objects.

left_button

Defined As: int left_button;

Description: After a call to the **readmouse** function, the **left_button** variable holds the mouse's left button status. If the left button is held down, **left_button** will be set to TRUE (1). Otherwise, **left_button** will be set to FALSE (0) to indicate a released left button.

mouse

Defined As: pointer mouse;

Description: The **mouse** variable is a globally defined **pointer** object that can be easily incorporated into an application program by simply accessing **mouse** object through its related functions.

mouse_col

Defined As: int mouse_col;

Description: After a call to the **readmouse** function, the **mouse_col** variable holds the mouse pointer's column coordinate.

mouse_row

Defined As: int mouse_row;

Description: After a call to the **readmouse** function, the **mouse_row** variable holds the mouse pointer's row coordinate.

mouse_x

Defined As: int mouse_x;

Description: After a call to the **readmouse** function, the **mouse_x** variable holds the mouse's graphical x-coordinate.

mouse_y
Defined As: int mouse_y;

Description: After a call to the **readmouse** function, the **mouse_y** variable holds the mouse's graphical y-coordinate.

STANDARD DATA TYPES

In **gwindows.hpp**, the GWINDOWS toolbox defines a number of useful data types. These include:

boolean
Defined As: typedef int boolean;

Description: The **boolean** data type is used to define logical variables. To assist in the use of the boolean data type, the following two constants are defined in **gwindows.hpp**:

Constant	Value
TRUE	1
FALSE	0

date
Defined As:
```
struct date {
    int month, day, year;
};
```

Description: The **date** structure is used to define dates for **date_string**, **display_date**, and **input_date** functions. **Date** structure is used as follows:

Data Type	Description
month	The date's month.
day	The date's day of the month.
year	The date's year.

MENU
Defined As:
```
struct MENU {
    char *string;
    int hotkey;
    void (*function)(void);
    void (*help)(void);
};
```

Description: The **MENU** structure is used to define menu items for the GWINDOWS toolbox menu objects. **MENU** structure is used, as follows:

Data Type	Description
string	Pointer to a string, which defines the menu item.
hotkey	Position in *string* of the menu item's hotkey character.
(**function*)()	Pointer to a function, which is executed if the menu item is selected.
(**help*)()	Pointer to a function, which is executed if help is requested for the highlighted menu item.

MENU_HEAD

Defined As:
```
struct MENU_HEAD {
    char *heading;
    int hotkey, number;
    MENU *mptr;
};
```

Description: The **MENU_HEAD** structure is used to define menus for pull-down menu objects. **MENU_HEAD** structure is used, as follows:

Data Type	Description
heading	Pointer to a string which defines the menu's heading.
hotkey	Position in *heading* of the menu's pull-down hotkey character.
number	Number of items in the pull-down menu.
mptr	Pointer to an array of **MENU** structures which defines the pull-down menu.

phone

Defined As:
```
struct phone {
    int area, exchange, no;
};
```

Description: The **phone** structure is used to define phone numbers for the **display_phone**, **input_phone**, and **phone_string** functions. The **phone** structure is used, as follows:

Data Type	Description
area	The phone number's area code.
exchange	The phone number's exchange.
no	The phone number's final four digits.

ssn

Defined As:
```
struct ssn {
    int no1, no2, no3;
};
```

Description: The **ssn** structure is used to define Social Security numbers for the **display_ssn**, **input_ssn**, and **ssn_string** functions. The **ssn** structure is used, as follows:

Data Type	Description
no1	The Social Security number's first three digits.
no2	The Social Security number's middle two digits.
no3	The Social Security number's final four digits.

OBJECTS

In **gwindows.hpp**, the GWINDOWS toolbox defines a variety of objects. These objects are used to implement features such as the graphical environment, fonts, display screen pointers, dynamic display screen windows, and a variety of menu systems.

dialog

Defined As:
```
class dialog {
    int row, col;
    boolean ESC_flag;
public:
    dialog(int, int, boolean e = FALSE);
    dialog(dialog &);
    int get(int, MENU *, int, ...);
};
```

Description: The **dialog** objects are used to implement dialog box style menus. The **dialog** constructor is used to define the display screen portion of a dialog box menu and, as an option, define the menu's **ESC** key flag (*ESC_flag*).

environment

Defined As:
```
class environment {
    static old_video_mode;
public:
    environment();
    ~environment();
};
```

Description: The **environment** objects are used to set the state of the video display adapter. The **environment** constructor sets the computer's display adapter for an appropriate graphics mode. The **environment** destructor restores the display adapter to the video mode that existed when the object was constructed. By defining a static **environment** object, **video**, in **lowlevel.cpp**, the GWINDOWS toolbox automatically initializes the operating environment using the construction and destruction features of the C++ programming language.

font

Defined As:
```
class font {
    boolean oflag;
    unsigned char *fontptr, *oldlptr, *olduptr;
public:
    font(unsigned char *fp);
    font(font &);
    ~font();
    void open(void);
    void close(void);
    unsigned char *getptr(void);
};
```

Description: The **font** objects are used to define display screen fonts. Also, the **font** constructor is used to define a pointer (*fontptr*) to the user-defined font table. The **font** destructor ensures that any opened fonts will be closed when they go out of scope.

menucolors

Defined As:
```
class menucolors {
    int col, high;
public:
    menucolors();
    menucolors(menucolors &);
    void setcolor(int);
    void sethighlight(int);
    int color(void);
    int highlight(void);
};
```

Description: The **menucolors** objects are used to define the colors for the GWINDOWS menu objects.

pointer

Defined As:
```
class pointer {
public:
    pointer();
    ~pointer();
    void on();
    void off();
    void read(void);
    int x(void);
    int y(void);
    int row(void);
    int col(void);
    int lbutton(void);
    int rbutton(void);
};
```

Description: The **pointer** objects are used to implement display screen pointing devices. The **pointer** constructor is used to reset a pointer object's device driver. The **pointer** destructor is used to ensure that a pointing device's display screen pointer is turned off when the object goes out of scope.

popup

Defined As:
```
class popup {
    int row, col1;
    boolean ESC_flag;
public:
    popup(int, int, boolean e = FALSE);
    popup(popup &);
    int get(int, MENU *);
};
```

Description: The **popup** objects are used to implement pop-up style menus. The **popup** constructor is used to define a pop-up menu's upper left corner (*row*, *col1*) and to optionally define the menu's **ESC** key flag (*ESC_flag*).

pulldown

Defined As:
```
class pulldown {
    int row, number, *tabs;
    char *hotkeys;
    MENU_HEAD *menus;
    void (*menu_help)(void);
public:
    pulldown(int, int, MENU_HEAD *,
        void(*m_h)(void) = NULL);
    pulldown(pulldown &);
    void display(void);
    int get(int);
};
```

Description: The **pulldown** objects are used to implement pull-down style menus. The **pulldown** constructor is used to define a pull-down menu's menu bar row (*row*), the number (*number*) of the menu's pull-down menus, a pointer (*menus*) to the menu's array of MENU_HEAD structures, and to optionally define the menu's general help function (*menu_help*).

window

Defined As:
```
class window {
    int row1, col1, row2, col2, watt, bflg;
    char *buffer;
    boolean oflag, sflag;
    int orow, ocol, ostart, oend;
    int crow, ccol;
    int b_adj(int cols);
    int urow();
    int lcol();
    int brow();
    int rcol();
public:
    windows(int r1 = 1, int c1 = 1, int r2 = 25,
        int c2 = 80, int w = 7, int b =
        NO_BORDER, int s = NO_SCROLL);
    window(window &);
    ~window();
    void draw(void);
    void open(void);
    void close(void);
    void setcurpos(int, int);
    int currow(void);
    int curcol(void);
    int p_row(int);
    int p_col(int);
    void cls(void);
```

```
            void clreol(void);
            void scroll(int, int, boolean);
            void horizontal_bar(int, int);
            void vertical_bar(int, int);
            void print(char *);
            void println(char *);
            void printat(int, int, char *);
            void printlnat(int, int, char *);
};
```

Description: The **window** objects are used to define dynamic display screen windows. The **window** constructor is used to specify the window's upper left corner (*row1, col1*), lower right corner (*row2, col2*), color attribute (*watt*), border type (*bflg*), and scroll type (*sflag*). The *bflg* parameter can be one of the following constants (defined in **gwindows.hpp**):

Constant	Action
NO_BORDER	When the window is opened, it is drawn without a border.
SINGLE_LINE	When the window is opened, it is drawn with a single-lined border.
DOUBLE_LINE	When the window is opened, it is drawn with a double-lined border.

The *sflag* parameter can be one of the following constants (defined in **gwindows.hpp**):

Constant	Action
SCROLL	Scrolls text sent to the window by the **window::print**, **window::println**, **window::printat**, and **window::print-lnat** functions.
NO_SCROLL	Truncates text sent to the window by the **window::print, window::println, window::printat**, and **window::print-lnat** functions.

FUNCTIONS

The GWINDOWS toolbox contains a variety of functions. To facilitate their use in application programs, this section describes the GWINDOWS functions in the following format:

Summary: Presents an exact syntactic model for each of the GWINDOWS functions.

Description: Describes a function's purpose and how it is used in an application program.

9 GWINDOWS Reference Guide

Return Value: Explains any of the possible return values for a GWINDOWS function.

See Also: Lists any similar or related GWINDOWS functions.

Example: Illustrates using a GWINDOWS function in an application program.

background

Summary:
```
#include "gwindows.hpp"
int background(color);
int color;        (EGA color value)
```

Description: The **background** function determines the background color for a specified EGA color value (*color*).

Return Value: The **background** function returns the EGA color value's background color.

Example: The following program demonstrates the **background** function by displaying the background value for a variety of EGA color values.

```
//
// background demo
//
#include <stdio.h>
#include <stdlib.h>
#include "gwindows.hpp"

main()
{
    displaycenter(1, 40, gmenu.highlight(), "background demo");
    setcurpos(2, 1);
    printf("%d\n", background(gmenu.color()));
    printf("%d\n", background(gmenu.highlight()));
    printf("%d\n", background(egacolor(BLUE, GREEN)));
    waitkey();
    exit(0);
}
```

clearcolumn

Summary:
```
#include "gwindows.hpp"
void clearcolumn(row1, col, row2, color);
    int row1;    (top row of the display screen column)
    int col;     (display screen column)
    int row2;    (bottom row of the display screen column)
    int color;   (color value)
```

Description: The **clearcolumn** function clears a display screen column (*col*) starting at the row specified by (*row1*) and ending with the row specified by (*row2*). Additionally, the cleared display screen column's color will be set to *color*.

Return Value: No value is returned.

See Also: **clearrow** and **clearwindow**

Example: The following program demonstrates the **clearcolumn** function by clearing the 40th display screen column.

```
//
// clearcolumn demo
//
#include <stdlib.h>
#include "gwindows.hpp"

main()
{
    displaycenter(1, 40, gmenu.highlight(), "clearcolumn Demo");
    waitkey();
    clearcolumn(1, 40, 25, BLUE);
    waitkey();
    exit(0);
}
```

clearrow

Summary:
```
#include "gwindows.hpp"
void clearrow(row, col1, col2, color);
int row;      (display screen row)
int col1;     (left column of the display screen row)
int col2;     (right column of the display screen row)
int color;    (color value)
```

Description: The **clearrow** function clears a display screen row (*row*) starting at the column specified by (*col1*) and ending with the column specified by (*col2*). Additionally, the cleared display screen row's color will be set to *color*.

Return Value: No value is returned.

See Also: **clearcolumn** and **clearwindow**

Example: The following program demonstrates the **clearrow** function by clearing the 2nd display screen row.

9 GWINDOWS Reference Guide

```
//
// clearrow demo
//
#include <stdlib.h>
#include "gwindows.hpp"

main()
{
    displaycenter(1, 40, gmenu.highlight(), "clearrow Demo");
    waitkey();
    clearrow(2, 1, 80, RED);
    waitkey();
    exit(0);
}
```

clearwindow

Summary: #include "gwindows.hpp"
void clearwindow(*row1*, *col1*, *row2*, *col2*, *color*);
int *row1*, *col1*;   (upper left corner of the display screen window)
int *row2*, *col2*;   (lower right corner of the display screen window)
int *color*;   (color value)

Description: The **clearwindow** function clears an area of the display screen defined by the coordinates (*row1*, *col1*) and (*row2*, *col2*). Additionally, the cleared display screen window's color is set to *color*.

Return Value: No value is returned.

See Also: **clearcolumn** and **clearrow**

Example: The following program demonstrates the **clearwindow** function by clearing the lower half of the display screen.

```
//
// clearwindow demo
//
#include <stdlib.h>
#include "gwindows.hpp"

main()
{
    displaycenter(1, 40, gmenu.highlight(), "clearwindow demo");
    waitkey();
    clearwindow(13, 1, 25, 80, BLUE);
    waitkey();
    exit(0);
}
```

cursorcolor

Summary:
```
#include "gwindows.hpp"
void cursorcolor(color);
int color;      (color value)
```

Description: The **cursorcolor** function sets the cursor character's color to the value specified by (*color*).

Return Value: No value is returned.

Example: The following program demonstrates the **cursorcolor** function by changing the cursor character's color from black to white.

```
//
// cursorcolor demo
//
#include <stdlib.h>
#include "gwindows.hpp"

main()
{
    clearwindow(1, 1, 25, 80, background(gmenu.highlight()));
    displaycenter(1, 40, gmenu.highlight(), "cursorcolor demo");
    displaystring(2, 1, gmenu.highlight(), "The cursor is now black");
    setcurpos(3, 1);
    cursoron();
    waitkey();
    displaystring(4, 1, gmenu.highlight(), "The cursor is now white");
    setcurpos(5, 1);
    cursorcolor(WHITE);
    waitkey();
    exit(0);
}
```

cursoroff, cursoron

Summary:
```
#include "gwindows.hpp"
void cursoroff(void);
void cursoron(void);
```

Description: The **cursoroff** function turns the cursor off. The **cursoron** function turns the cursor on.

Return Value: No value is returned.

Example: The following program demonstrates the **cursoroff** and **cursoron** functions by first turning the cursor on and then turn the cursor back off again.

9 GWINDOWS Reference Guide

```
//
// cursoroff/cursoron demo
//
#include <stdlib.h>
#include "gwindows.hpp"

main()
{
    clearwindow(1, 1, 25, 80, background(gmenu.highlight()));
    displaycenter(1, 40, gmenu.highlight(), "cursoroff/cursoron
        demo");
    displaystring(2, 1, gmenu.highlight(),
        "Press any key to turn the cursor on....");
    waitkey();
    setcurpos(3, 1);
    cursoron();
    displaystring(4, 1, gmenu.highlight(),
        "Press any key to turn the cursor off....");
    waitkey();
    cursoroff();
    waitkey();
    exit(0);
}
```

date_string

Summary: #include "gwindows.hpp"
char *date_string(*string*, *date*);
char **string*;   (storage location for the date string)
date &*date*;   (date structure)

Description: The **date_string** function constructs an eight-character date string (*string* = "mm/dd/yy") for the date defined by *date*.

Return Value: The **date_string** function returns a pointer to the resulting date string.

See Also: **display_date** and **input_date**

Example: The following program demonstrates the **date_string** function by displaying a constructed date string on the third line of the display screen.

```
//
// date_string demo
//
#include <stdlib.h>
#include "gwindows.hpp"

main()
{
    static date d = {10, 3, 61};
    char line[80];

    displaycenter(1, 40, gmenu.highlight(), "date_string demo");
    displaystring(3, 1, gmenu.highlight(), date_string(line, d));
    waitkey();
    exit(0);
}
```

dialog::get

Summary:

```
#include "gwindows.hpp"
object.get(nitems, menu, ntitles, [title, ...]);
dialog object;       (dialog box menu object)
int nitems;          (number of menu items)
MENU *menu;          (pointer to an array of MENU structures)
int ntitles;         (number of titles)
char *title;         (title pointer)
```

Description: The **dialog::get** function displays the dialog box menu defined by (*object*). If any titles are specified, they are displayed above the menu items pointed to by *menu*. A menu item can be selected by pressing the indicated hotkey. Furthermore, the double-lined menu item can be selected by simply pressing **ENTER**. If available, help can be accessed for the highlighted menu item by pressing **F1**. The double-lined highlighting is moved from one menu item to the next by pressing either the **LEFT** or **RIGHT ARROW** key.

Return Value: If the menu item has a NULL function pointer, the **dialog::get** function returns the value of the selected item's hotkey. Otherwise, the **dialog::get** function returns a value of zero.

Example: The following program demonstrates the **dialog::get** function by asking whether or not a file should be saved. If instructed, the **dialog::get** function executes the simulated save file function.

```
//
// dialog::get demo
//
#include <stdlib.h>
#include "gwindows.hpp"

void save_file(void);

static MENU menu[3] = {
    {"Yes", 0, save_file, NULL},
    {"No", 0, NULL, NULL},
    {"Cancel", 0, NULL, NULL} };

main()
{
    int key;

    clearwindow(1, 1, 25, 80, background(gmenu.highlight()));
    mouse.on();
    do {
        key = dialog(13, 40, TRUE).get(3, menu, 2,
            "The file hasn't been saved!",
            "Do you want me to save it?");
    } while (key != 27 && key != 'C');
    exit(0);
}

void save_file(void)
{
    displaycenter(13, 40, gmenu.highlight(),
        "The file has been saved");
    waitkey();
    clearrow(13, 1, 80, background(gmenu.highlight()));
}
```

display_date

Summary:	`#include "gwindows.hpp"`
	`void display_date(row, col, color, date);`
	`int row, col;` (screen position)
	`int color;` (color value)
	`date &date;` (date structure)

Description:	The **display_date** function displays a date (*date*) at the display screen position defined by (*row, col*) in the color specified by (*color*).
Return Value:	No value is returned.
See Also:	**date_string** and **input_date**

Example: The following program demonstrates the **display_date** function by displaying a variety of dates on the display screen.

```
//
// display_date demo
//
#include <stdlib.h>
#include "gwindows.hpp"

main()
{
    static date d1 = {02, 04, 81} ;
    static date d2 = {03, 12, 83} ;

    clearwindow(1, 1, 25, 80, background(gmenu.highlight()));
    displaycenter(1, 40, gmenu.highlight(), "display_date demo");
    display_date(3, 10, gmenu.highlight(), d1);
    display_date(3, 20, gmenu.highlight(), d2);
    waitkey();
    exit(0);
}
```

display_dollar

Summary:
```
#include "gwindows.hpp"
void display_dollar(row, col, length, color, dollar)
int row, col;         (screen position)
int length;           (field length)
int color;            (color value)
double &dollar;       (dollar value)
```

Description: The **display_dollar** function displays a right-justified dollar value (*dollar*) with a field length of *length* at the display screen position defined by (*row*, *col*) in the color specified by (*color*).

Return Value: No value is returned.

See Also: **input_dollar**

Example: The following program demonstrates the **display_dollar** function by displaying a variety of dollar values on the screen.

9 GWINDOWS Reference Guide

```
//
// display_dollar demo
//
#include <stdlib.h>
#include "gwindows.hpp"

main()
{
    double n1 = 32.376, n2 = -55.23;

    clearwindow(1, 1, 25, 80, background(gmenu.highlight()));
    displaycenter(1, 40, gmenu.highlight(), "display_dollar demo");
    display_dollar(3, 1, 10, gmenu.highlight(), n1);
    display_dollar(4, 1, 10, gmenu.highlight(), n2);
    display_dollar(5, 1, 10, gmenu.highlight(), 67.328);
    waitkey();
    exit(0);
}
```

display_number

Summary: #include "gwindows.hpp"
void display_number(*row*, *col*, *length*, *color*, *number*);
int *row*, *col*;   (screen position)
int *length*;   (field length)
int *color*;   (color value)
unsigned long &*number*;   (numeric value)

Description: The **display_number** function displays a right-justified unsigned numeric value (*number*) with a field length of *length* at the display screen position defined by (*row*, *col*) in the color specified by *color*.

Return Value: No value is returned.

See Also: **input_number**

Example: The following program demonstrates the **display_number** function by displaying a variety of numeric values on the display screen.

```
//
// display_number demo
//
#include <stdlib.h>
#include "gwindows.hpp"

main()
{
    unsigned long n1 = 456789, n2 = 6789999;

    clearwindow(1, 1, 25, 80, background(gmenu.highlight()));
    displaycenter(1, 40, gmenu.highlight(), "display_number demo");
    display_number(3, 1, 10, gmenu.highlight(), n1);
    display_number(4, 1, 10, gmenu.highlight(), 32767);
    display_number(5, 1, 10, gmenu.highlight(), n2);
    waitkey();
    exit(0);
}
```

display_phone

Summary: #include "gwindows.hpp"
void display_phone(*row*, *col*, *color*, *number*);
int *row*, *col*;   (screen position)
int *color*;   (color value)
phone &*number*;   (phone number structure)

Description: The **display_phone** function displays a phone number (*number*) at the display screen position defined by (*row*, *col*) in the color specified by *color*.

Return Value: No value is returned.

See Also: **input_phone** and **phone_string**

Example: The following program demonstrates the **display_phone** function by displaying an assortment of phone numbers on the display screen.

9 GWINDOWS Reference Guide

```
//
// display_phone demo
//
#include <stdlib.h>
#include "gwindows.hpp"

main()
{
    static phone pn1 = {800, 555, 6678} ;
    static phone pn2 = {207, 555, 3277} ;

    clearwindow(1, 1, 25, 80, background(gmenu.highlight()));
    displaycenter(1, 40, gmenu.highlight(), "display_phone demo");
    display_phone(3, 1, gmenu.highlight(), pn1);
    display_phone(4, 1, gmenu.highlight(), pn2);
    waitkey();
    exit(0);
}
```

display_ssn

Summary:
```
#include "gwindows.hpp"
void display_ssn(row, col, color, number);
int row, col;          (screen position)
int color;             (color value)
ssn &number;           (Social Security number structure)
```

Description: The **display_ssn** function displays a Social Security number (*number*) at the display screen position defined by (*row*, *col*) in the color specified by *color*.

Return Value: No value is returned.

See Also: **input_ssn** and **ssn_string**

Example: The following program demonstrates the **display_ssn** function by displaying an assortment of Social Security numbers on the display screen.

```
//
// display_ssn demo
//
#include <stdlib.h>
#include "gwindows.hpp"

main()
{
    static ssn sn1 = {007, 25, 5687} ;
    static ssn sn2 = {101, 55, 3535} ;
```

continued...

```
            clearwindow(1, 1, 25, 80, background(gmenu.highlight()));
            displaycenter(1, 40, gmenu.highlight(), "display_ssn demo");
            display_ssn(3, 1, gmenu.highlight(), sn1);
            display_ssn(4, 1, gmenu.highlight(), sn2);
            waitkey();
            exit(0);
        }
```

display_string

Summary:
```
#include "gwindows.hpp"
void display_string(row, col, length, color, string);
int row, col;        (screen position)
int length;          (field length)
int color;           (color value)
char *string;        (string pointer)
```

Description: The **display_string** function displays a left-justified alphanumeric string (*string*) with a field length of *length* at the display screen position defined by (*row*, *col*) in the color specified by *color*.

Return Value: No value is returned.

See Also: **input_string**

Example: The following program demonstrates the **display_string** function by displaying an assortment of strings on the screen.

```
//
// display_string demo
//
#include <stdlib.h>
#include "gwindows.hpp"

main()
{
    char *s1 = "This is demo string 1";
    char *s3 = "This is demo string 3";

    clearwindow(1, 1, 25, 80, background(gmenu.highlight()));
    displaycenter(1, 40, gmenu.highlight(), "display_string demo");
    display_string(3, 1, 25, gmenu.highlight(), s1);
    display_string(4, 1, 25, gmenu.highlight(),
        "This is demo string 2");
    display_string(5, 1, 25, gmenu.highlight(), s3);
    waitkey();
    exit(0);
}
```

displaycenter

Summary:	#include "gwindows.hpp" void displaycenter(*row, col, color, string*); int *row*; (screen row) int *col*; (column to center the string on) int *color*; (color value) char **string*; (string pointer)
Description:	The **displaycenter** function displays a string (*string*) on the display screen row defined by *row* and centered on the column defined by *col*. Additionally, the string will be displayed in the color specified by *color*.
Return Value:	No value is returned.
Example:	The following program demonstrates the **displaycenter** function by centering a string on the top line of the screen.

```
//
// displaycenter demo
//
#include <stdlib.h>
#include "gwindows.hpp"

main()
{
    displaycenter(1, 40, gmenu.highlight(),
        "This message is centered on the top display line");
    waitkey();
    exit(0);
}
```

displaychar

Summary:	#include "gwindows.hpp" void displaychar(*row, col, color, chr*); int *row, col*; (screen position) int *color*; (color value); int *chr*; (character)
Description:	The **displaychar** function displays a character (*chr*) at the display screen position defined by (*row, col*) in the color defined by *color*.
Return Value:	No value is returned.
Example:	The following program demonstrates the **displaychar** function by displaying a black-on-white **M** at screen position (4,10).

```
//
// displaychar demo
//
#include <stdlib.h>
#include "gwindows.hpp"

main()
{
    displaycenter(1, 40, gmenu.highlight(), "displaychar demo");
    displaychar(4, 10, egacolor(WHITE, BLACK), 'M');
    waitkey();
    exit(0);
}
```

displaystring

Summary:	#include "gwindows.hpp" void displaystring(*row*, *col*, *color*, *string*); int *row*, *col*; (screen position) int *color*; (color value) char *string; (string pointer)
Description:	The **displaystring** function displays a string (*string*) at the display screen position defined by (*row*, *col*) in the color specified by *color*.
Return Value:	No value is returned.
Example:	The following program demonstrates the **displaystring** function by displaying a string at screen position (3,10).

```
//
// displaystring demo
//
#include <stdlib.h>
#include "gwindows.hpp"

main()
{
    displaycenter(1, 40, gmenu.highlight(), "displaystring demo");
    displaystring(3, 10, gmenu.highlight(),
        "This message starts at row 3, column 10");
    waitkey();
    exit(0);
}
```

drawborder

Summary:
```
#include "gwindows.hpp"
void drawborder(row1, col1, row2, col2, color, btype)
int row1, col1;   (upper left corner of the display screen window)
int row2, col2;   (lower right corner of the display screen window)
int color;        (color value)
int btype;        (border type flag)
```

Description: The **drawborder** function draws a border around a display screen window in which coordinates are defined by the points (*row1*, *col1*) and (*row2*, *col2*). Additionally, the border is drawn with the color specified by *color*.

The *btype* parameter can be one of the following constants (defined in **gwindows.hpp**):

Constant	Action
SINGLE_LINE	Draws a single-lined border around the display screen window.
DOUBLE_LINE	Draws a double lined border around the display screen window.

Return Value: No value is returned.

Example: The following program demonstrates the **drawborder** function by drawing a double-lined border around the right half of the screen.

```
//
// drawborder demo
//
#include <stdlib.h>
#include "gwindows.hpp"

main()
{
    clearwindow(1, 1, 25, 80, background(gmenu.highlight()));
    drawborder(1, 41, 25, 80, gmenu.highlight(), DOUBLE_LINE);
    waitkey();
    exit(0);
}
```

egacolor

Summary:
```
#include "gwindows.hpp"
int egacolor(background, foreground);
int background;    (background color value)
int foreground;    (foreground color value)
```

Description: The **egacolor** function constructs an EGA color value from a specified background color (*background*) and a specified foreground color (*foreground*).

Return Value: The **egacolor** function returns the constructed EGA color value.

Example: The following program demonstrates the **egacolor** function by displaying a variety of multi-colored strings.

```
//
// egacolor demo
//
#include <stdlib.h>
#include "gwindows.hpp"

main()
{
    displaycenter(1, 40, egacolor(GREEN, YELLOW),
        "egacolor demo");
    displaystring(3, 1, egacolor(RED, BLUE),
        "This is a blue-on-red string");
    displaystring(4, 1, egacolor(BROWN, YELLOW),
        "This is a yellow-on-brown string");
    displaystring(5, 1, egacolor(CYAN, MAGENTA),
        "This is a magenta-on-cyan string");
    waitkey();
    exit(0);
}
```

egamode

Summary:
```
#include "gwindows.hpp"
int egamode(void);
```

Description: The **egamode** function determines the video mode setting.

Return Value: If the video mode is set for the 640-by-350 16-color EGA graphics mode, the **egamode** function returns TRUE (1). Otherwise, the **egamode** function returns FALSE (0) to indicate the 640-by-200 2-color CGA graphics mode.

Example: The following program demonstrates the **egamode** function by displaying the video display type.

```
//
// egamode demo
//
#include <stdio.h>
#include <stdlib.h>
#include "gwindows.hpp"

main()
{
    setcurpos(1, 1);
    if (egamode())
        printf("This is an EGA display\n");
    else
        printf("This is a CGA display\n");
    waitkey();
    exit(0);
}
```

fillcolumn

Summary:
```
#include "gwindows.hpp"
void fillcolumn(row1, col, row2, color, chr);
int row1;    (top row of the display screen column)
int col;     (display screen column)
int row2;    (bottom row of the display screen column)
int color;   (color value)
int chr;     (character)
```

Description: The **fillcolumn** function fills a display screen column (*col*) starting at the row specified by *row1* and ending with the row specified by *row2* with the character defined by *chr*. Additionally, the screen column's color is set to *color*.

Return Value: No value is returned.

See Also: **fillrow** and **fillwindow**

Example: The following program demonstrates the **fillcolumn** function by filling the first display screen column with *s.

```
//
// fillcolumn demo
//
#include <stdlib.h>
#include "gwindows.hpp"
```

continued...

```
main()
{
    displaycenter(1, 40, gmenu.highlight(), "fillcolumn demo");
    fillcolumn(1, 1, 25, gmenu.highlight(), '*');
    waitkey();
    exit(0);
}
```

fillrow

Summary:

```
#include "gwindows.hpp"
void fillrow(row, col1, col2, color, chr);
int row;      (display screen row)
int col1;     (left column of the display screen row)
int col2;     (right column of the display screen row)
int color;    (color value)
int chr;      (character)
```

Description: The **fillrow** function fills a display screen row (*row*) starting at the column specified by *col1* and ending with the column specified by *col2* with the character defined by *chr*. Additionally, the display screen row's color is set to *color*.

Return Value: No value is returned.

See Also: **fillcolumn** and **fillwindow**

Example: The following program demonstrates the **fillrow** function by filling the second screen row with *s.

```
//
// fillrow demo
//
#include <stdlib.h>
#include "gwindows.hpp"

main()
{
    displaycenter(1, 40, gmenu.highlight(), "fillrow demo");
    fillrow(2, 1, 80, gmenu.highlight(), '*');
    waitkey();
    exit(0);
}
```

fillwindow

Summary:
```
#include "gwindows.hpp"
void fillwindow(row1, col1, row2, col2, color, chr);
int row1,col1;   (upper left corner of the display screen window)
int row2,col2;   (lower right corner of the display screen window)
int color;       (color value)
int chr;         (character)
```

Description: The **fillwindow** function fills the display screen window defined by the coordinates (*row1*, *col1*) and (*row2*, *col2*) with the character specified by *chr*. Additionally, the screen window will be filled with the color specified by *color*.

Return Value: No value is returned.

See Also: **fillcolumn** and **fillrow**

Example: The following program demonstrates the **fillwindow** function by filling the bottom half of the display screen with Ms.

```
//
// fillwindow demo
//
#include <stdlib.h>
#include "gwindows.hpp"

main()
{
    displaycenter(1, 40, gmenu.highlight(), "fillwindow.demo");
    fillwindow(13, 1, 25, 80, gmenu.highlight(), 'M');
    waitkey();
    exit(0);
}
```

font::close

Summary:
```
#include "gwindows.hpp"
object.close(void);
font object;   (font object)
```

Description: The **font::close** function closes the previously opened text font defined by *object*.

Return Value: No value is returned.

See Also: **font::open**

Example: The following program demonstrates the **font::close** function by closing a previously opened sans serif font.

```
//
// font::close demo
//
#include <stdlib.h>
#include "gwindows.hpp"

extern font sansega;

main()
{
    clearwindow(1, 1, 25, 80, background(gmenu.highlight()));
    displaycenter(1, 40, gmenu.highlight(), "font::close demo");
    sansega.open();
    displaystring(3, 1, gmenu.highlight(),
        "This string is displayed using a sans serif font");
    sansega.close();
    displaystring(4, 1, gmenu.highlight(),
        "This string is displayed using the system font");
    waitkey();
    exit(0);
}
```

font::getptr

Summary:
#include "gwindows.hpp"
unsigned char *object.getptr(void);
font object;   (font object)

Description: The **font::getptr** function retrieves a font object's (*object*) font table pointer.

Return Value: The **font::getptr** function returns an **unsigned char** pointer to the font object's font table.

Example: The following program demonstrates the **font::getptr** function by displaying a font object's font table pointer.

```
//
// font::getptr
//
#include <stdio.h>
#include <stdlib.h>
#include "gwindows.hpp"

extern font sansega;
```

continued...

9 GWINDOWS Reference Guide

```
main()
{
    displaycenter(1, 40, gmenu.highlight(), "font::getptr demo");
    setcurpos(3, 1);
    printf("Sans Serif font begins at memory location: %lp\n",
        sansega.getptr());
    waitkey();
    exit(0);
}
```

font::open

Summary: #include "gwindows.hpp"
object.open(void);
font *object*;   (font object)

Description: The **font::open** function opens the text font defined by *object*.

Return Value: No value is returned.

See Also: **font::close**

Example: The following program demonstrates the **font::open** function by opening a sans serif font.

```
//
// font::open demo
//
#include <stdlib.h>
#include "gwindows.hpp"

extern font sansega;

main()
{
    clearwindow(1, 1, 25, 80, background(gmenu.highlight()));
    displaycenter(1, 40, gmenu.highlight(), "font::open demo");
    displaystring(3, 1, gmenu.highlight(),
        "This string is displayed using the system font");
    sansega.open();
    displaystring(4, 1, gmenu.highlight(),
        "This string is displayed using a sans serif font");
    sansega.close();
    waitkey();
    exit(0);
}
```

getcurpos

Summary:	#include "gwindows.hpp" void getcurpos(*row*, *col*); int **row*; (cursor row position) int **col*; (cursor column position)
Description:	The **getcurpos** function retrieves the cursor position by returning the cursor's row position in *row* and the cursor's column position in *col*.
Return Value:	No value is returned.
Example:	The following program demonstrates the **getcurpos** function by retrieving and displaying the current cursor position.

```
//
// getcurpos demo
//
#include <stdio.h>
#include <stdlib.h>
#include "gwindows.hpp"

main()
{
    int row, col;
    char line[80];

    setcurpos(23, 8);
    getcurpos(&row, &col);
    clearwindow(1, 1, 25, 80, background(gmenu.highlight()));
    displaycenter(1, 40, gmenu.highlight(), "getcurpos demo");
    sprintf(line, "Row: %2d  Column: %2d", row, col);
    displaystring(3, 1, gmenu.highlight(), line);
    waitkey();
    exit(0);
}
```

getfontvectors

Summary:	#include "gwindows.hpp" void getfontvectors(*lowerhalf*, *upperhalf*); unsigned char ***lowerhalf*; (lower font table pointer) unsigned char ***upperhalf*; (upper font table pointer)
Description:	The **getfontvectors** function retrieves the current font table pointers by returning the lower-half font table pointer in *lowerhalf* and the upper-half font table pointer in *upperhalf*.
Return Value:	No value is returned.
See Also:	**setfontvectors**

Example: The following program demonstrates the **getfontvectors** function by retrieving and displaying the current font table pointers.

```
//
// getfontvectors demo
//
#include <stdio.h>
#include <stdlib.h>
#include "gwindows.hpp"

main()
{
    char line[80];
    unsigned char *lowerhalf, *upperhalf;

    clearwindow(1, 1, 25, 80, background(gmenu.highlight()));
    displaycenter(1, 40, gmenu.highlight(), "getfontvectors demo");
    getfontvectors(&lowerhalf, &upperhalf);
    if (egamode()) {
        sprintf(line, "Current font table pointer: %lp", lowerhalf);
        displaystring(3, 1, gmenu.highlight(), line);
    }
    else {
        sprintf(line, "Current lower font table pointer: %lp", lowerhalf);
        displaystring(3, 1, gmenu.highlight(), line);
        sprintf(line, "Current upper font table pointer: %lp", upperhalf);
        displaystring(4, 1, gmenu.highlight(), line);
    }
    waitkey();
    exit(0);
}
```

hidemouse

Summary:
```
#include "gwindows.hpp"
void hidemouse(void);
```

Description: The **hidemouse** function turns off the mouse pointer.

Return Value: No value is returned.

See Also: **showmouse**

Example: The following program demonstrates the **hidemouse** function by turning off the mouse pointer.

```
//
// hidemouse demo
//
#include <stdlib.h>
#include "gwindows.hpp"

main()
{
    clearwindow(1, 1, 25, 80, background(gmenu.highlight()));
    displaycenter(1, 40, gmenu.highlight(), "hidemouse demo");
    resetmouse();
    showmouse();
    do {
        readmouse();
    } while (!keypressed() && !left_button);
    hidemouse();
    if (keypressed())
        waitkey();
    exit(0);
}
```

hotstring

Summary:

```
#include "gwindows.hpp"
void hotstring(row, col, hotkey, color, string);
int row, col;           (screen position)
int hotkey;             (hotkey position)
int color;              (color value)
char *string;           (string pointer)
```

Description: The **hotstring** function displays a string at the display screen position defined by (*row, col*) in the color specified by *color*. Additionally, the string's *hotkey* character is underlined.

Return Value: No value is returned.

Example: The following program demonstrates the **hotstring** function by displaying a hotstring at the beginning of the tenth display screen line.

```
//
// hotstring demo
//
#include <stdlib.h>
#include "gwindows.hpp"

main()
{
    displaycenter(1, 40, gmenu.color(), "hotstring demo");
    hotstring(10, 1, 10, gmenu.color(), "This is a HOTSTRING");
    waitkey();
    exit(0);
}
```

input_date

Summary:
```
#include "gwindows.hpp"
int input_date(row, col, color, date);
int row, col;          (screen position)
int color;             (data entry field's color)
date &date;            (data entry field's contents)
```

Description: The **input_date** function displays and inputs an eight-character date (*date* = "mm/dd/yy") at the display screen position defined by (*row, col*) in the color specified by *color*. The following control keys are active during the **input_date** function:

Control Key	Action
HOME	Move to the first character in the data entry field.
END	Move to the last character in the data entry field.
LEFT ARROW	Move to the previous character in the data entry field.
RIGHT ARROW	Move to the next character in the data entry field.

Return Value: The **input_date** function returns the value of the last key pressed.

See Also: **date_string** and **display_date**

Example: The following program demonstrates the **input_date** function by requesting the current date.

```
//
// input_date demo
//
#include <stdlib.h>
#include "gwindows.hpp"

main()
{
    static date d;

    clearwindow(1, 1, 25, 80, background(gmenu.highlight()));
    displaycenter(1, 40, gmenu.highlight(), "input_date demo");
    displaystring(10, 1, gmenu.highlight(),
        "Please Enter Today's Date:");
    while (input_date(10, 28, gmenu.highlight(), d) != 27) ;
    exit(0);
}
```

input_dollar

Summary:
```
#include "gwindows.hpp"
int input_dollar(row, col, length, color, dollar);
int row, col;           (screen position)
int length;             (data entry field's length)
int color;              (data entry field's color)
double &dollar;         (data entry field's contents)
```

Description: The **input_dollar** function displays and inputs a right-justified dollar value (*dollar*) with a field length of *length* at the display screen position defined by (*row*, *col*) in the color specified by *color*. The following control keys are active during the **input_dollar** function:

Control Key	Action
HOME	Clear the data entry field's contents.
BACKSPACE	Erase the last digit entered.

Return Value: The **input_dollar** function returns the value of the last key pressed.

See Also: **display_dollar**

Example: The following program demonstrates the **input_dollar** function by requesting an account balance.

```
//
// input_dollar demo
//
#include <stdlib.h>
#include "gwindows.hpp"

main()
{
    double n = 0;

    clearwindow(1, 1, 25, 80, background(gmenu.highlight()));
    displaycenter(1, 40, gmenu.highlight(), "input_dollar demo");
    displaystring(10, 1, gmenu.highlight(),
        "Please Enter The Account Balance:");
    while (input_dollar(10, 35, 10, gmenu.highlight(), n) != 27) ;
    exit(0);
}
```

input_number

Summary:
```
#include "gwindows.hpp"
int input_number(row, col, length, color, number);
int row, col;              (screen position)
int length;                (data entry field's length)
int color;                 (data entry field's color)
unsigned long &number;     (data entry field's contents)
```

9 GWINDOWS Reference Guide

Description: The **input_number** function displays and inputs a right-justified numeric value (*number*) with a field length of *length* at the display screen position defined by (*row, col*). The following control keys are active during the **input_number** function:

Control Key	Action
HOME	Clear the data entry field's contents.
BACKSPACE	Erase the last digit entered.

Return Value: The **input_number** function returns the value of the last key pressed.

See Also: display_number

Example: The following program demonstrates the **input_number** function by requesting an account number.

```
//
// input_number demo
//
#include <stdlib.h>
#include "gwindows.hpp"

main()
{
    unsigned long n = 0;

    clearwindow(1, 1, 25, 80, background(gmenu.highlight()));
    displaycenter(1, 40, gmenu.highlight(), "input_number demo");
    displaystring(10, 1, gmenu.highlight(),
        "Please Enter The Account Number:");
    while (input_number(10, 34, 6, gmenu.highlight(), n) != 27) ;
    exit(0);
}
```

input_phone

Summary:
```
#include "gwindows.hpp"
int input_phone(row, col, color, number);
int row, col;          (screen position)
int color;             (data entry field's color)
phone &number;         (data entry field's contents)
```

Description: The **input_phone** function displays and inputs a 14-character telephone number (*number* = "(xxx) xxx-xxxx") at the display screen position defined by (*row, col*) in the color specified by *color*. The following control keys are active during the **input_phone** function:

GWINDOWS Reference Guide 9

	Control Key	Action
	HOME	Move to the first character in the data entry field.
	END	Move to the last character in the data entry field.
	LEFT ARROW	Move to the previous character in the data entry field.
	RIGHT ARROW	Move to the next character in the data entry field.

Return Value: The **input_phone** function returns the value of the last key pressed.

See Also: **phone_string** and **display_phone**

Example: The following program demonstrates the **input_phone** function by requesting the operator's telephone number.

```
//
// input_phone demo
//
#include <stdlib.h>
#include "gwindows.hpp"

main()
{
    static phone n;

    clearwindow(1, 1, 25, 80, background(gmenu.highlight()));
    displaycenter(1, 40, gmenu.highlight(), "input_phone demo");
    displaystring(10, 1, gmenu.highlight(),
        "Please Enter Your Phone Number:");
    while (input_phone(10, 33, gmenu.highlight(), n) != 27) ;
    exit(0);
}
```

input_ssn

Summary:
```
#include "gwindows.hpp"
int input_ssn(row, col, color, number);
int row, col;          (screen position)
int color;             (data entry field's color)
ssn &number;           (data entry field's contents)
```

Description: The **input_ssn** function displays and inputs an 11-character Social Security number (*number* = "xxx-xx-xxxx") at the display screen position defined by (*row*, *col*) in the color specified by *color*. The following control keys are active during the **input_ssn** function:

243

9 GWINDOWS Reference Guide

Control Key	**Action**
HOME	Move to the first character in the data entry field.
END	Move to the last character in the data entry field.
LEFT ARROW	Move to the previous character in the data entry field.
RIGHT ARROW	Move to the next character in the data entry field.

Return Value: The **input_ssn** function returns the value of the last key pressed.

See Also: **ssn_string** and **display_ssn**

Example: The following program demonstrates the **input_ssn** function by requesting the operator's Social Security number.

```
//
// input_ssn demo
//
#include <stdlib.h>
#include "gwindows.hpp"

main()
{
    static ssn n;

    clearwindow(1, 1, 25, 80, background(gmenu.highlight()));
    displaycenter(1, 40, gmenu.highlight(), "input_ssn demo");
    displaystring(10, 1, gmenu.highlight(),
        "Please Enter Your Social Security Number:");
    while (input_ssn(10, 43, gmenu.highlight(), n) != 27) ;
    exit(0);
}
```

input_string

Summary:
```
#include "gwindows.hpp"
int input_string(row, col, length, color, string);
int row, col;          (screen position)
int length;            (data entry field's length)
int color;             (data entry field's color)
char *string;          (data entry field's contents)
```

Description: The **input_string** function displays and inputs a left-justified alphanumeric string (*string*) with a field length of *length* at the display screen position defined by (*row*, *col*). The following control keys are active during the **input_string** function:

GWINDOWS Reference Guide **9**

Control Key	**Action**
HOME	Clear the data entry field's contents.
BACKSPACE	Erase the last digit entered.

Return Value: The **input_string** function returns the value of the last key pressed.

See Also: **display_string**

Example: The following program demonstrates the **input_string** function by requesting the operator's name.

```
//
// input_string demo
//
#include <stdlib.h>
#include "gwindows.hpp"

main()
{
    static char string[31];

    clearwindow(1, 1, 25, 80, background(gmenu.highlight()));
    displaycenter(1, 40, gmenu.highlight(), "input_string demo");
    displaystring(10, 1, gmenu.highlight(),
        "Please Enter Your Name:");
    while (input_string(10, 25, 30, gmenu.highlight(), string) != 27) ;
    exit(0);
}
```

keypressed

Summary:
```
#include "gwindows.hpp"
int keypressed(void);
```

Description: The **keypressed** function determines whether or not a key has been pressed.

Return Value: If a key has been pressed, the **keypressed** function returns a value of TRUE (1). Otherwise, the **keypressed** function returns a value of FALSE (0) to indicate a key hasn't been pressed.

See Also: **waitkey**

Example: The following program demonstrates the **keypressed** function by performing a continuous loop until a key is pressed.

9 GWINDOWS Reference Guide

```
//
// keypressed demo
//
#include <stdlib.h>
#include "gwindows.hpp"

main()
{
    clearwindow(1, 1, 25, 80, background(gmenu.highlight()));
    displaycenter(1, 40, gmenu.highlight(), "keypressed demo");
    displaystring(3, 1, gmenu.highlight(),
        "Press any key to exit the program....");
    while (!keypressed()) ;
    waitkey();

    exit(0);
}
```

max

Summary:	#include "gwindows.hpp" int max(*first*, *second*); int *first*; (integer value) int *second*; (integer value)
Description:	The **max** function compares two integer values (*first*, *second*) to see which one is the largest.
Return Value:	The **max** function returns the largest of the two integer values.
See Also:	**min**
Example:	The following program demonstrates the **max** function by determining the longest string in an array of strings.

```
//
// max demo
//
#include <stdio.h>
#include <stdlib.h>
#include <string.h>
#include "gwindows.hpp"

static char *test[3] = {
    "This is the first string",
    "This is the second string",
    "This is the third string"};
```

continued...

```
main()
{
    int i, longest = 0;
    char line[81];

    clearwindow(1, 1, 25, 80, background(gmenu.highlight()));
    displaycenter(1, 40, gmenu.highlight(), "max demo");
    for (i = 0; i < 3; i++)
        longest = max(longest, strlen(test[i]));
    sprintf(line, "The longest string has a length of %d character.",
        longest;
    displaystring(3, 1, gmenu.highlight(), line);
    waitkey();
    exit(0);
}
```

menucolors::color

Summary: #include "gwindows.hpp"
int *object*.color(void);

Description: The **menucolors::color** function retrieves a menucolors object's (*object*) main color value.

Return Value: The **menucolors::color** function returns the object's main color value.

See Also: **menucolors::setcolor**

Example: The following program demonstrates the **menucolors::color** function by displaying a message using a menucolors object's main color value.

```
//
// menucolors::color demo
//
#include <stdlib.h>
#include "gwindows.hpp"

main()
{
    clearwindow(1, 1, 25, 80, background(gmenu.color()));
    displaycenter(1, 40, gmenu.color(),
        "This message is displayed usingthe gmenu.color() colors");
    waitkey();
}
```

menucolors::highlight

Summary: #include "gwindows.hpp"
int *object*.highlight(void);

Description:	The **menucolors::highlight** function retrieves a menucolors object's (*object*) highlight color value.
Return Value:	The **menucolors::highlight** function returns the object's highlight color value.
See Also:	**menucolors::sethighlight**
Example:	The following program demonstrates the **menucolors::highlight** function by displaying a message using a menucolors object's highlight color value.

```
//
// menucolors::highlight demo
//
#include <stdlib.h>
#include "gwindows.hpp"

main()
{
    clearwindow(1, 1, 25, 80, background(gmenu.highlight()));
    displaycenter(1, 40, gmenu.highlight(),
        "This message is displayed using the gmenu.highlight()
            colors");
    waitkey();
}
```

menucolors::setcolor

Summary:	#include "gwindows.hpp" void *object*.setcolor(*color*); int *color*; (color value)
Description:	The **menucolors::setcolor** function sets a menucolors object's (*object*) main color value to the color specified by *color*.
Return Value:	No value is returned.
See Also:	**menucolors::color**
Example:	The following program demonstrates the **menucolors::setcolor** function by setting a menucolors object's main color value to a variety of colors.

```
//
// menucolors::setcolor demo
//
#include <stdlib.h>
#include "gwindows.hpp"
```

continued...

```
main()
{
    clearwindow(1, 1, 25, 80, background(gmenu.color()));
    displaycenter(1, 40, gmenu.color(),
        "This string is displayed using the gmenu.color() colors");
    gmenu.setcolor(egacolor(YELLOW, GREEN));
    displaycenter(2, 40, gmenu.color(),
        "This string is displayed using the new gmenu.color() colors");
    waitkey();
    exit(0);
}
```

menucolors::sethighlight

Summary: #include "gwindows.hpp"
void *object*.sethighlight(*color*);
int *color*;   (color value)

Description: The **menucolors::sethighlight** function sets a menucolors object's (*object*) highlight color value to the color specified by *color*.

Return Value: No value is returned.

See Also: **menucolors::highlight**

Example: The following program demonstrates the **menucolors::sethighlight** function by setting a menucolors object's highlight color value to a variety of colors.

```
//
// menucolors::sethighlight demo
//
#include <stdlib.h>
#include "gwindows.hpp"

main()
{
    clearwindow(1, 1, 25, 80, background(gmenu.highlight()));
    displaycenter(1, 40, gmenu.highlight(),
        "This stringisdisplayedusingthegmenu.highlight()colors");
    gmenu.sethighlight(egacolor(BLUE, WHITE));
    displaycenter(2, 40, gmenu.highlight(),
        "This string is displayed using the new gmenu.highlight()
            colors");
    waitkey();
    exit(0);
}
```

min

Summary:
```
#include "gwindows.hpp"
int min(first, second);
int first;        (integer value)
int second;       (integer value)
```

Description: The **min** function compares two integer values (*first*, *second*) to see which one is the smallest.

Return Value: The **min** function returns the smallest of the two integer values.

See Also: **max**

Example: The following program demonstrates the **min** function by determining the shortest string in an array of strings.

```
//
// min demo
//
#include <stdio.h>
#include <stdlib.h>
#include <string.h>
#include "gwindows.hpp"

static char *test[3] = {
    "This is the first string",
    "This is the second string",
    "This is the third string"};

main()
{
    int i, shortest = 9999;
    char line[81];

    clearwindow(1, 1, 25, 80, background(gmenu.highlight()));
    displaycenter(1, 40, gmenu.highlight(), "min demo");
    for (i = 0; i < 3; i++)
        shortest = min(shortest, strlen(test[i]));
    sprintf(line, "The shortest string has a length of %d character.",
        shortest);
    displaystring(3, 1, gmenu.highlight(), line);
    waitkey();
    exit(0);
}
```

movewindow

Summary:
```
#include "gwindows.hpp"
void movewindow(row1, col1, row2, col2, row3, col3);
int row1, col1;(source window's upper left corner)
int row2, col2;(source window's lower right corner)
int row3, col3;(destination window's upper left corner)
```

Description: The **movewindow** function moves the display screen window defined by the coordinates (*row1*, *col1*) and (*row2*, *col2*) to a new location starting at the coordinates defined by (*row3*, *col3*).

Return Value: No value is returned.

Example: The following program demonstrates the **movewindow** function by moving the lower right quarter of the screen to the upper left quarter of the screen.

```
//
// movewindow demo
//
#include <stdlib.h>
#include "gwindows.hpp"

main()
{
    clearwindow(1, 1, 25, 80, background(gmenu.highlight()));
    displaycenter(1, 40, gmenu.highlight(), "movewindow demo");
    fillwindow(13, 41, 25, 80, gmenu.color(), '*');
    waitkey();
    movewindow(13, 41, 25, 80, 1, 1);
    waitkey();
    exit(0);
}
```

phone_string

Summary:
```
#include "gwindows.hpp"
char *phone_string(string, number);
char *string;          (storage location for the phone number string)
phone &number;         (phone number structure)
```

Description: The **phone_string** function constructs a 14-character phone number string (*string* = "(xxx) xxx-xxxx") for the phone number defined by *number*.

Return Value: The **phone_string** function returns a pointer to the resulting phone number string.

See Also: **display_phone** and **input_phone**

9 GWINDOWS Reference Guide

Example: The following program demonstrates the **phone_string** function by displaying a constructed phone number string on the tenth line of the display screen.

```
//
// phone_string demo
//
#include <stdlib.h>
#include "gwindows.hpp"

main()
{
    static phone n = {207, 555, 3235};
    char line[81];

    clearwindow(1, 1, 25, 80, background(gmenu.highlight()));
    displaycenter(1, 40, gmenu.highlight(), "phone_string demo");
    displaystring(10, 1, gmenu.highlight(), phone_string(line, n));
    waitkey();
    exit(0);
}
```

pointer::col

Summary:
```
#include "gwindows.hpp"
int object.col(void);
pointer object;          (display screen pointer object)
```

Description: The **pointer::col** function determines a display screen pointer object's (*object*) column position. (**Note:** To obtain the display screen pointer's current column position, a call to the **pointer::read** function must be performed before a call to the **pointer::col** function.)

Return Value: The **pointer::col** function returns the display screen pointer's column position.

See Also: **pointer::read**

Example: The following program demonstrates the **pointer::col** function by continuously displaying the display screen pointer's column position.

```
//
// pointer::col demo
//
#include <stdio.h>
#include <stdlib.h>
#include "gwindows.hpp"
```

continued...

```
main()
{
    char line[81];

    clearwindow(1, 1, 25, 80, background(gmenu.highlight()));
    displaycenter(1, 40, gmenu.highlight(), "pointer::col demo");
    mouse.on();
    do {
        mouse.read();
        sprintf(line, "Pointer Column: %3d", mouse.col());
        displaystring(3, 1, gmenu.highlight(), line);
    } while (!keypressed() && !mouse.lbutton() &&
        !mouse.rbutton());
    if (keypressed())
        waitkey();
    exit(0);
}
```

pointer::lbutton

Summary: #include "gwindows.hpp"
int *object*.lbutton(void);
pointer *object*;   (display screen pointer object)

Description: The **pointer::lbutton** function determines a display screen pointer object's (*object*) left button status. (**Note:** To obtain the display screen pointer's current left button status, a call to the **pointer::read** function must be performed before a call to the **pointer::lbutton** function.)

Return Value: The **pointer::lbutton** function returns the display screen pointer's left button status. If the display screen pointer's left button is being pressed, the **pointer::lbutton** function will return TRUE (1). If not, the **pointer::lbutton** function will return FALSE (0) to indicate a released left button.

See Also: **pointer::read**

Example: The following program demonstrates the **pointer::lbutton** function by continuously displaying the display screen pointer's left button status.

```
//
// pointer::lbutton demo
//
#include <stdio.h>
#include <stdlib.h>
#include "gwindows.hpp"
```

continued...

9 GWINDOWS Reference Guide

```
main()
{
    char line[81];

    clearwindow(1, 1, 25, 80, background(gmenu.highlight()));
    displaycenter(1, 40, gmenu.highlight(), "pointer::lbutton demo");
    mouse.on();
    do {
        mouse.read();
        sprintf(line, "Pointer Left Button Status: %d",
            mouse.lbutton());
        displaystring(3, 1, gmenu.highlight(), line);
    } while (!keypressed() && !mouse.rbutton());
    if (keypressed())
        waitkey();
    exit(0);
}
```

pointer::off

Summary: #include "gwindows.hpp"
void *object*.off(void);
pointer *object*;   (display screen pointer object)

Description: The **pointer::off** function turns off a display screen pointer object (*object*).

Return Value: No value is returned.

See Also: **pointer::on**

Example: After waiting for a key or the display screen pointer's left button to be pressed, the following program demonstrates the **pointer::off** function by turning the display screen pointer off.

```
//
// pointer::off demo
//
#include <stdlib.h>
#include "gwindows.hpp"

main()
{
    clearwindow(1, 1, 25, 80, background(gmenu.highlight()));
    displaycenter(1, 40, gmenu.highlight(), "pointer::off demo");
    mouse.on();
```

continued...

```
            do {
                mouse.read();
            } while (!keypressed() && !mouse.lbutton());
            mouse.off();
            if (keypressed())
                waitkey();
            exit(0);
        }
```

pointer::on

Summary: include "gwindows.hpp"
void *object*.on(void);
pointer *object*;   (display screen pointer object)

Description: The **pointer::on** function turns on a display screen pointer object (*object*).

Return Value: No value is returned.

See Also: **pointer::off**

Example: The following program demonstrates the **pointer::on** function by turning the display screen pointer off.

```
        //
        // pointer::on demo
        //
        #include <stdlib.h>
        #include "gwindows.hpp"

        main()
        {
            clearwindow(1, 1, 25, 80, background(gmenu.highlight()));
            displaycenter(1, 40, gmenu.highlight(), "pointer::on demo");
            mouse.on();
            do {
                mouse.read();
            } while (!keypressed() && !mouse.lbutton());
            if (keypressed())
                waitkey();
            exit(0);
        }
```

pointer::rbutton

Summary: #include "gwindows.hpp"
int *object*.rbutton(void);
pointer *object*;   (display screen pointer object)

Description:	The **pointer::rbutton** function determines a display screen pointer object's (*object*) right button status. (**Note:** To obtain the screen pointer's current right button status, a call to the **pointer::read** function must be performed before a call to the **pointer::rbutton** function.)
Return Value:	The **pointer::rbutton** function returns the display screen pointer's right button status. If the screen pointer's right button is being pressed, the **pointer::rbutton** function will return TRUE (1). If not, the **pointer::rbutton** function will return FALSE (0) to indicate a released right button.
See Also:	**pointer::read**
Example:	The following program demonstrates the **pointer::rbutton** function by continuously displaying the screen pointer's right button status.

```
//
// pointer::rbutton demo
//
#include <stdio.h>
#include <stdlib.h>
#include "gwindows.hpp"

main()
{
    char line[81];

    clearwindow(1, 1, 25, 80, background(gmenu.highlight()));
    displaycenter(1, 40, gmenu.highlight(), "pointer::rbutton demo");
    mouse.on();
    do {
        mouse.read();
        sprintf(line, "Pointer Right Button Status: %d", mouse.rbutton());
        displaystring(3, 1, gmenu.highlight(), line);
    } while (!keypressed() && !mouse.lbutton());
    if (keypressed())
        waitkey();
    exit(0);
}
```

pointer::read

Summary:	#include "gwindows.hpp" void *object*.read(void); pointer *object*; (display screen pointer object)
Description:	The **pointer::read** function determines a display screen pointer object's (*object*) row position, column position, x-coordinate position, y-coordinate position, left button status, and right button status.

GWINDOWS Reference Guide 9

Return Value:	No value is returned.
See Also:	**pointer::col, pointer::lbutton, pointer::rbutton, pointer::row, pointer::x,** and **pointer::y**
Example:	The following program demonstrates the **pointer::read** function by continuously displaying the screen pointer's row position, column position, x-coordinate position, y-coordinate position, left button status, and right button status.

```
//
// pointer::read demo
//
#include <stdio.h>
#include <stdlib.h>
#include "gwindows.hpp"

main()
{
    char line[81];

    clearwindow(1, 1, 25, 80, background(gmenu.highlight()));
    displaycenter(1, 40, gmenu.highlight(), "pointer::read demo");
    mouse.on();
    do {
        mouse.read();
        sprintf(line, "Pointer Row: %3d", mouse.row());
        displaystring(3, 1, gmenu.highlight(), line);
        sprintf(line, "Pointer Column: %3d", mouse.col());
        displaystring(4, 1, gmenu.highlight(), line);
        sprintf(line, "Pointer X: %3d", mouse.x());
        displaystring(5, 1, gmenu.highlight(), line);
        sprintf(line, "Pointer Y: %3d", mouse.y());
        displaystring(6, 1, gmenu.highlight(), line);
        sprintf(line, "Pointer Left Button Status: %d",
                mouse.lbutton());
        displaystring(7, 1, gmenu.highlight(), line);
        sprintf(line, "Pointer Right Button Status: %d",
                mouse.rbutton());
        displaystring(8, 1, gmenu.highlight(), line);
    } while (!keypressed()) ;
    waitkey();
    exit(0);
}
```

pointer::row

Summary: #include "gwindows.hpp"
int *object*.row(void);
pointer *object*; (display screen pointer object)

Description: The **pointer::row** function determines a screen pointer object's (*object*) row position. (**Note:** To obtain the screen pointer's current row position, a call to the **pointer::read** function must be performed before a call to the **pointer::row** function.)

Return Value: The **pointer::row** function returns the screen pointer's row position.

See Also: **pointer::read**

Example: The following program demonstrates the **pointer::row** function by continuously displaying the display screen pointer's row position.

```
//
// pointer::row demo
//
#include <stdio.h>
#include <stdlib.h>
#include "gwindows.hpp"

main()
{
    char line[81];

    clearwindow(1, 1, 25, 80, background(gmenu.highlight()));
    displaycenter(1, 40, gmenu.highlight(), "pointer::row demo");
    mouse.on();
    do {
        mouse.read();
        sprintf(line, "Pointer Row: %3d", mouse.row());
        displaystring(3, 1, gmenu.highlight(), line);
    } while (!keypressed() && !mouse.lbutton() &&
        !mouse.rbutton()) ;
    if (keypressed())
        waitkey();
    exit(0);
}
```

pointer::x

Summary: #include "gwindows.hpp"
int *object*.x(void);
pointer *object*; (display screen pointer object)

Description: The **pointer::x** function determines a display screen pointer object's (*object*) x-coordinate position. (**Note:** To obtain the display screen pointer's current x-coordinate position, a call to the **pointer::read** function must be performed before a call to the **pointer::x** function.)

Return Value: The **pointer::x** function returns the display screen pointer's x-coordinate position.

See Also: **pointer::read**

Example: The following program demonstrates the **pointer::x** function by continuously displaying the screen pointer's x-coordinate position.

```
//
// pointer::x demo
//
#include <stdio.h>
#include <stdlib.h>
#include "gwindows.hpp"

main()
{
    char line[81];

    clearwindow(1, 1, 25, 80, background(gmenu.highlight()));
    displaycenter(1, 40, gmenu.highlight(), "pointer::x demo");
    mouse.on();
    do {
        mouse.read();
        sprintf(line, "Pointer X: %3d", mouse.x());
        displaystring(3, 1, gmenu.highlight(), line);
    } while (!keypressed() && !mouse.lbutton() &&
        !mouse.rbutton()) ;
    if (keypressed())
        waitkey();
    exit(0);
}
```

pointer::y

Summary:
#include "gwindows.hpp"
int *object*.y(void);
pointer *object*;   (display screen pointer object)

Description: The **pointer::y** function determines a display screen pointer object's (*object*) y-coordinate position. (**Note:** To obtain the screen pointer's current y-coordinate position, a call to the **pointer::read** function must be performed before a call to the **pointer::y** function.)

9 GWINDOWS Reference Guide

Return Value: The **pointer::y** function returns the display screen pointer's y-coordinate position.

See Also: **pointer::read**

Example: The following program demonstrates the **pointer::y** function by continuously displaying the screen pointer's y-coordinate position.

```
//
// pointer::y demo
//
#include <stdio.h>
#include <stdlib.h>
#include "gwindows.hpp"

main()
{
    char line[81];

    clearwindow(1, 1, 25, 80, background(gmenu.highlight()));
    displaycenter(1, 40, gmenu.highlight(), "pointer::y demo");
    mouse.on();
    do {
        mouse.read();
        sprintf(line, "Pointer Y: %3d", mouse.y());
        displaystring(3, 1, gmenu.highlight(), line);
    } while (!keypressed() && !mouse.lbutton() &&
        !mouse.rbutton()) ;
    if (keypressed())
        waitkey();
    exit(0);
}
```

popup::get

Summary:
```
#include "gwindows.hpp"
int object.get(nitems, menu);
popup object;        (pop-up menu object)
int nitems;          (number of menu items)
MENU *menu;          (pointer to an array of MENU structures)
```

Description: The **popup::get** function displays the pop-up menu defined by *object*. Selection of a menu item is accomplished by pressing that item's indicated hotkey. Also, the highlighted menu item can be selected by pressing the **ENTER** key. Help, if it's available, can be requested for the highlighted menu item by pressing **F1**. The highlighting can be moved by pressing either the **UP** or **DOWN ARROW** key.

Return Value: If the pop-up menu object's **ESC_flag** is TRUE and the ESC key is pressed, the **popup::get** function returns a value of 27. Otherwise, the **popup::get** function will return a value of 0.

Example: The following program demonstrates the **popup::get** function by displaying a three-item pop-up menu. The pop-up menu will be continuously displayed until the "Exit the Program" menu item is selected by the operator.

```
//
// popup demo
//
#include <stdlib.h>
#include "gwindows.hpp"

void save_file(void);
void load_file(void);
void exit_prog(void);
void sf_help(void);
void lf_help(void);
void ep_help(void);

static MENU menu[3] = {
    {"Save the File", 0, save_file, sf_help},
    {"Load the File", 0, load_file, lf_help},
    {"Exit the Program", 0, exit_prog, ep_help} };

main()
{
    clearwindow(1, 1, 25, 80, background(gmenu.highlight()));
    mouse.on();
    while (!((popup)popup(3, 30, TRUE)).get(3, menu)) ;
    exit(0);
}

void save_file(void)
{
    displaycenter(19, 40, gmenu.highlight(), "Save File Function");
    waitkey();
    clearwindow(19, 1, 19, 80, background(gmenu.highlight()));
}
```

continued...

```
void load_file(void)
{
    displaycenter(19, 40, gmenu.highlight(), "Load File Function");
    waitkey();
    clearwindow(19, 1, 19, 80, background(gmenu.highlight()));
}

void exit_prog(void)
{
    exit(0);
}

void sf_help(void)
{
    displaycenter(19, 40, gmenu.highlight(),
        "Save File Help Function");
    waitkey();
    clearwindow(19, 1, 19, 80, background(gmenu.highlight()));
}

void lf_help(void)
{
    displaycenter(19, 40, gmenu.highlight(),
        "Load File Help Function");
    waitkey();
    clearwindow(19, 1, 19, 80, background(gmenu.highlight()));
}

void ep_help(void)
{
    displaycenter(19, 40, gmenu.highlight(),
        "Exit Program Help Function");
    waitkey();
    clearwindow(19, 1, 19, 80, background(gmenu.highlight()));
}
```

pulldown::display

Summary: #include "gwindows.hpp"
void *object*.display(void);
pulldown *object*;   (pull-down menu object)

Description: The **pulldown::display** function displays a pull-down menu bar for the pull-down menu defined by *object*.

Return Value: No value is returned.

See Also: **pulldown::get**

GWINDOWS Reference Guide **9**

Example: For a complete demonstration of the pull-down menu functions, see the example under **pulldown::get**.

pulldown::get

Summary:
```
#include "gwindows.hpp"
int object.get(ikey);
pulldown object;      (pull-down menu object)
int ikey;             (initial key value)
```

Description: The **pulldown::get** function is used to implement multiple pull-down menus. The **pulldown::get** function recognizes the following control keys:

Control Key	Action
ALT + Heading Hotkey	Pulls down the indicated menu.
ESC	Removes the current menu from the display screen.
LEFT ARROW	Removes the current menu from the display screen and pulls down the next menu to the left.
RIGHT ARROW	Removes the current menu from the display screen and pulls down the next menu to the right.
Menu Item Hotkey	Executes the selected menu item's function.
ENTER	Executes the highlighted menu item's function.
F1	If a menu hasn't been pulled down, executes the overall help function. Otherwise, executes the highlighted menu item's help function.
UP ARROW	Moves the highlight bar up to the previous menu item.
DOWN ARROW	Moves the highlight bar down to the next menu item.

An initial key value can be sent to the **pulldown::get** function by placing the appropriate value in the *ikey* parameter. Otherwise, the *ikey* parameter must equal zero to indicate no initial key.

Return Value: If a menu item isn't selected, the **pulldown::get** function returns the value of the last key pressed. Otherwise, the **pulldown::get** function returns a value of 0.

See Also: **pulldown::display**

Example: The following program demonstrates the **pulldown::display** and **pulldown::get** functions by implementing a series of pull-down menus for a simple general ledger program.

```c
//
// pulldown demo
//
#include <stdlib.h>
#include "gwindows.hpp"

void save_file(void);
void read_file(void);
void exit_prog(void);
void add_acc(void);
void del_acc(void);
void add_tra(void);
void del_tra(void);
void prt_coa(void);
void led_upd(void);
void fin_stat(void);
void read_func(void);
void sf_help(void);
void rf_help(void);
void aa_help(void);
void da_help(void);
void at_help(void);
void dt_help(void);
void pc_help(void);
void lu_help(void);
void fs_help(void);
void main_help(void);

static MENU file[3] = {
    {"Save the File", 0, save_file, sf_help},
    {"Read the File", 0, read_file, rf_help},
    {"Exit the Program", 0, exit_prog, NULL} };

static MENU accounts[2] = {
    {"Add an Account", 0, add_acc, aa_help},
    {"Delete an Account", 0, del_acc, da_help} };

static MENU transact[2] = {
    {"Add a Transaction", 0, add_tra, at_help},
    {"Delete a Transaction", 0, del_tra, dt_help} };

static MENU print[3] = {
    {"Print a Chart of Accounts", 8, prt_coa, pc_help},
    {"Print a Ledger Update", 15, led_upd, lu_help},
    {"Print Financial Statements", 6, fin_stat, fs_help} };

static MENU read[1] = { {"", 0, read_func, NULL} };
```

continued...

```c
static MENU_HEAD heads[5] = {
    {"File", 0, 3, file},
    {"Accounts", 0, 2, accounts},
    {"Transactions", 0, 2, transact},
    {"Print", 0, 3, print},
    {"Read", 0, 1, read} };

main()
{
    pulldown menu(1, 5, heads, main_help);

    cursorcolor(gmenu.highlight() & 0xff);
    clearwindow(1, 1, 25, 80, background(gmenu.highlight()));
    mouse.on();
    setcurpos(15, 1);
    cursoron();
    menu.display();
    while (TRUE) {
        int key = menu.get(0);
    }
}

void save_file(void)
{
    displaycenter(19, 40, gmenu.highlight(), "Save File Function");
    waitkey();
    clearwindow(19, 1, 19, 80, background(gmenu.highlight()));
}

void read_file(void)
{
    displaycenter(19, 40, gmenu.highlight(), "Read File Function");
    waitkey();
    clearwindow(19, 1, 19, 80, background(gmenu.highlight()));
}

void exit_prog(void)
{
    exit(0);
}

void add_acc(void)
{
    displaycenter(19, 40, gmenu.highlight(),
        "Add Account Function");
    waitkey();
    clearwindow(19, 1, 19, 80, background(gmenu.highlight()));
}
```

continued...

9 GWINDOWS Reference Guide

```
void del_acc(void)
{
    displaycenter(19, 40, gmenu.highlight(),
        "Delete Account Function");
    waitkey();
    clearwindow(19, 1, 19, 80, background(gmenu.highlight()));
}

void add_tra(void)
{
    displaycenter(19, 40, gmenu.highlight(), "Add Transaction Function");
    waitkey();
    clearwindow(19, 1, 19, 80, background(gmenu.highlight()));
}

void del_tra(void)
{
    displaycenter(19, 40, gmenu.highlight(),
        "Delete Transaction Function");
    waitkey();
    clearwindow(19, 1, 19, 80, background(gmenu.highlight()));
}

void prt_coa(void)
{
    displaycenter(19, 40, gmenu.highlight(),
        "Print Chart of Accounts Function");
    waitkey();
    clearwindow(19, 1, 19, 80, background(gmenu.highlight()));
}

void led_upd(void)
{
    displaycenter(19, 40, gmenu.highlight(),
        "Ledger Update Function");
    waitkey();
    clearwindow(19, 1, 19, 80, background(gmenu.highlight()));
}

void fin_stat(void)
{
    displaycenter(19, 40, gmenu.highlight(), "Financial Statements Function");
    waitkey();
    clearwindow(19, 1, 19, 80, background(gmenu.highlight()));
}
```

continued...

```c
void read_func(void)
{
    displaycenter(19, 40, gmenu.highlight(), "Read Test Function");
    waitkey();
    clearwindow(19, 1, 19, 80, background(gmenu.highlight()));
}

void sf_help(void)
{
    displaycenter(20, 40, gmenu.highlight(),
        "Save File Help Function");
    waitkey();
    clearwindow(20, 1, 20, 80, background(gmenu.highlight()));
}

void rf_help(void)
{
    displaycenter(20, 40, gmenu.highlight(),
        "Read File Help Function");
    waitkey();
    clearwindow(20, 1, 20, 80, background(gmenu.highlight()));
}

void aa_help(void)
{
    displaycenter(20, 40, gmenu.highlight(),
        "Add Account Help Function");
    waitkey();
    clearwindow(20, 1, 20, 80, background(gmenu.highlight()));
}

void da_help(void)
{
    displaycenter(20, 40, gmenu.highlight(),
        "Delete Account Help Function");
    waitkey();
    clearwindow(20, 1, 20, 80, background(gmenu.highlight()));
}

void at_help(void)
{
    displaycenter(20, 40, gmenu.highlight(),
        "Add Tranaction Help Function");
    waitkey();
    clearwindow(20, 1, 20, 80, background(gmenu.highlight()));
}
```

continued...

9 GWINDOWS Reference Guide

```
void dt_help(void)
{
    displaycenter(20, 40, gmenu.highlight(),
        "Delete Transaction Help Function");
    waitkey();
    clearwindow(20, 1, 20, 80, background(gmenu.highlight()));
}

void pc_help(void)
{
    displaycenter(20, 40, gmenu.highlight(),
        "Print Chart of Accounts Help Function");
    waitkey();
    clearwindow(20, 1, 20, 80, background(gmenu.highlight()));
}

void lu_help(void)
{
    displaycenter(20, 40, gmenu.highlight(),
        "Ledger Update Help Function");
    waitkey();
    clearwindow(20, 1, 20, 80, background(gmenu.highlight()));
}

void fs_help(void)
{
    displaycenter(20, 40, gmenu.highlight(),
        "Financial Statements Help Function");
    waitkey();
    clearwindow(20, 1, 20, 80, background(gmenu.highlight()));
}

void main_help(void)
{
    displaycenter(20, 40, gmenu.highlight(), "Main Help Function");
    waitkey();
    clearwindow(20, 1, 20, 80, background(gmenu.highlight()));
}
```

readmouse

Summary: #include "gwindows.hpp"
void readmouse(void);

Description: The **readmouse** function determines the mouse's row position, column position, x-coordinate position, y-coordinate position, left button status, and right button status.

Return Value: No value is returned.

See Also:	**left_button, mouse_col, mouse_row, mouse_x, mouse_y,** and **right_button**
Example:	The following program demonstrates the **read_mouse** function by continuously displaying the mouse's row position, column position, x-coordinate position, y-coordinate position, left button status, and right button status.

```
//
// readmouse demo
//
#include <stdio.h>
#include <stdlib.h>
#include "gwindows.hpp"

main()
{
    char line[80];

    clearwindow(1, 1, 25, 80, background(gmenu.highlight()));
    displaycenter(1, 40, gmenu.highlight(), "readmouse demo");
    resetmouse();
    showmouse();
    do {
        readmouse();
        sprintf(line, "Mouse Row: %3d", mouse_row);
        displaystring(3, 1, gmenu.highlight(), line);
        sprintf(line, "Mouse Column: %3d", mouse_col);
        displaystring(4, 1, gmenu.highlight(), line);
        sprintf(line, "Mouse X: %3d", mouse_x);
        displaystring(5, 1, gmenu.highlight(), line);
        sprintf(line, "Mouse Y: %3d", mouse_y);
        displaystring(6, 1, gmenu.highlight(), line);
        sprintf(line, "Mouse Left Button Status: %d", left_button);
        displaystring(7, 1, gmenu.highlight(), line);
        sprintf(line, "Mouse Right Button Status: %d", right_button);
        displaystring(8, 1, gmenu.highlight(), line);
    } while (!keypressed()) ;
    hidemouse();
    waitkey();
    exit(0);
}
```

9 GWINDOWS Reference Guide

resetmouse

Summary: #include "gwindows.hpp"
void resetmouse(void);

Description: The **resetmouse** function resets the mouse driver.

Return Value: No value is returned.

Example: The following program demonstrates the **resetmouse** function by resetting the mouse driver.

```
//
// resetmouse demo
//
#include <stdlib.h>
#include "gwindows.hpp"

main()
{
    clearwindow(1, 1, 25, 80, background(gmenu.highlight()));
    displaycenter(1, 40, gmenu.highlight(), "resetmouse demo");
    resetmouse();
    showmouse();
    do {
        readmouse();
    } while (!keypressed() && !left_button);
    hidemouse();
    if (keypressed())
        waitkey();
    exit(0);
}
```

restorewindow

Summary: #include "gwindows.hpp"
void restorewindow(*row1, col1, row2, col2, buffer*);
int *row1, col1*;   (upper left corner of the display
                                            screen window)
int *row2, col2*;   (lower right corner of the display
                                            screen window)
char **buffer*;   (buffer pointer)

Description: The **restorewindow** function displays a display screen window, which has been previously saved in *buffer*, at the coordinates defined by (*row1, col1*) and (*row2, col2*). Because each of the display screen window's characters requires more that one byte of storage, the buffer must be ((*row2 - row1* + 1) * (*col2 - col1* + 1) * 8) bytes long in CGA mode and ((*row2 - row1* + 1) * (*col2 - col1*) * 56) bytes long in EGA mode.

Return Value: No value is returned.

See Also: **savewindow**

Example: The following program demonstrates the **restorewindow** function by displaying a previously saved display screen window.
```
//
// restorewindow demo
//
#include <stdlib.h>
#include "gwindows.hpp"

static char vbuff[22400];

main()
{
    savewindow(1, 1, 10, 40, vbuff);
    clearwindow(1, 1, 25, 80, background(gmenu.highlight()));
    displaycenter(1, 40, gmenu.highlight(), "restorewindow demo");
    waitkey();
    restorewindow(1, 1, 10, 40, vbuff);
    waitkey();
    exit(0);
}
```

savewindow

Summary:
```
#include "gwindows.hpp"
void savewindow(row1, col1, row2, col2, buffer);
int row1, col1;      (upper left corner of the display
                      screen window)
int row2, col2;      (lower right corner of the display
                      screen window)
char *buffer;        (buffer pointer)
```

Description: The **savewindow** function buffers a display screen window at the coordinates defined by (*row1*, *col1*) and (*row2*, *col2*). Because each of the display screen window's characters requires more that one byte of storage, *buffer* must be ((*row2* - *row1* + 1) * (*col2* - *col1* + 1) * 8) bytes long in CGA mode and ((*row2* - *row1* + 1) * (*col2* - *col1*) * 56) bytes long in EGA mode.

Return Value: No value is returned.

See Also: **restorewindow**

Example: The following program demonstrates the **savewindow** function by duplicating the upper left ten lines of the display screen onto the upper right ten lines of the display screen.

9 GWINDOWS Reference Guide

```
//
// savewindow demo
//
#include <stdlib.h>
#include "gwindows.hpp"

static char vbuff[22400];

main()
{
    clearwindow(1, 1, 25, 80, background(gmenu.highlight()));
    displaycenter(1, 40, gmenu.highlight(), "savewindow demo");
    savewindow(1, 1, 10, 40, vbuff);
    waitkey();
    restorewindow(1, 41, 10, 80, vbuff);
    waitkey();
    exit(0);
}
```

setcurpos

Summary: #include "gwindows.hpp"
void setcurpos(*row, col*);
int *row, col*;   (cursor position)

Description: The **setcurpos** function moves the cursor to the display screen position defined by (*row, col*).

Return Value: No value is returned.

Example: The following program demonstrates the **setcurpos** function by moving the cursor to the right half of the display screen's center line.

```
//
// setcurpos demo
//
#include <stdio.h>
#include <stdlib.h>
#include "gwindows.hpp"

main()
{
    setcurpos(13, 41);
    printf("This message starts at the right half of the center line");
    waitkey();
    exit(0);
}
```

setfontvectors

Summary: #include "gwindows.hpp"
void setfontvectors(*lowerhalf*, *upperhalf*);
unsigned char **lowerhalf*;   (lower font table pointer)
unsigned char **upperhalf*;   (upper font table pointer)

Description: The **setfontvectors** function sets the current font table pointers to the lower-half font table pointer defined by *lowerhalf* and the upper-half font table pointer defined by *upperhalf*.

Return Value: No value is returned.

See Also: **getfontvectors**

Example: The following program demonstrates the **setfontvectors** function by manually setting and resetting the font table pointers.

```
//
// setfontvectors demo
//
#include <stdlib.h>
#include "gwindows.hpp"

extern font sansega;

unsigned char *oldlower, *oldupper;

main()
{
    clearwindow(1, 1, 25, 80, background(gmenu.highlight()));
    displaycenter(1, 40, gmenu.highlight(), "setfontvectors data");
    displaystring(3, 1, gmenu.highlight(),
        "This is displayed using the system font");
    getfontvectors(&oldlower, &oldupper);
    setfontvectors(sansega.getptr(), sansega.getptr() + 1792);
    displaystring(4, 1, gmenu.highlight(),
        "This is displayed using the sans serif font");
    setfontvectors(oldlower, oldupper);
    displaystring(5, 1, gmenu.highlight(),
        "This is displayed using the system font");
    waitkey();
    exit(0);
}
```

showmouse

Summary: #include "gwindows.hpp"
void showmouse(void);

Description: The **showmouse** function turns on the mouse pointer.

Return Value: No value is returned.

See Also: **hidemouse**

Example: The following program demonstrates the **showmouse** function by turning on the mouse pointer.

```
//
// showmouse demo
//
#include <stdlib.h>
#include "gwindows.hpp"

main()
{
    clearwindow(1, 1, 25, 80, background(gmenu.highlight()));
    displaycenter(1, 40, gmenu.highlight(), "showmouse demo");
    resetmouse();
    showmouse();
    do {
        readmouse();
    } while (!keypressed() && !left_button);
    hidemouse();
    if (keypressed())
        waitkey();
    exit(0);
}
```

ssn_string

Summary: #include "gwindows.hpp"
char *ssn_string(*string*, *number*);
char **string*;   (storage location for the Social Security number string)
ssn &*number*;   (Social Security number structure)

Description: The **ssn_string** function constructs an 11-character Social Security number string (*string* = "xxx-xx-xxxx") for the Social Security number defined by *number*.

Return Value: The **ssn_string** function returns a pointer to the resulting Social Security number string.

See Also: **display_ssn** and **input_ssn**

Example: The following program demonstrates the **ssn_string** function by displaying a constructed Social Security number string on the tenth line of the display screen.

```
//
// ssn_string demo
//
#include <stdlib.h>
#include "gwindows.hpp"

main()
{
    static ssn n = {007, 55, 3535};
    char line[81];

    clearwindow(1, 1, 25, 80, background(gmenu.highlight()));
    displaycenter(1, 40, gmenu.highlight(), "ssn_string demo");
    displaystring(10, 1, gmenu.highlight(), ssn_string(line, n));
    waitkey();
    exit(0);
}
```

ucursoroff, ucursoron

Summary:
```
#include "gwindows.hpp"
void ucursoroff(void);
void ucursoron(void);
```

Description: The **ucursoroff** function unconditionally turns the cursor off. The **ucursoron** function unconditionally turns the cursor on.

Return Value: No value is returned.

Example: The following program demonstrates the **ucursoroff** and **ucursoron** functions by first turning the cursor on and then turn the cursor back off again.

```
//
// ucursoroff/ucursoron demo
//
#include <stdlib.h>
#include "gwindows.hpp"

main()
{
    clearwindow(1, 1, 25, 80, background(gmenu.highlight()));
    displaycenter(1, 40, gmenu.highlight(),
        "ucursoroff/ucursoron demo");
```

continued...

```
            displaystring(2, 1, gmenu.highlight(),
                "Press any key to turn the cursor on....");
            waitkey();
            setcurpos(3, 1);
            ucursoron();
            displaystring(4, 1, gmenu.highlight(),
                "Press any key to turn the cursor off....");
            waitkey();
            ucursoroff();
            waitkey();
            exit(0);
        }
```

underline

Summary:
```
#include "gwindows.hpp"
void underline(row, col, color);
int row, col;   (screen position)
int color;      (color value)
```

Description: The **underline** function underlines the character displayed at the position defined by (*row*, *col*) in the color specified by *color*.

Return Value: No value is returned.

Example: The following program demonstrates the **underline** function by underlining all of the characters on the second display screen row.

```
//
// underline demo
//
#include <stdlib.h>
#include "gwindows.hpp"

main()
{
    int i;

    clearwindow(1, 1, 25, 80, background(gmenu.highlight()));
    displaycenter(1, 40, gmenu.highlight(), "underline demo");
    fillrow(2, 1, 80, gmenu.highlight(), '*');
    waitkey();
    for (i = 1; i < 81; i++)
        underline(2, i, gmenu.highlight());
    waitkey();
    exit(0);
}
```

waitkey

Summary: #include "gwindows.hpp"
    int waitkey(void);

Description: The **waitkey** function waits for the operator to press a key.

Return Value: The **waitkey** function returns the ASCII code for all nonextended-keyboard keys. Extended-keyboard keys return a value of their scan code + 256.

Example: The following program demonstrates the **waitkey** function by returning the values for an assortment of key presses. Program execution will continue until the **ESC** key is pressed.

```
//
// waitkey demo
//
#include <stdio.h>
#include <stdlib.h>
#include "gwindows.hpp"

main()
{
    int key;
    char line[81];

    clearwindow(1, 1, 25, 80, background(gmenu.highlight()));
    displaycenter(1, 40, gmenu.highlight(), "waitkey demo");
    while (TRUE) {
        if ((key = waitkey()) == 27)
            exit(0);
        sprintf(line, "Key Value: %3d", key);
        displaystring(3, 1, gmenu.highlight(), line);
    }
}
```

window::close

Summary: #include "gwindows.hpp"
    void *object*.close(void);
    window *object*;   (dynamic display screen window object)

Description: The **window::close** function closes the previously opened display screen window defined by *object*.

Return Value: No value is returned.

See Also: **window::open**

Example: The following program demonstrates the **window::close** function by closing the display screen window at the coordinates (1,20) and (15,50).

```
//
// window::close demo
//
#include <stdlib.h>
#include "gwindows.hpp"

main()
{
    window w(1, 20, 15, 50, gmenu.color(), SINGLE_LINE);

    w.open();
    waitkey();
    w.close();
    exit(0);
}
```

window::clreol

Summary:
```
#include "gwindows.hpp"
void object.clreol(void);
window object;          (dynamic display screen window object)
```

Description: The **window::clreol** function clears the current display screen window line from the cursor's current column position to the display screen window's right border. The display screen window is defined by *object*.

Return Value: No value is returned.

Example: The following program demonstrates the **window::clreol** function by erasing a portion of the display screen window's top line.

```
//
// window::clreol demo
//
#include <stdlib.h>
#include "gwindows.hpp"

main()
{
    int i;
    window w(1, 20, 15, 50, gmenu.color(), SINGLE_LINE);

    w.open();
    for (i = 0; i < 10; i++)
        w.println("This is another string");
    waitkey();
    w.setcurpos(1, 2);
    w.clreol();
    waitkey();
    exit(0);
}
```

window::cls

Summary:	#include "gwindows.hpp" void *object*.cls(void); window *object*; (dynamic display screen window object)
Description:	The **window::cls** function clears the dynamic display screen window object defined by *object*.
Return Value:	No value is returned.
Example:	The following program demonstrates the **window::cls** function by clearing the contents of a display screen window.

```
//
// window::cls demo
//
#include <stdlib.h>
#include "gwindows.hpp"

main()
{
    int i;
    window w(1, 20, 15, 50, gmenu.color(), SINGLE_LINE);

    w.open();
    for (i = 0; i < 10; i++)
        w.println("This is another string");
    waitkey();
    w.cls();
    waitkey();
    exit(0);
}
```

window::curcol

Summary:	#include "gwindows.hpp" int *object*.curcol(void); window *object*; (dynamic display screen window object)
Description:	The **window::curcol** function retrieves a dynamic display screen window object's (*object*) cursor column.
Return Value:	The **window::curcol** function returns the dynamic display screen window's cursor column.
See Also:	**window::currow**
Example:	The following program demonstrates the **window::curcol** function by displaying a dynamic screen window's cursor column.

9 GWINDOWS Reference Guide

```
//
// windows::curcol demo
//
#include <stdio.h>
#include <stdlib.h>
#include "gwindows.hpp"

main()
{
    int i;
    char line[81];
    window w(1, 20, 15, 50, gmenu.color(), SINGLE_LINE);

    w.open();
    w.setcurpos(10, 5);
    sprintf(line, "Current Window Column: %d", w.curcol());
    displaystring(20, 1, gmenu.color(), line);
    waitkey();
    exit(0);
}
```

window::currow

Summary: `#include "gwindows.hpp"`
int *object*.currow(void);
window *object*;   (dynamic display screen window object)

Description: The **window::currow** function retrieves a dynamic display screen window object's (*object*) cursor row.

Return Value: The **window::currow** function returns the dynamic display screen window's cursor row.

See Also: **window::curcol**

Example: The following program demonstrates the **window::currow** function by displaying a dynamic display screen window's cursor row.

```
//
// windows::currow demo
//
#include <stdio.h>
#include <stdlib.h>
#include "gwindows.hpp"

main()
{
    int i;
    char line[81];
    window w(1, 20, 15, 50, gmenu.color(), SINGLE_LINE);
```
continued...

```
            w.open();
            w.setcurpos(10, 5);
            sprintf(line, "Current Window Row: %d", w.currow());
            displaystring(20, 1, gmenu.color(), line);
            waitkey();
            exit(0);
        }
```

window::draw

Summary:
```
#include "gwindows.hpp"
void object.draw(void);
window object;       (dynamic display screen window object)
```

Description: The **window::draw** function draws the dynamic display screen window defined by *object*.

Return Value: No value is returned.

See Also: **window::open**

Example: The following program demonstrates the **window::draw** function by drawing a double-lined display screen window at the coordinates (10,30) and (15,50).

```
//
// window::draw demo
//
#include <stdlib.h>
#include "gwindows.hpp"

main()
{
    window(10, 30, 15, 50, gmenu.color(), DOUBLE_LINE).draw();
    waitkey();
    exit(0);
}
```

window::horizontal_bar

Summary:
```
#include "gwindows.hpp"
void object.horizontal_bar(curpos, total);
window object;      (dynamic display screen window object)
int curpos;         (current line position)
int total;          (line length)
```

Description: The **window::horizontal_bar** function draws a horizontal scroll bar on the bottom line of a dynamic display screen window (*object*). The scroll bar setting is derived by dividing *curpos* by *total*.

Return Value: No value is returned.

9 GWINDOWS Reference Guide

See Also: **window::vertical_bar**

Example: The following program demonstrates the **window::horizontal_bar** function by displaying a variety of line positions.

```
//
// window::horizontal_bar demo
//
#include <stdlib.h>
#include "gwindows.hpp"

main()
{
    window w(1, 30, 10, 70, gmenu.highlight(), SINGLE_LINE);

    w.open();
    w.horizontal_bar(0, 100);
    waitkey();
    w.horizontal_bar(50, 100);
    waitkey();
    w.horizontal_bar(100, 100);
    waitkey();
    exit(0);
}
```

window::open

Summary: #include "gwindows.hpp"
void *object*.open(void);
window *object*;   (dynamic display screen window object)

Description: The **window::open** function dynamically opens and draws the display screen window defined by *object*.

Return Value: No value is returned.

See Also: **window::close** and **window::draw**

Example: The following program demonstrates the **window::open** function by opening and drawing a dynamic display screen window at the coordinates (1,20), and (15,50).

```
//
// window::open demo
//
#include <stdlib.h>
#include "gwindows.hpp"
```

    continued...

```
main()
{
    window w(1, 20, 15, 50, gmenu.highlight(), DOUBLE_LINE);

    w.open();
    waitkey();
    w.close();
    exit(0);
}
```

window::p_col

Summary:
```
#include "gwindows.hpp"
int object.p_col(column);
window object;        (dynamic display screen window object)
int column;           (logical column)
```

Description: The **window::p_col** function determines the physical display screen column for a dynamic display screen window object's (*object*) logical column (*column*).

Return Value: The **window::p_col** function returns the logical column's corresponding physical display screen column.

See Also: **window::p_row**

Example: The following program demonstrates the **window::p_col** function by displaying the physical display screen column for a dynamic screen window's logical column.

```
//
// windows::p_col demo
//
#include <stdio.h>
#include <stdlib.h>
#include "gwindows.hpp"

main()
{
    int i;
    char line[81];
    window w(1, 20, 15, 50, gmenu.color(), SINGLE_LINE);

    w.open();
    sprintf(line, "Logical Column: 5 = Physical Column: %d",
w.p_col(5));
    displaystring(20, 1, gmenu.color(), line);
    waitkey();
    exit(0);
}
```

window::p_row

Summary: #include "gwindows.hpp"
int *object*.p_row(*row*);
window *object*;   (dynamic display screen window object)
int *row*;   (logical row)

Description: The **window::p_row** function determines the physical display screen row for a dynamic display screen window object's (*object*) logical row (*row*).

Return Value: The **window::p_row** function returns the logical row's corresponding physical display screen row.

See Also: **window::p_col**

Example: The following program demonstrates the **window::p_row** function by displaying the physical display screen row for a dynamic screen window's logical row.

```
//
// windows::p_row demo
//
#include <stdio.h>
#include <stdlib.h>
#include "gwindows.hpp"

main()
{
    int i;
    char line[81];
    window w(1, 20, 15, 50, gmenu.color(), SINGLE_LINE);

    w.open();
    sprintf(line, "Logical Row: 7 = Physical Row: %d" , w.p_row(7));
    displaystring(20, 1, gmenu.color(), line);
    waitkey();
    exit(0);
}
```

window::print

Summary: #include "gwindows.hpp"
void *object*.print(*string*);
window *object*;   (dynamic display screen window object)
char **string*;   (string pointer)

Description: The **window::print** function displays a *string* at a dynamic display screen window object's (*object*) current cursor position.

Return Value: No value is returned.

See Also: **window::printat, window::println,** and **window::printlnat**

Example: The following program demonstrates the **window::print** function by displaying an assortment of strings in a dynamic display screen window.

```
//
// window::print demo
//
#include <stdlib.h>
#include "gwindows.hpp"

main()
{
    int i;
    window w(1, 20, 15, 50, gmenu.highlight(), SINGLE_LINE,
        SCROLL);

    w.open();
    w.print("This is message 1");
    w.print("This is message 2");
    w.print("This is message 3");
    waitkey();
    exit(0);
}
```

window::printat

Summary:
#include "gwindows.hpp"
void *object*.printat(*row*, *col*, *string*);
window *object*;   (dynamic display screen window object)
int *row*, *col*;   (window position)
char *string;   (string pointer)

Description: The **window::printat** function displays a *string* at the dynamic display screen window position defined by (*row*, *col*). The dynamic display screen window is defined by *object*.

Return Value: No value is returned.

See Also: **window::print, window::println,** and **window::printlnat**

Example: The following program demonstrates the **window::printat** function by displaying a variety of strings in a dynamic screen window.

```
//
// window::printat demo
//
#include <stdlib.h>
#include "gwindows.hpp"
```

continued...

```
main()
{
    int i;
    window w(1, 20, 15, 50, gmenu.highlight(), SINGLE_LINE,
        SCROLL);

    w.open();
    w.printat(2, 1, "This is message 1");
    w.printat(1, 1, "This is message 2");
    w.printat(5, 1, "This is message 3");
    waitkey();
    exit(0);
}
```

window::println

Summary: #include "gwindows.hpp"
void *object*.println(*string*);
window *object*;   (dynamic display screen window object)
char **string*;   (string pointer)

Description: The **window::println** function displays a *string* and a carriage return at a dynamic display screen window object's (*object*) current cursor position.

Return Value: No value is returned.

See Also: **window::print, window::printat,** and **window::printlnat**

Example: The following program demonstrates the **window::println** function by displaying an assortment of strings in a display screen window.

```
//
// window::println demo
//
#include <stdlib.h>
#include "gwindows.hpp"

main()
{
    int i;
    window w(1, 20, 15, 50, gmenu.highlight(), SINGLE_LINE,
        SCROLL);

    w.open();
    w.println("This is message 1");
    w.println("This is message 2");
    w.println("This is message 3");
    waitkey();
    exit(0);
}
```

window::printlnat

Summary:
```
#include "gwindows.hpp"
void object.printlnat(row, col, string);
window object;      (dynamic display screen window object)
int row, col;       (window position)
char *string;       (string pointer)
```

Description: The **window::printlnat** function displays a *string* and a carriage return at the dynamic display screen window position defined by (*row*, *col*). The dynamic display screen window is defined by *object*.

Return Value: No value is returned.

See Also: **window::print, window::printat,** and **window::println**

Example: The following program demonstrates the **window ::printlnat** function by displaying a variety of strings in a display screen window.

```
//
// window::printlnat demo
//
#include <stdlib.h>
#include "gwindows.hpp"

main()
{
    int i;
    window w(1, 20, 15, 50, gmenu.highlight(), SINGLE_LINE,
        SCROLL);

    w.open();
    w.printlnat(2, 1, "This is message 1");
    w.printlnat(1, 1, "This is message 2");
    w.printlnat(5, 1, "This is message 3");
    waitkey();
    exit(0);
}
```

window::scroll

Summary:
```
#include "gwindows.hpp"
void object.scroll(nlines, direction, cflag);
window object;      (dynamic display screen window object)
int nlines;         (number of lines to be scrolled)
int directions;     (scroll direction)
int cflag;          (clear lines flag)
```

Description: The **window::scroll** function scrolls the contents of the dynamic display screen window defined by *object*. If *cflag* is TRUE (1), the *nlines* at the beginning of the scroll are cleared. If not, the beginning scroll lines are left intact. The *direction* parameter can be one of the following constants (defined in **gwindows.hpp**):

Constant	Action
UP	Scroll the dynamic display screen window's contents up *nlines*.
DOWN	Scroll the dynamic display screen window's contents down *nlines*.
LEFT	Scroll the dynamic display screen window's contents left *nlines*.
RIGHT	Scroll the dynamic display screen window's contents right *nlines*.

Return Value: No value is returned.

Example: The following program demonstrates the **window::scroll** function by performing a variety of scroll operations.

```
//
// window::scroll demo
//
#include <stdlib.h>
#include "gwindows.hpp"

main()
{
    int i;
    window w(1, 20, 15, 50, gmenu.color(), SINGLE_LINE);

    w.open();
    for (i = 0; i < 10; i++)
        w.println("This is another string");
    waitkey();
    w.scroll(1, UP, CLEAR);
    waitkey();
    w.scroll(1, DOWN, CLEAR);
    waitkey();
    w.scroll(1, LEFT, CLEAR);
    waitkey();
    w.scroll(1, RIGHT, CLEAR);
    waitkey();
    exit(0);
}
```

window::setcurpos

Summary:
```
#include "gwindows.hpp"
void object.setcurpos(row, col);
window object;      (dynamic display screen window object)
int row, col;       (window position)
```

Description: The **window::setcurpos** function moves the cursor to the dynamic display screen window position defined by (*row*, *col*). The dynamic display screen window is defined by *object*.

Return Value: No value is returned.

Example: The following program demonstrates the **window::setcurpos** function by moving the cursor to a variety of positions.

```
//
// window::setcurpos demo
//
#include <stdlib.h>
#include "gwindows.hpp"

main()
{
    int i;
    window w(1, 20, 15, 50, gmenu.highlight(), SINGLE_LINE);

    w.open();
    ucursoron();
    waitkey();
    w.setcurpos(10, 5);
    waitkey();
    w.setcurpos(6, 17);
    waitkey();
    exit(0);
}
```

window::vertical_bar

Summary:
```
#include "gwindows.hpp"
void object.vertical_bar(curpos, total);
window object;      (dynamic display screen window object)
int curpos;         (current file position)
int total;          (file length)
```

Description: The **window::vertical_bar** function draws a vertical scroll bar on the right side of a dynamic display screen window (*object*). The scroll bar setting is derived by dividing *curpos* by *total*.

Return Value: No value is returned.

See Also: **window::horizontal_bar**

Example: The following program demonstrates the **window::vertical_bar** function by displaying a variety of file positions.

```
//
// window::vertical_bar demo
//
#include <stdlib.h>
#include "gwindows.hpp"

main()
{
    window w(1, 30, 10, 70, gmenu.highlight(), SINGLE_LINE);

    w.open();
    w.vertical_bar(0, 100);
    waitkey();
    w.vertical_bar(50, 100);
    waitkey();
    w.vertical_bar(100, 100);
    waitkey();
    exit(0);
}
```

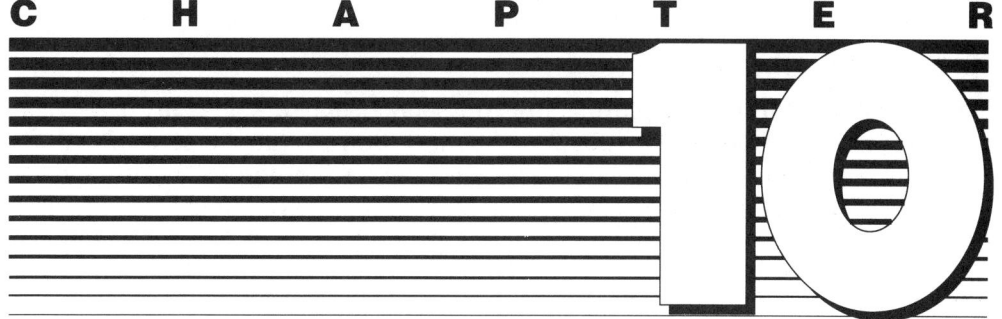

IBM PC AND EGA ROM BIOS VIDEO SERVICES

As explained in Chapter 1, the IBM PC and EGA ROM BIOS video functions place a wide variety of display input/output routines at a programmer's disposal. This chapter presents a detailed look at the ROM BIOS video functions that are common to all IBM PCs and compatibles. The chapter further presents a detailed look at the ROM BIOS video functions that are provided by the EGA display adapter. Each of the ROM BIOS video functions is presented as follows.

10 IBM PC and EGA ROM BIOS Video Services

Register Summary

The register summary explains how the 8086 registers are used to pass parameters to a ROM BIOS video function and return values back to the calling program. An 8086 register model is presented for each of the ROM BIOS video functions. All of the shaded registers in the 8086 register summaries indicate registers that are used either by the calling program to pass parameters to the ROM BIOS video function or by the ROM BIOS video function to return values back to the calling program. Parameter passing is summarized in an appropriate **Call With** section. Returned values are summarized in an appropriate **Returns** section.

Function Description

A description of the ROM BIOS function's purpose is presented for each of the ROM BIOS video functions. Furthermore, any notes of special interest are provided.

Suggested Macro Definition

A suggested assembly language macro definition is presented for each of the ROM BIOS video functions. Although the use of such a macro is strictly optional, macros can save programmers a great deal of time in developing programs that continuously use the same function calls over and over.

Programming Example

A program fragment is presented for each of the ROM BIOS video functions. These examples are intended to illustrate how each of the ROM BIOS video functions are used in an application program.

SET VIDEO MODE (FUNCTION 00H)

Register Summary

AX: | AH | AL |
BX: | BH | BL |
CX: | CH | CL |
DX: | DH | DL |

| SP |
| BP |
| SI |
| DI |

| IP |
| FLAGS |

| CS |
| DS |
| SS |
| ES |

Call With

AH = 00H

AL = Video Mode

Returns

Nothing

10 IBM PC and EGA ROM BIOS Video Services

Function Description

ROM BIOS video function 00H sets the currently active video mode as follows:

Display Mode	Description	Adapter(s)
00H	40 x 25 black and white text	CGA, EGA, PCjr
01H	40 x 25 color text	CGA, EGA, PCjr
02H	80 x 25 black and white text	CGA, EGA, PCjr
03H	80 x 25 color text	CGA, EGA, PCjr
04H	320 x 200 4 color graphics	CGA, EGA, PCjr
05H	320 x 200 4 color (color off)	CGA, EGA, PCjr
06H	640 x 200 2 color graphics	CGA, EGA, PCjr
07H	80 x 25 black and white text	MDA, EGA
08H	160 x 200 16 color graphics	PCjr
09H	320 x 200 16 color graphics	PCjr
0AH	640 x 200 4 color graphics	PCjr
0DH	320 x 200 16 color graphics	EGA
0EH	640 x 200 16 color graphics	EGA
0FH	640 x 350 2 color graphics	EGA
10H	640 x 350 4/16 color graphics	EGA

Suggested Macro Definition

```
setvidmode   macro   vidmode
             mov     ah,0
             mov     al,vidmode
             int     10h
             endm
```

Programming Example

The following program fragment demonstrates how ROM BIOS video function 00H is used to set the current video mode to the 80-column by 25-row color text mode:

```
            .
            .
            .
            mov   ah,0    ;AH = Set video mode function code
            mov   al,3    ;Set video mode to
            int   10h     ; 80 x 25 color mode
            .
            .
            .
```

SET CURSOR TYPE (FUNCTION 01H)

Register Summary

Call With

AH = 01H

CH = Starting cursor line

CL = Ending cursor line

Returns

Nothing

10 IBM PC and EGA ROM BIOS Video Services

Function Description

ROM BIOS video function 01H sets the starting and ending lines for the blinking cursor character. The default values used by most application programs are as follows:

Cursor Type	Starting Line	Ending Line
Mode 07H	11	12
Modes 00H - 03H	6	7
Turn cursor off	32	0

Suggested Macro Definition

```
setcurtype    macro    sline,eline
              mov      ah,1
              mov      ch,sline
              mov      cl,eline
              int      10h
              endm
```

Programming Example

The following program fragment demonstrates how ROM BIOS video function 01H is used to turn the cursor off:

```
        .
        .
        .
        mov    ah,1         ;AH = Set cursor type function
        mov    cx,2000h     ;CX = Turn off cursor values
        int    10H          ;Turn off the cursor
        .
        .
        .
```

IBM PC and EGA ROM BIOS Video Services 10

SET CURSOR POSITION (FUNCTION 02H)

Register Summary

AX: | AH | AL |
BX: | BH | BL |
CX: | CH | CL |
DX: | DH | DL |

SP
BP
SI
DI

IP
FLAGS

CS
DS
SS
ES

Call With

AH = 02H

BH = Page number

DH = Cursor row

DL = Cursor column

Returns

Nothing

10 IBM PC and EGA ROM BIOS Video Services

Function Description

ROM BIOS video function 02H sets the current cursor position. In graphics modes, the page number passed in BH must be zero. The upper left hand corner of the screen is 0,0. The lower right hand corner of the screen is 24,79 in 80-column modes and 24,39 in 40-column modes.

Suggested Macro Definition

```
setcurpos    macro    page,row,column
             mov      ah,2
             mov      bh,page
             mov      dh,row
             mov      dl,column
             endm
```

Programming Example

The following program fragment demonstrates how ROM BIOS video function 02H is used to home the cursor:

```
        .
        .
        .
        mov     ah,2        ;AH = Set cursor position function code
        mov     bh,0        ;BH = Page 0
        xor     dx,dx       ;Set cursor to upper left hand corner
        int     10h         ;Position the cursor
        .
        .
        .
```

READ CURSOR VALUES (FUNCTION 03H)

Register Summary

Call With

AH = 03H

BH = Page number

Returns

CH = Cursor starting line

CL = Cursor ending line

DH = Cursor row position

DL = Cursor column position

10 IBM PC and EGA ROM BIOS Video Services

Function Description

ROM BIOS video function 03H retrieves the cursor character's starting line, the cursor character's ending line, the cursor row position, and the cursor column position. In graphics modes, the page number passed in BH must be zero.

Suggested Macro Definition

```
readcurval    macro    page
              mov      ah,3
              mov      bh,page
              endm
```

Programming Example

The following program fragment demonstrates how ROM BIOS video function 03H is used to retrieve the page zero cursor values:

```
        .
        .
        .
        mov     ah,3        ;AH = Read cursor values function code
        mov     bh,0        ;BH = Page 0
        int     10h         ;Go get the values
        .
        .
        .
```

READ LIGHT PEN VALUES (FUNCTION 04H)

Register Summary

Call With

AH = 04H

Returns

AH = 0 if light pen isn't triggered
     1 if light pen is triggered

CH = Pixel row

BX = Pixel column

DH = Character row

DL = Character column

10 IBM PC and EGA ROM BIOS Video Services

Function Description

ROM BIOS video function 04H returns the light pen's trigger status, pixel position, and character position.

Suggested Macro Definition

```
readpen      macro
             mov      ah,4
             int      10h
             int      10h
             endm
```

Programming Example

The following program fragment demonstrates how ROM BIOS video function 04H is used to retrieve the light pen values. Note that the following code fragment will perform a continuous loop until the light pen is triggered:

```
               .
               .
               .
loop:     mov      ah,4      ;AH = Read light pen function code
          int      10h       ;Get the light pen values
          test     ah,1      ;Loop till the
          jz       loop      ; pen is triggered
               .
               .
               .
```

SELECT DISPLAY PAGE (FUNCTION 05H)

Register Summary

Call With

AH = 05H

AL = Page number

Returns

Nothing

10 IBM PC and EGA ROM BIOS Video Services

Function Description

ROM BIOS video function 05H selects the currently active display page. The maximum allowable page number varies according to the video mode and the display adapter as follows:

Mode(s)	Adapter	Allowable Page Numbers
00H and 01H	CGA	0 to 7
02H and 03H	CGA	0 to 3
02H, 03H, and 0DH	EGA	0 to 7
0EH	EGA	0 to 3
0FH and 10H	EGA	0 to 1

Suggested Macro Definition

```
seldisppag  macro   page
            mov     ah,5
            mov     al,page
            int     10h
            endm
```

Programming Example

The following program fragment demonstrates how ROM BIOS video function 05H is used to select display page 1.

```
            .
            .
            .
            mov     ah,5        ;AH = Select page function code
            mov     al,1        ;Select
            int     10h         ; page 1
            .
            .
            .
```

304

SCROLL WINDOW UP (FUNCTION 06H)

Register Summary

AX: | AH | AL |
BX: | BH | BL |
CX: | CH | CL |
DX: | DH | DL |

SP
BP
SI
DI

IP
FLAGS

CS
DS
SS
ES

Call With

AH = 06H

AL = Number of scroll lines

BH = Attribute for the cleared area

CH = Upper left row

CL = Upper left column

DH = Lower right row

DL = Lower right column

Returns

Nothing

10 IBM PC and EGA ROM BIOS Video Services

Function Description

ROM BIOS video function 06H scrolls a display screen window's contents upward. If the number of lines passed in AL is equal to zero, the entire window will be cleared. Otherwise, only the specified number of lines in AL will be scrolled and cleared.

Suggested Macro Definition

```
windowup    macro   row1,col1,row2,col2,lines,att
            mov     ah,6
            mov     al,lines
            mov     bh,att
            mov     ch,row1
            mov     cl,col1
            mov     dh,row2
            mov     dl,col2
            int     10h
            endm
```

Programming Example

The following program fragment demonstrates how ROM BIOS video function 06H is used to clear the left half of the display screen:

```
        .
        .
        .
        mov     ah,6        ;AH = Scroll window up function code
        mov     al,0        ;AL = Clear the whole window
        mov     bh,7        ;BH = Normal attribute
        mov     ch,0        ;CH = Upper left row
        mov     cl,0        ;CL = Upper left column
        mov     dh,24       ;DH = Lower right row
        mov     dl,39       ;DL = Lower right column
        int     10h         ;Clear the screen
        .
        .
        .
```

SCROLL WINDOW DOWN (FUNCTION 07H)

Register Summary

AX: | AH | AL |
BX: | BH | BL |
CX: | CH | CL |
DX: | DH | DL |

SP
BP
SI
DI

IP
FLAGS

CS
DS
SS
ES

Call With

AH = 07H

AL = Number of scroll lines

BH = Attribute for the cleared area

CH = Upper left row

CL = Upper left column

DH = Lower right row

DL = Lower right column

Returns

Nothing

10 IBM PC and EGA ROM BIOS Video Services

Function Description

ROM BIOS video function 07H scrolls a display screen window's contents downward. If the number of lines passed in AL is equal to zero, the window will be completely cleared. Otherwise, only the specified number of lines in AL will be scrolled and cleared.

Suggested Macro Definition

```
windowdown  macro   row1,col1,row2,col2,lines,att
            mov     ah,7
            mov     al,lines
            mov     bh,att
            mov     ch,row1
            mov     cl,col1
            mov     dh,row2
            mov     dl,col2
            int     10h
            endm
```

Programming Example

The following program fragment demonstrates how ROM BIOS video function 07H is used to clear the right half of the display screen's top ten lines:

```
            .
            .
            .
            mov     ah,7        ;AH = Scroll window down function code
            mov     al,0        ;AL = Clear the whole window
            mov     bh,7        ;BH = Normal attribute
            mov     ch,0        ;CH = Upper left row
            mov     cl,40       ;CL = Upper left column
            mov     dh,9        ;DH = Lower right row
            mov     dl,79       ;DL = Lower right column
            int     10h         ;Clear the window
            .
            .
            .
```

IBM PC and EGA ROM BIOS Video Services 10

READ CHARACTER/ATTRIBUTE PAIR (FUNCTION 08H)

Register Summary

AX: | AH | AL |
BX: | BH | BL |
CX: | CH | CL |
DX: | DH | DL |

SP
BP
SI
DI

IP
FLAGS

CS
DS
SS
ES

Call with

AH = 08H

BH = Page number

Returns

AH = Attribute

AL = ASCII code

10 IBM PC and EGA ROM BIOS Video Services

Function Description

ROM BIOS video function 08H retrieves the character/attribute pair located at the current cursor position. While in graphics modes, the page number passed in BH must be zero.

Suggested Macro Definition

```
readpair    macro   page
            mov     ah,8
            mov     bh,page
            int     10h
            endm
```

Programming Example

The following program fragment demonstrates how ROM BIOS video function 08H is used to read the character/attribute pair in the upper left corner of the display screen:

```
        .
        .
        .
        mov     ah,2        ;AH = Set cursor function code
        mov     bh,0        ;BH = Page 0
        mov     dh,0        ;DH = Cursor row position
        mov     dl,0        ;DL = Cursor column position
        int     10h         ;Home the cursor
        mov     ah,8        ;AH = Read pair function code
        mov     bh,0        ;BH = Page 0
        int     10h         ;Get the char/att pair
        .
        .
        .
```

IBM PC and EGA ROM BIOS Video Services 10

WRITE CHARACTER/ATTRIBUTE PAIR (FUNCTION 09H)

Register Summary

AX: | AH | AL |
BX: | BH | BL |
CX: | CH | CL |
DX: | DH | DL |

SP
BP
SI
DI

IP
FLAGS

CS
DS
SS
ES

Call With

AH = 09H

AL = ASCII code

BH = Page number

BL = Attribute

CX = Number of characters

Returns

Nothing

10 IBM PC and EGA ROM BIOS Video Services

Function Description

ROM BIOS video function 09H displays a specified number of character/attribute pairs, beginning at the current cursor position. The cursor position is not updated by ROM BIOS video function 09H. In graphics modes, the page number passed in BH must equal zero.

Suggested Macro Definition

```
writepair    macro    page,char,att,number
             mov      ah,9
             mov      al,char
             mov      bh,page
             mov      bl,att
             mov      cx,number
             int      10h
             endm
```

Programming Example

The following program fragment demonstrates how ROM BIOS video function 09H is used to completely fill the bottom line of the display screen with an underline character:

```
        .
        .
        .
        mov     ah,2        ;AH = Set cursor function code
        mov     bh,0        ;BH = Page 0
        mov     dh,24       ;DH = Cursor row position
        mov     dl,0        ;DL = Cursor column position
        int     10h         ;Move the cursor
        mov     ah,9        ;AH = Write pair function code
        mov     al,'_'      ;AL = Underline character
        mov     bh,0        ;BH = Page 0
        mov     bl,7        ;BL = Normal attribute
        mov     cx,80       ;CX = Line length
        int     10h         ;Display the line
        .
        .
        .
```

IBM PC and EGA ROM BIOS Video Services 10

WRITE CHARACTERS (FUNCTION 0AH)

Register Summary

AX:	AH	AL
BX:	BH	BL
CX:	CH	CL
DX:	DH	DL

SP
BP
SI
DI

IP
FLAGS

CS
DS
SS
ES

Call With

AH = 0AH

AL = ASCII code

BH = Page number

BL = Color (Graphics only)

CX = Number of characters

Returns

Nothing

10 IBM PC and EGA ROM BIOS Video Services

Function Description

ROM BIOS video function 0AH writes a specified number of characters, beginning at the current cursor position. The cursor position is not updated by ROM BIOS video function 0AH. In graphics modes, the page number passed in BH must be zero.

Suggested Macro Definition

```
writechar      macro      page,char,number,color
               mov        ah,0ah
               mov        al,char
               mov        bh,page
               ifnb       <color>
               mov        bl,color
               endif
               mov        cx,number
               int        10h
               endm
```

Programming Example

The following program fragment demonstrates how ROM BIOS video function 0AH is used to display 40 * (asterisk) characters, starting at the upper left corner of the display screen:

```
       .
       .
       .
       mov     ah,2         ;AH = Set cursor function code
       mov     bh,0         ;BH = Page 0
       mov     dh,0         ;DH = Cursor row position
       mov     dl,0         ;DL = Cursor column position
       int     10h          ;Home the cursor
       mov     ah,0ah       ;AH = Write characters function code
       mov     al,'*'       ;AL = Asterisk character
       mov     bh,0         ;BH = Page 0
       mov     cx,40        ;CX = Number of characters
       int     10h          ;Display the characters
       .
       .
       .
```

SET COLOR PALETTE (0BH)

Register Summary

Call With

AH = 0BH

BH = Function code

BL = Color or Palette code

Returns

Nothing

10 IBM PC and EGA ROM BIOS Video Services

Function Description

ROM BIOS video function 0BH selects either a color palette or the background and border colors. If the function code in BH is equal to zero, ROM BIOS video function 0BH sets the background and border colors. While in graphics modes, the background and the border colors will be set to the color passed in BL. While in text modes, only the border color will be set to the color passed in BL. If the function code in BH is equal to one, the new color palette code is passed in BL as follows:

Palette	Pixel Value	Color
0	0	Current Background Color
0	1	Green
0	2	Red
0	3	Brown
1	0	Current Background Color
1	1	Cyan
1	2	Magenta
1	3	White

Suggested Macro Definition

```
setpalette   macro   func,color
             mov     ah,0bh
             mov     bh,func
             mov     bl,color
             endm
```

Programming Example

The following program fragment demonstrates how ROM BIOS video function 0BH is used to set a display screen's background to white.

```
        .
        .
        .
        mov   ah,0bh    ;AH = Set palette function
        mov   bh,0      ;BH = Set border color function
        mov   bl,7      ;BL = White color value
        int   10h       ;Set border to white
        .
        .
        .
```

WRITE GRAPHICS PIXEL (FUNCTION 0CH)

Register Summary

Call With

AH = 0CH

AL = Color value

CX = Pixel column

DX = Pixel row

Returns

Nothing

Function Description

ROM BIOS video function 0CH sets a graphics pixel to the color passed in AL. For video modes 04H and 05H, the legitimate range for color values is 0 to 3. Video mode 06H allows only color values 0 and 1. Whenever bit 7 of the color value is set, the color value is **xor**ed with the pixel's current color value.

Suggested Macro Definition

```
writepixel      macro   pixelx,pixely,color
                mov     ah,0ch
                mov     al,color
                mov     cx,pixelx
                mov     dx,pixely
                endm
```

Programming Example

The following program fragment demonstrates how ROM BIOS video function 0CH is used to draw a graphics line across the center of the display screen:

```
                .
                .
                .
        mov     cx,0        ;CX = Starting x-coordinate
        mov     dx,120      ;DX = Y-coordinate
loop:   mov     ah,0ch      ;AH = Write pixel function code
        mov     al,1        ;AL = Color value
        int     10h         ;Turn on the pixel
        inc     cx          ;Bump the x-coordinate
        cmp     cx,640      ;Loop
        jb      loop        ; till done
                .
                .
                .
```

READ GRAPHICS PIXEL (FUNCTION 0DH)

Register Summary

AX: | AH | AL |
BX: | BH | BL |
CX: | CH | CL |
DX: | DH | DL |

SP
BP
SI
DI

IP
FLAGS

CS
DS
SS
ES

Call With

AH = 0DH

CX = Pixel column

DX = Pixel row

Returns

AL = Color value

10 IBM PC and EGA ROM BIOS Video Services

Function Description
ROM BIOS video function 0DH retrieves the color value for a specified graphics pixel. The range of the retrieved color value is dependent upon the current video mode.

Suggested Macro Definition

```
readpixel    macro    pixelx,pixely
             mov      ah,0dh
             mov      cx,pixelx
             mov      dx,pixely
             int      10h
             endm
```

Programming Example
The following program fragment demonstrates how ROM BIOS video function 0DH is used to retrieve the color value of pixel 0,25:

```
        .
        .
        .
        mov     ah,0dH      ;AH = Read pixel function code
        mov     cx,0        ;CX = Pixel x-coordinate
        mov     dx,25       ;DX = Pixel y-coordinate
        int     10h         ;Retrieve the color value
        .
        .
        .
```

WRITE CHARACTER IN TELETYPE MODE (FUNCTION 0EH)

Register Summary

Call With

AH = 0EH

AL = ASCII code

BH = Page number

BL = Color value for graphics modes

Returns

Nothing

Function Description

ROM BIOS video function 0EH displays a character by using a teletype mode. The ASCII codes for bell, backspace, carriage return, and linefeed are all recognized by the teletype mode. All other ASCII codes display their corresponding characters.

Suggested Macro Definition

```
writetty     macro     char,page,color
             mov       ah,0eh
             mov       al,char
             mov       bh,page
             ifnb      <color>
             mov       bl,color
             endif
             int       10h
             endm
```

Programming Example

The following program fragment demonstrates how ROM BIOS video function 0EH is used to perform a carriage return:

```
        .
        .
        .
        mov     ah,0eh      ;AH = Write teletype function code
        mov     al,13       ;AL = Carriage return
        mov     bh,0        ;BH = Page number
        int     10h         ;Do a carriage return
        .
        .
        .
```

GET VIDEO MODE (FUNCTION 0FH)

Register Summary

AX: | AH | AL |
BX: | BH | BL |
CX: | CH | CL |
DX: | DH | DL |

Call With

AH = 0FH

Return

AH = Line length

AL = Video Mode

BH = Page Number

10 IBM PC and EGA ROM BIOS Video Services

Function Description

ROM BIOS video function 0FH retrieves the number of columns per display line, the currently active page number, and the current video mode as follows:

Display Mode	Description	Adapter(s)
00H	40 x 25 black and white text	CGA, EGA, PCjr
01H	40 x 25 color text	CGA, EGA, PCjr
02H	80 x 25 black and white text	CGA, EGA, PCjr
03H	80 x 25 color text	CGA, EGA, PCjr
04H	320 x 200 4 color graphics	CGA, EGA, PCjr
05H	320 x 200 4 color (color off)	CGA, EGA, PCjr
06H	640 x 200 2 color graphics	CGA, EGA, PCjr
07H	80 x 25 black and white text	MDA, EGA
08H	160 x 200 16 color graphics	PCjr
09H	320 x 200 16 color graphics	PCjr
0AH	640 x 200 4 color graphics	PCjr
0DH	320 x 200 16 color graphics	EGA
0EH	640 x 200 16 color graphics	EGA
0FH	640 x 350 2 color graphics	EGA
10H	640 x 350 4/16 color graphics	EGA

Suggested Macro Definition

```
getvidmode   macro
             mov      ah,0fh
             int      10h
             endm
```

Programming Example

The following program fragment demonstrates how ROM BIOS video function 0FH is used to retrieve the current video mode, the current display page, and the number of columns per line:

```
        .
        .
        .
        mov    ah,0fh    ;AH = Get video mode function code
        int    10h       ;Get the video mode
        .
        .
        .
```

SET PALETTE REGISTER
(FUNCTION 10H, SUBFUNCTION 00H)

Register Summary

Call With

AH = 10H

AL = 00H

BH = Color value

BL = Palette register

Return

Nothing

10 IBM PC and EGA ROM BIOS Video Services

Function Description
EGA ROM BIOS video function 10H (subfunction 00H) sets the palette register specified in register BL (00H to 0FH) to the color value passed in register BH.

Suggested Macro Definition

```
setpalreg    macro    color,register
             mov      ax,1000h
             mov      bh,color
             mov      bl,register
             endm
```

Programming Example
The following program fragment demonstrates EGA ROM BIOS video function 10H (subfunction 00H) by setting palette register 01H to color value 32H:

```
            .
            .
            .
            mov    bh,1          ;BH = Palette register
            mov    bl,32h        ;BL = Color value
            mov    ax,1000h      ;Set the
            int    10h           ; palette register
            .
            .
            .
```

SET BORDER COLOR
(FUNCTION 10H, SUBFUNCTION 01H)

Register Summary

AX: | AH | AL |
BX: | BH | BL |
CX: | CH | CL |
DX: | DH | DL |

SP
BP
SI
DI

IP
FLAGS

CS
DS
SS
ES

Call With

AH = 10H

AL = 01H

BH = Color value

Returns

Nothing

10 IBM PC and EGA ROM BIOS Video Services

Function Description

EGA ROM BIOS video function 10H (subfunction 01H) sets the border color to the color passed in register BH.

Suggested Macro Definition

```
setborder    macro    color
             mov      ax,1001h
             mov      bh,color
             endm
```

Programming Example

The following program fragment demonstrates EGA ROM BIOS video function 10H (subfunction 01H) by setting the border color to red:

```
        .
        .
        .
        mov    bh,04h      ;BH = Red color value
        mov    ax,1001h    ;Set the
        int    10h         ; border color
        .
        .
        .
```

IBM PC and EGA ROM BIOS Video Services 10

SET ALL PALETTE REGISTERS AND THE BORDER COLOR (FUNCTION 10H, SUBFUNCTION 02H)

Register Summary

Call With

AH = 10H

AL = 02H

ES:DX = Address of a seventeen-byte color list

Returns

Nothing

10 IBM PC and EGA ROM BIOS Video Services

Function Description

EGA ROM BIOS video function 10H (subfunction 02H) sets all of the palette registers to the first 16 bytes contained in the list pointed to by registers ES:DX. Additionally, the border color is set to the value specified by the color list's 17th byte.

Suggested Macro Definition

```
setall     macro   colorlist
           mov     ax,seg colorlist
           mov     es,ax
           mov     dx,offset colorlist
           mov     ax,1002h
           int     10h
           endm
```

Programming Example

The following program fragment demonstrates EGA ROM BIOS video function 10H (subfunction 02H) by setting the palette registers and the border color:

```
    .
    .
    .
    mov     ax,seg newcolors     ;AX = New color list's address
    mov     es,ax                ;Put it in ES
    mov     dx,offset newcolors  ;ES:DX = New color list's address
    mov     ax,1002h             ;Set the
    int     10h                  ; new color values
    .
    .
    .
```

TOGGLE BLINK/INTENSITY FLAG (FUNCTION 10H, SUBFUNCTION 03H)

Register Summary

AX: | AH | AL |
BX: | BH | BL |
CX: | CH | CL |
DX: | DH | DL |

SP
BP
SI
DI

IP
FLAGS

CS
DS
SS
ES

Call With

AH = 10H

AL = 03H

BL = Blink/intensity flag

Returns

Nothing

10 IBM PC and EGA ROM BIOS Video Services

Function Description

EGA ROM BIOS video function 10H (subfunction 03H) sets the blink/intensity flag to the value passed in register BL as follows:

Value	Action
0	Intensify characters with their most significant bits set.
1	Blink characters with their most significant bits set.

Suggested Macro Definition

```
setblink     macro    flag
             mov      bl,flag
             mov      ax,1003h
             int      10h
             endm
```

Programming Example

The following program fragment demonstrates EGA ROM BIOS video function 10H (subfunction 03H) by setting the blink/intensity flag for blinking:

```
        .
        .
        .
        mov     bl,1         ;BL = Blink specifier
        mov     ax,1003h     ;Set the
        int     10h          ; blink/intensity flag
        .
        .
        .
```

IBM PC and EGA ROM BIOS Video Services 10

LOAD USER FONT (FUNCTION 11H, SUBFUNCTION 00H)

Register Summary

AX: | AH | AL |
BX: | BH | BL |
CX: | CH | CL |
DX: | DH | DL |

SP
BP
SI
DI

IP
FLAGS

CS
DS
SS
ES

Call With

AH = 11H

AL = 00H

BH = Number of bytes per character

BL = Block to load

CX = Number of characters in the font table

DX = First character code in the font table

ES:BP = Address of the font table

Returns

Nothing

10 IBM PC and EGA ROM BIOS Video Services

Function Description

EGA ROM BIOS video function 11H (subfunction 00H) loads the user-defined font table pointed to by registers ES:BP into the character generator RAM block defined by register BL. EGA ROM BIOS video function 11H (subfunction 00H) is only valid for text display modes.

Suggested Macro Definition

```
loaduserfont1  macro   bytes,block,chars,first,tableptr
               mov     bh,bytes
               mov     bl,block
               mov     cx,chars
               mov     dx,first
               mov     ax,seg tableptr
               mov     es,ax
               mov     bp,offset tableptr
               mov     ax,1100h
               int     10h
               endm
```

Programming Example

The following program fragment demonstrates EGA ROM BIOS video function 11H (subfunction 00H) by loading a user-defined font table into character generator RAM:

```
     .
     .
     .
     mov    bh,8                  ;BH = Number of bytes per character
     mov    bl,0                  ;BL = Character Generator RAM block
     mov    cx,256                ;CX = Number of characters
     mov    dx,0                  ;DX = First character code
     mov    ax,seg fonttable      ;AX = Font table offset
     mov    es,ax                 ;Put it in ES
     mov    bp,offset fonttable   ;ES:BP = Font table pointer
     mov    ax,1100h              ;Load the
     int    10h                   ; user-defined font
     .
     .
     .
```

LOAD ROM BIOS 8-BY-14 FONT (FUNCTION 11H, SUBFUNCTION 01H)

Register Summary

Call With

AH = 11h

AL = 01H

BL = Block to load

Returns

Nothing

10　IBM PC and EGA ROM BIOS Video Services

Function Description

EGA ROM BIOS video function 11H (subfunction 01H) loads the default 8-by-14 font table into the character generator RAM block specified by register BL. EGA ROM BIOS video function 11H (subfunction 01H) is only valid for text display modes.

Suggested Macro Definition

```
load8by14font1  macro   block
                mov     bl,block
                mov     ax,1101h
                int     10h
                endm
```

Programming Example

The following program fragment demonstrates EGA ROM BIOS video function 11H (subfunction 01H) by loading the default 8-by-14 font table into character generator RAM:

```
        .
        .
        .
        mov     bl,0        ;BL = Character generator RAM block
        mov     ax,1101h    ;Load the
        int     10h         ; 8-by-14 font
        .
        .
        .
```

LOAD ROM BIOS 8-BY-8 FONT (FUNCTION 11H, SUBFUNCTION 02H)

Register Summary

Call With

AH = 11H

AL = 02H

BL = Block to load

Returns

Nothing

10 IBM PC and EGA ROM BIOS Video Services

Function Description

EGA ROM BIOS video function 11H (subfunction 02H) loads the default 8-by-8 font table into the character generator RAM block specified by register BL. EGA ROM BIOS video function 11H (subfunction 02H) is only valid for text display modes.

Suggested Macro Definition

```
load8by8font1   macro   block
                mov     bl,block
                mov     ax,1102h
                int     10h
                endm
```

Programming Example

The following program fragment demonstrates EGA ROM BIOS video function 11H (subfunction 02H) by loading the default 8-by-8 font table into character generator RAM:

```
        .
        .
        .
        mov     bl,0            ;BL = Character generator RAM block
        mov     ax,1102h        ;Load the
        int     10h             ; 8-by-8 font
        .
        .
        .
```

SELECT CHARACTER GENERATOR RAM BLOCK (FUNCTION 11H, SUBFUNCTION 03H)

Register Summary

Call With

AH = 11H

AL = 03H

BL = Character generator RAM block

Return

Nothing

10 IBM PC and EGA ROM BIOS Video Services

Function Description

EGA ROM BIOS video function 11H (subfunction 03H) sets the character generator RAM block to the value passed in register BL as follows:

Bits	Action
0 - 1	Character RAM block to be selected when bit 3 of the character's attribute byte is equal to 0.
2 - 3	Character RAM block to be selected when bit 3 of the character's attribute byte is equal to 1.
4 - 7	Not used.

EGA ROM BIOS video function 11H (subfunction 03H) is only valid during text display modes.

Suggested Macro Definition:

```
selectblock   macro   block
              mov     bl,block
              mov     ax,1103h
              int     10h
              endm
```

Programming Example

The following program fragment demonstrates EGA ROM BIOS video function 11H (subfunction 03H) by selecting the character generator RAM blocks:

```
        .
        .
        .
        mov     bl,0            ;BL = Block select values
        mov     ax,1103h        ;Select the
        int     10h             ; character generator RAM blocks
        .
        .
        .
```

LOAD USER FONT (FUNCTION 11H, SUBFUNCTION 10H)

Register Summary

AX: | AH | AL |
BX: | BH | BL |
CX: | CH | CL |
DX: | DH | DL |

SP
BP
SI
DI

IP
FLAGS

CS
DS
SS
ES

Call With

AH = 11H

AL = 10H

BH = Number of bytes per character

BL = Block to load

CX = Number of characters in the font table

DX = First character code in the font table

ES:BP = Address of the font table

Returns

Nothing

10 IBM PC and EGA ROM BIOS Video Services

Function Description

Like EGA ROM BIOS video function 11H (subfunction 00H), EGA ROM BIOS video function 11H (subfunction 10H) loads the user-defined font table pointed to by registers ES:BP into the character generator RAM block defined by register BL. Furthermore, the video controller is reprogrammed as follows:

Controller Setting	Value
Maximum scan line	number of bytes per character - 1
Cursor start	number of bytes per character - 2
Cursor end	number of bytes per character - 1
Vertical display end	(rows * number of bytes per character) - 1
Underline location	number of bytes per character - 1

EGA ROM BIOS video function 11H (subfunction 10H) is only valid for text display modes and should only be called after a mode set.

Suggested Macro Definition

```
loaduserfont2   macro   bytes,block,chars,first,tableptr
                mov     bh,bytes
                mov     bl,block
                mov     cx,chars
                mov     dx,first
                mov     ax,seg tableptr
                mov     es,ax
                mov     bp,offset tableptr
                mov     ax,1110h
                int     10h
                endm
```

Programming Example

The following program fragment demonstrates EGA ROM BIOS video function 11H (subfunction 10H) by loading a user-defined font table into character generator RAM:

```
        .
        .
        .
        mov     bh,8                    ;BH = Number of bytes per character
        mov     bl,0                    ;BL = Character Generator RAM block
        mov     cx,256                  ;CX = Number of characters
        mov     dx,0                    ;DX = First character code
        mov     ax,seg fonttable        ;AX = Font table offset
        mov     es,ax                   ;Put it in ES
        mov     bp,offset fonttable     ;ES:BP = Font table pointer
        mov     ax,1110h                ;Load the
        int     10h                     ; user-defined font
        .
        .
        .
```

LOAD ROM BIOS 8-BY-14 FONT (FUNCTION 11H, SUBFUNCTION 11H)

Register Summary

AX: | AH | AL |
BX: | BH | BL |
CX: | CH | CL |
DX: | DH | DL |

SP
BP
SI
DI

IP
FLAGS

CS
DS
SS
ES

Call With

AH = 11H

AL = 11H

BL = Block to load

Returns

Nothing

Function Description

Like EGA ROM BIOS video function 11H (subfunction 01H), EGA ROM BIOS video function 11H (subfunction 11H) loads the default 8-by-14 font table into the character generator RAM block specified by register BL. Furthermore, the video controller is reprogrammed as follows:

Controller Setting	Value
Maximum scan line	number of bytes per character - 1
Cursor start	number of bytes per character - 2
Cursor end	number of bytes per character - 1
Vertical display end	(rows * number of bytes per character) - 1
Underline location	number of bytes per character - 1

EGA ROM BIOS video function 11H (subfunction 11H) is only valid for text display modes and should only be called after a mode set.

Suggested Macro Definition

```
load8by14font2 macro   block
                mov    bl,block
                mov    ax,1111h
                int    10h
                endm
```

Programming Example

The following program fragment demonstrates EGA ROM BIOS video function 11H (subfunction 11H) by loading the default 8-by-14 font table into character generator RAM:

```
       .
       .
       .
       mov   bl,0         ;BL = Character generator RAM block
       mov   ax,1111h     ;Load the
       int   10h          ; 8-by-14 font
       .
       .
       .
```

LOAD ROM BIOS 8-BY-8 FONT (FUNCTION 11H, SUBFUNCTION 12H)

Register Summary

Call With

AH = 11H

AL = 12H

BL = Block to load

Returns

Nothing

IBM PC and EGA ROM BIOS Video Services 10

Function Description

Like EGA ROM BIOS video function 11H (subfunction 02H), EGA ROM BIOS video function 11H (subfunction 12H) loads the default 8-by-8 font table into the character generator RAM block specified by register BL. Furthermore, the video controller is reprogrammed as follows:

Controller Setting	Value
Maximum scan line	number of bytes per character - 1
Cursor start	number of bytes per character - 2
Cursor end	number of bytes per character - 1
Vertical display end	(rows * number of bytes per character) - 1
Underline location	number of bytes per character - 1

EGA ROM BIOS video function 11H (subfunction 12H) is only valid for text display modes and should only be called after a mode set.

Suggested Macro Definition

```
load8by8font2   macro   block
                mov     bl,block
                mov     ax,1112h
                int     10h
                endm
```

Programming Example

The following program fragment demonstrates EGA ROM BIOS video function 11H (subfunction 12H) by loading the default 8-by-8 font table into character generator RAM:

```
        .
        .
        .
        mov     bl,0        ;BL = Character generator RAM block
        mov     ax,1112h    ;Load the
        int     10h         ; 8-by-8 font
        .
        .
        .
```

SET THE UPPER FONT TABLE POINTER (FUNCTION 11H, SUBFUNCTION 20H)

Register Summary

Call With

AH = 11H

AL = 20H

ES:BP = Address of the font table

Returns

Nothing

IBM PC and EGA ROM BIOS Video Services 10

Function Description

EGA ROM BIOS video function 11H (subfunction 20H) sets the upper font table pointer (INT 1FH) to the address passed in registers ES:BP. The upper font table is used for character codes 80H to FFH and is only valid for video modes 04H to 06H.

Suggested Macro Definition:

```
setuppertable  macro   tableptr
               mov     ax,seg tableptr
               mov     es,ax
               mov     bp,offset tableptr
               mov     ax,1120h
               int     10h
               endm
```

Programming Example

The following program fragment demonstrates EGA ROM BIOS video function 11H (subfunction 20H) by setting the upper font table pointer:

```
        .
        .
        .
        mov     ax,seg newupper     ;AX = New upper font table's segment
        mov     es,ax                ;Put it in ES
        mov     bp,offset newupper  ;ES:BP = New font table's address
        mov     ax,1120h             ;Set the new
        int     10h                  ; upper font table pointer
        .
        .
        .
```

SET FONT TABLE POINTER
(FUNCTION 11H, SUBFUNCTION 21H)

Register Summary

Call With

AH = 11H

AL = 21H

BL = Number of character rows flag

CX = Bytes per character

DL = User-defined number of character rows per screen

ES:BP = Address of the font table

Returns

Nothing

IBM PC and EGA ROM BIOS Video Services 10

Function Description

EGA ROM BIOS video function 11H (subfunction 21H) sets the font table pointer (INT 43H) to the address passed in registers ES:BP. Additionally, the number of character rows per screen is passed in register BL as follows:

Value	Number of Character Rows Per Screen
0	Actual number of rows per screen is passed in register DL.
1	14 rows per screen.
2	25 rows per screen.
3	43 rows per screen.

EGA ROM BIOS video function 11H (subfunction 21H) is only valid for graphic display modes.

Suggested Macro Definition

```
setfonttable   macro   rowflag,bytes,rows,tableptr
               mov     bl,rowflag
               mov     cx,bytes
               mov     dl,rows
               mov     ax,seg tableptr
               mov     es,ax
               mov     bp,offset tableptr
               mov     ax,1121h
               int     10h
               endm
```

Programming Example

The following program fragment demonstrates EGA ROM BIOS video function 11H (subfunction 21H) by setting the font table pointer to a user-defined font:

```
        .
        .
        .
        mov     bl,2                ;BL = 25 rows per screen flag
        mov     cx,14               ;CX = Number of bytes per character
        mov     ax,seg userfont     ;AX = User-defined font's segment
        mov     es,ax               ;Put it in ES
        mov     bp,offset userfont  ;ES:BP = User-defined font pointer
        mov     ax,1121h            ;Set the new
        int     10h                 ; font table pointer
        .
        .
        .
```

SET FONT TABLE POINTER TO ROM BIOS 8-BY-14 FONT (FUNCTION 11H, SUBFUNCTION 22H)

Register Summary

Call With

AH = 11H

AL = 22H

BL = Number of character rows flag

DL = User-defined number of character rows per screen

Returns

Nothing

Function Description

EGA ROM BIOS video function 11H (subfunction 22H) points the font table pointer (INT 43H) to the ROM BIOS 8-by-14 font table. Additionally, the number of character rows per screen is passed in register BL as follows:

Value	Number of Character Rows Per Screen
0	Actual number of rows per screen is passed in register DL.
1	14 rows per screen.
2	25 rows per screen.
3	43 rows per screen.

EGA ROM BIOS video function 11H (subfunction 22H) is only valid for graphic display modes.

Suggested Macro Definition

```
setfont8by14   macro   rowflag,row
               mov     bl,rowflag
               mov     dl,row
               mov     ax,1122h
               int     10h
               endm
```

Programming Example

The following program fragment demonstrates EGA ROM BIOS video function 11H (subfunction 22H) by pointing the font table pointer to the ROM BIOS 8-by-14 font table:

```
        .
        .
        .
        mov     bl,2         ;BL=25 rows per screen flag
        mov     ax,1122h     ;Set the new
        int     10h          ; font table pointer
        .
        .
        .
```

SET FONT TABLE POINTER TO ROM BIOS
8-BY-8 FONT (FUNCTION 11H, SUBFUNCTION 23H)

Register Summary

Call With

AH = 11H

AL = 23H

BL = Number of character rows flag

DL = User-defined number of character rows per screen

Returns

Nothing

IBM PC and EGA ROM BIOS Video Services 10

Function Description

EGA ROM BIOS video function 11H (subfunction 23H) points the font table pointer (INT 43H) to the ROM BIOS 8-by-8 font table. Additionally, the number of character rows per screen is passed in register BL as follows:

Value	Number of Character Rows Per Screen
0	Actual number of rows per screen is passed in register DL.
1	14 rows per screen.
2	25 rows per screen.
3	43 rows per screen.

EGA ROM BIOS video function 11H (subfunction 23H) is only valid for graphic display modes.

Suggested Macro Definition

```
setfont8by8    macro    rowflag,row
               mov      bl,rowflag
               mov      dl,row
               mov      ax,1123h
               int      10h
               endm
```

Programming Example

The following program fragment demonstrates EGA ROM BIOS video function 11H (subfunction 23H) by pointing the font table pointer to the ROM BIOS 8-by-8 font table:

```
         .
         .
         .
         mov    bl,2         ;BL=25 rows per screen flag
         mov    ax,1123h     ;Set the new
         int    10h          ; font table pointer
         .
         .
         .
```

GET FONT INFORMATION
(FUNCTION 11H, SUBFUNCTION 30H)

Register Summary

AX: | AH | AL |
BX: | BH | BL |
CX: | CH | CL |
DX: | DH | DL |

SP
BP
SI
DI

IP
FLAGS

CS
DS
SS
ES

Call With

AH = 11H

AL = 30H

BH = Font code

Returns

CX = Bytes per character

DL = Number of rows per screen - 1

ES:BP = Address of the font table

IBM PC and EGA ROM BIOS Video Services 10

Function Description

EGA ROM BIOS video function 11H (subfunction 30H) retrieves the font information for the font specified in register BH as follows:

Font Code	Font
0	Current INT 1FH font
1	Current INT 43H font
2	ROM BIOS 8-by-14 font
3	ROM BIOS 8-by-8 font (codes 00H to 7FH)
4	ROM BIOS 8-by-8 font (codes 80H to FFH)
5	Alternate ROM BIOS 9-by-14 font

Suggested Macro Definition

```
getfontinfo   macro   font
              mov     bh,font
              mov     ax,1130h
              int     10h
              endm
```

Programming Example

The following program fragment demonstrates EGA ROM BIOS video function 11H (subfunction 30H) by retrieving the INT 1FH font information:

```
        .
        .
        .
        mov     bh,0        ;BH = INT 1FH font code
        mov     ax,1130h    ;Get the
        int     10h         ; font information
        .
        .
        .
```

GET CONFIGURATION INFORMATION (FUNCTION 12H, SUBFUNCTION 10H)

Register Summary

Call With

AH = 12H

BL = 10H

Returns

BH = Display type

BL = Amount of video memory

CH = Feature bits

CL = Switch settings

IBM PC and EGA ROM BIOS Video Services 10

Function Description

EGA ROM BIOS video function 12H (subfunction 10H) retrieves the display adapter configuration information. The display type is returned in register BH as follows:

Value	Display Type
0	Color display
1	Monochrome display

Additionally, EGA ROM BIOS video function 12H (subfunction 10H) returns the amount of video memory in register BL as follows:

Value	Amount of Video Memory
0	64K
1	128K
2	192K
3	256K

Suggested Macro Definition

```
getconfiginfo  macro
               mov    bl,10h
               mov    ah,12h
               int    10h
               endm
```

Programming Example

The following program fragment demonstrates EGA ROM BIOS video function 12H (subfunction 10H) by retrieving the display adapter's configuration information:

```
        .
        .
        .
        mov    bl,10h     ;Get the
        mov    ah,12h     ;  configuration
        int    10h        ;  information
        .
        .
        .
```

359

SELECT ALTERNATE SCREEN PRINT ROUTINE (FUNCTION 12H, SUBFUNCTION 20H)

Register Summary

AX:	**AH**	AL
BX:	BH	**BL**
CX:	CH	CL
DX:	DH	DL

```
SP
BP
SI
DI
```

```
IP
FLAGS
```

```
CS
DS
SS
ES
```

Call With

AH = 12H

BL = 20H

Returns

Nothing

IBM PC and EGA ROM BIOS Video Services 10

Function Description

EGA ROM BIOS video function 12H (subfunction 20H) sets the screen print routine to an alternate routine, which will correctly print screens longer that 25 lines.

Suggested Macro Definition

```
printscreen   macro
              mov       bl,20h
              mov       ah,12h
              int       10h
              endm
```

Programming Example

The following program fragment demonstrates EGA ROM BIOS video function 12H (subfunction 20H) by setting the screen print routine to the alternate EGA routine:

```
            .
            .
            .
            mov     bl,20h      ;Set the
            mov     ah,12h      ; alternate
            int     10h         ; print screen routine
            .
            .
            .
```

10 IBM PC and EGA ROM BIOS Video Services

WRITE STRING IN TELETYPE MODE (FUNCTION 13H)

Register Summary

Call With

AH = 13H

AL = Write mode

BH = Video page

BL = Attribute

CX = String length

DH = Row

DL = Column

ES:BP = Address of the string

Returns

Nothing

IBM PC and EGA ROM BIOS Video Services 10

Function Description

EGA ROM BIOS video function 13H displays the string pointed to by registers ES:BP using the mode specified in register AL as follows:

Value	Description
0	The string is composed of character codes only and the cursor position isn't updated.
1	The string is composed of character codes only and the cursor position is updated.
2	The string is composed of character/attribute pairs and the cursor position isn't updated.
3	The string is composed of character/attribute pairs and the cursor position is updated.

Suggested Macro Definition

```
writestring   macro   mode,page,att,length,row,col,string
              mov     bh,page
              mov     bl,att
              mov     cx,length
              mov     dh,row
              mov     dl,col
              mov     ax,seg string
              mov     es,ax
              mov     bp,offset string
              mov     al,mode
              mov     ah,13h
              int     10h
              endm
```

Programming Example

The following program fragment demonstrates EGA ROM BIOS video function 13H by displaying a string in the upper left corner of the display screen:

10 IBM PC and EGA ROM BIOS Video Services

.
.
.

```
mov     bh,0              ;BH = Video page
mov     bl,7              ;BL = Display attribute
mov     cx,20             ;CX = String length
xor     dx,dx             ;DH = Row 0, DL = Column 0
mov     ax,seg string     ;AX = String's segment
mov     es,ax             ;Put it in ES
mov     bp,offset string  ;ES:BP = String pointer
mov     al,0              ;AL = Write mode
mov     ah,13h            ;Display
int     10h               ; the string
```

.
.
.

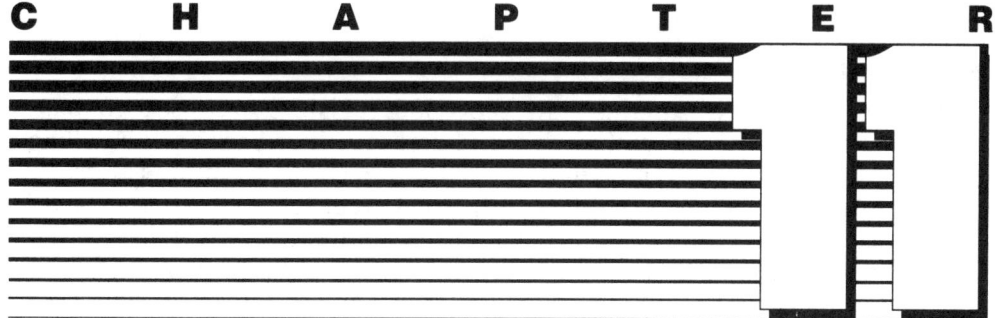

THE MICROSOFT MOUSE DRIVER ROUTINES

A s explained in Chapter 4, the Microsoft mouse driver offers a wide variety of routines for controlling a Microsoft-compatible mouse. This chapter presents a detailed look at the routines that are contained in the Microsoft mouse driver. Each of the Microsoft mouse-driver functions is described by a register summary, a function description, a suggested macro description, and a programming example.

11 The Microsoft Mouse Driver Routines

Register Summary

The register summary explains how the 8086 registers are used to pass parameters to a mouse driver function and return values back to the calling program. An 8086 register model is presented for each of the mouse driver functions. All of the shaded registers in the 8086 register summaries indicate registers that are used either by the calling program to pass parameters to the mouse driver function or by the mouse driver function to return values back to the calling program. Parameter passing is summarized in an appropriate **Call With** section. Returned values are summarized in an appropriate **Returns** section.

Function Description

A description of the mouse driver function's purpose is presented for each of the mouse driver functions. Furthermore, notes of special interest are provided.

Suggested Macro Definition

A suggested assembly language macro definition is presented for each of the mouse driver functions. Although the use of such a macro is strictly optional, macros can save programmers a great deal of time in developing programs that continuously use the same function calls over and over.

Programming Example

A program fragment is presented for each of the mouse driver functions. These examples are intended to illustrate how each of the mouse driver functions are used in an application program.

RESET THE MOUSE DRIVER (FUNCTION 00H)

Register Summary

AX: | AH | AL |
BX: | BH | BL |
CX: | CH | CL |
DX: | DH | DL |

SP
BP
SI
DI

IP
FLAGS

CS
DS
SS
ES

Call With

AX = 00H

Returns

AX = Mouse status

BX = Number of mouse buttons

11 The Microsoft Mouse Driver Routines

Function Description

Mouse driver function 00H resets the mouse driver by turning off the mouse pointer and disabling any event handlers. If a mouse is available, function 00H will return a value of 0FFFFH in register AX. Otherwise, function 00H will return a value of 0000H in register AX.

Suggested Macro Definition:

```
resetdriver   macro
              mov       ax,0
              int 33h
              endm
```

Programming Example

The following program fragment demonstrates how mouse driver function 00H is used to reset the mouse driver and save the driver's returned status:

```
        .
        .
        .
        mov     ax,0          ;Reset the
        int     33h           ; mouse driver
        mov     mstatus,ax    ;Save the driver's status
        .
        .
        .
```

TURN ON THE MOUSE POINTER (FUNCTION 01H)

Register Summary:

AX: **AH** | **AL**
BX: BH | BL
CX: CH | CL
DX: DH | DL

SP
BP
SI
DI

IP
FLAGS

CS
DS
SS
ES

Call With

AX = 0001H

Returns

Nothing

11 The Microsoft Mouse Driver Routines

Description
Mouse driver function 01H turns on the mouse pointer.

Suggested Macro Definition

```
pointeron    macro
             mov      ax,1
             int      33h
             endm
```

Programming Example
The following program fragment demonstrates mouse driver function 01H by turning on the mouse pointer:

```
        .
        .
        .
        mov     ax,1        ;Turn on the
        int     33h         ; mouse pointer
        .
        .
        .
```

The Microsoft Mouse Driver Routines 11

TURN OFF THE MOUSE POINTER (FUNCTION 02H)

Register Summary

Call With

AX = 0002H

Returns

Nothing

11 The Microsoft Mouse Driver Routines

Description
Mouse driver function 02H turns off the mouse pointer.

Suggested Macro Definition

```
pointeroff    macro
              mov     ax,2
              int     33h
              endm
```

Example
The following program fragment demonstrates mouse driver function 02H by turning off the mouse pointer:

```
        .
        .
        .
        mov     ax,2        ;Turn off the
        int     33h         ; mouse pointer
        .
        .
        .
```

GET BUTTON STATUS AND POINTER POSITION (FUNCTION 03H)

Register Summary

AX: | AH | AL |
BX: | BH | BL |
CX: | CH | CL |
DX: | DH | DL |

SP
BP
SI
DI

IP
FLAGS

CS
DS
SS
ES

Call With

AX = 0003H

Returns

BX = Button status

CX = Pointer x-coordinate

DX = Pointer y-coordinate

11 The Microsoft Mouse Driver Routines

Description

Mouse driver function 03H returns the mouse pointer's x-coordinate in register CX, the mouse pointer's y-coordinate in register DX, and the mouse buttons' status in register BX as follows:

Bit	True (1)	False(0)
0	Left button down	Left button released
1	Right button down	Right button released
2	Center button down	Center button released

Suggested Macro Definition

```
getstatus    macro
             mov    ax,3
             int    33h
             endm
```

Example

The following program fragment demonstrates mouse driver function 03H by continuously looping until the left mouse button is pressed:

```
           .
           .
           .
loop:     mov    ax,3       ;Get the
          int    33h        ; mouse status
          and    bx,1       ;Loop till the
          jz     loop       ; left button is pressed
           .
           .
           .
```

SET POINTER POSITION (FUNCTION 04H)

Register Summary:

Call With

AX = 0004H

CX = X-coordinate

DX = Y-coordinate

Returns

Nothing

11   The Microsoft Mouse Driver Routines

Description
Mouse driver function 04H moves the mouse pointer to the coordinates defined by registers CX and DX.

Suggested Macro Definition:

```
setpointerpos   macro   x,y
                mov     cx,x
                mov     dx,y
                mov     ax,4
                int     33h
                endm
```

Example
The following program fragment demonstrates mouse driver function 04H by moving the mouse pointer to the upper left corner of the display screen:

```
        .
        .
        .
        mov     cx,0        ;X-coordinate = 0
        mov     dx,0        ;Y-coordinate = 0
        mov     ax,4        ;Move the
        int     33h         ; mouse pointer
        .
        .
        .
```

GET BUTTON PRESS STATUS (FUNCTION 05H)

Register Summary

AX: | AH | AL |
BX: | BH | BL |
CX: | CH | CL |
DX: | DH | DL |

SP
BP
SI
DI

IP
FLAGS

CS
DS
SS
ES

Call With

AX = 0005H

BX = Button number

Returns

AX = Mouse buttons' status

BX = Button press count

CX = X-coordinate of last press

DX = Y-coordinate of last press

11 The Microsoft Mouse Driver Routines

Description

Mouse driver function 05H returns the press count, since function 05H was previously called, and the pointer position of the last press for the mouse button specified in register BX as follows:

Button	Value
Left	0
Right	1
Center	2

Additionally, mouse driver function 05H returns the mouse buttons' status in register AX as follows:

Bit	True (1)	False(0)
0	Left button down	Left button released
1	Right button down	Right button released
2	Center button down	Center button released

Suggested Macro Definition:

```
buttonpress   macro   button
              mov     bx,button
              mov     ax,5
              int     33h
              endm
```

Example

The following program fragment demonstrates mouse driver function 05H by continuously looping until the left button is pressed with the mouse pointer located on the top line of the display screen:

```
          .
          .
          .
loop:     mov   bx,0      ;Get the
          mov   ax,5      ; left
          int   33h       ;   button values
          and   ax,1      ;Loop if
          jz    loop      ; button not pressed
          cmp   dx,8      ;Loop if not
          jb    loop      ; on top line
          .
          .
          .
```

GET BUTTON RELEASE STATUS (FUNCTION 06H)

Register Summary

AX: | AH | AL |
BX: | BH | BL |
CX: | CH | CL |
DX: | DH | DL |

SP
BP
SI
DI

IP
FLAGS

CS
DS
SS
ES

Call With

AX = 0006H

BX = Button number

Returns

AX = Mouse buttons' status

BX = Button release count

CX = X-coordinate of last release

DX = Y-coordinate of last release

11 The Microsoft Mouse Driver Routines

Description

Mouse driver function 06H returns the release count, since function 06H was previously called, and the pointer position of the last release for the mouse button specified in register BX as follows:

Button	Value
Left	0
Right	1
Center	2

Additionally, mouse driver function 06H returns the mouse buttons' status in register AX as follows:

Bit	True (1)	False(0)
0	Left button down	Left button released
1	Right button down	Right button released
2	Center button down	Center button released

Suggested Macro Definition

```
buttonrelease  macro  button
               mov    bx,button
               mov    ax,6
               int    33h
               endm
```

Example

The following program fragment demonstrates mouse driver function 06H by continuously looping until the left button is released with the mouse pointer located on the top line of the display screen:

```
             .
             .
             .
loop:   mov    bx,0      ;Get the
        mov    ax,6      ; left
        int    33h       ;  button values
        and    ax,1      ;Loop if
        jnz    loop      ; button is pressed
        cmp    dx,8      ;Loop if not
        jb     loop      ; on top line
             .
             .
             .
```

The Microsoft Mouse Driver Routines **11**

SET HORIZONTAL LIMITS (FUNCTION 07H)

Register Summary:

AX: | AH | AL |
BX: | BH | BL |
CX: | CH | CL |
DX: | DH | DL |

SP
BP
SI
DI

IP
FLAGS

CS
DS
SS
ES

Call With

AX = 0007H

CX = Minimum x-coordinate

DX = Maximum x-coordinate

Returns

Nothing

11 The Microsoft Mouse Driver Routines

Description

Mouse driver function 07H limits the mouse pointer's display area to the horizontal coordinates specified in registers CX and DX.

Suggested Macro Definition

```
horlimits    macro    min,max
             mov      cx,min
             mov      dx,max
             mov      ax,7
             int      33h
             endm
```

Example

The following program fragment demonstrates mouse driver function 07H by limiting the mouse pointer to the right half of the display screen:

```
        .
        .
        .
        mov    cx,320    ;CX = Minimum x-coordinate
        mov    dx,639    ;DX = Maximum x-coordinate
        mov    ax,7      ;Go set
        int    33h       ; the limits
        .
        .
        .
```

SET VERTICAL LIMITS (FUNCTION 08H)

Register Summary

AX: | AH | AL |
BX: | BH | BL |
CX: | CH | CL |
DX: | DH | DL |

SP
BP
SI
DI

IP
FLAGS

CS
DS
SS
ES

Call With

AX = 0008H

CX = Minimum y-coordinate

DX = Maximum y-coordinate

Returns

Nothing

11 The Microsoft Mouse Driver Routines

Description
Mouse driver function 08H limits the mouse pointer's display area to the vertical coordinates specified in registers CX and DX.

Suggested Macro Definition

```
verlimits    macro    min,max
             mov      cx,min
             mov      dx,max
             mov      ax,8
             int      33h
             endm
```

Example
The following program fragment demonstrates mouse driver function 08H by limiting the mouse pointer to the top thirteen lines of the display screen:

```
        .
        .
        .
        mov    cx,0       ;CX = Minimum y-coordinate
        mov    dx,103     ;DX = Maximum y-coordinate
        mov    ax,8       ;Go set
        int    33h        ; the limits
        .
        .
        .
```

The Microsoft Mouse Driver Routines 11

SET GRAPHIC SHAPE (FUNCTION 09H)

Register Summary

AX: | AH | AL |
BX: | BH | BL |
CX: | CH | CL |
DX: | DH | DL |

SP
BP
SI
DI

IP
FLAGS

CS
DS
SS
ES

Call With

AX = 0009H

BX = Hot spot's left offset

CX = Hot spot's top offset

ES:DX = Shape buffer pointer

Returns

Nothing

11 The Microsoft Mouse Driver Routines

Description

Mouse driver function 09H changes the graphic pointer's shape to the shapes defined in the buffer pointed to by ES:DX as follows:

Buffer Bytes	Type of Mask
00H to 20H	ANDed with the display screen's image
21H to 40H	XORed with the display screen's image

Additionally, mouse driver function 09H defines the graphic pointer's hot spot to the relative offsets passed in registers BX and CX. These offsets are relative to the upper left corner of the graphic pointer's image and must be in the range -16 to 16.

Suggested Macro Definition

```
setgraphic   macro   left,top,buffer
             mov     bx,left
             mov     cx,right
             mov     ax,seg buffer
             mov     es,ax
             mov     dx,offset buffer
             mov     ax,9
             int     33h
             endm
```

Example

The following program demonstrates mouse driver function 09H by setting the graphic pointer to a new shape:

```
            .
            .
            .
    mov     bx,0              ;BX = Hot spot's left offset
    mov     cx,0              ;CX = Hot spot's right offset
    mov     ax,seg pointer    ;AX = Pointer buffer's segment
    mov     es,ax             ;Put it into ES
    mov     dx,offset pointer ;ES:DX = Pointer buffer pointer
    mov     ax,9              ;Set the
    int     33h               ; new pointer
            .
            .
            .
```

The Microsoft Mouse Driver Routines 11

SET TEXT POINTER TYPE (FUNCTION 0AH)

Register Summary

Call With

AX = 000AH

BX = Pointer type

CX = AND mask or starting cursor line

DX = XOR mask or ending cursor line

Returns

Nothing

11 The Microsoft Mouse Driver Routines

Description

Mouse driver function 0AH sets the type and shape for the mouse's text pointer. If register BX = 1, the mouse's text pointer will be set to the hardware text cursor and the cursor's starting and ending lines will be set to the values passed in registers CX and DX respectively. Otherwise, the mouse's text pointer will be set to a software cursor and the cursor's character/attribute AND and XOR bit masks be set to the values passed in registers CX and DX respectively.

Suggested Macro Definition:

```
settext    macro    type,amask,xmask
           mov      bx,type
           mov      cx,amask
           mov      dx,xmask
           mov      ax,0ah
           int      33h
           endm
```

Example

The following program fragment demonstrates mouse driver function 0AH by setting the mouse's text pointer to the hardware cursor:

```
    .
    .
    .
    mov    bx,1        ;Hardware cursor flag
    mov    cx,6        ;CX = Starting cursor line
    mov    dx,7        ;DX = Ending cursor line
    mov    ax,0ah      ;Set the new
    int    33h         ; text pointer
    .
    .
    .
```

GET MOTION COUNT (FUNCTION 0BH)

Register Summary

AX: | AH | AL |
BX: | BH | BL |
CX: | CH | CL |
DX: | DH | DL |

SP
BP
SI
DI

IP
FLAGS

CS
DS
SS
ES

Call With

AX = 000BH

Returns

CX = Horizontal mickey count

DX = Vertical mickey count

11 The Microsoft Mouse Driver Routines

Description

Mouse driver function 0BH returns the number of mickeys (1/200") the mouse has moved since function 0BH was last called.

Suggested Macro Definition

```
getmotion       macro
                mov     ax,0bh
                int     33h
                endm
```

Example

The following program fragment demonstrates mouse driver function 0BH by continuously looping until the mouse is moved up and to the left:

```
        .
        .
        .
loop:   mov     ax,0bh      ;Get the
        int     33h         ; motion count
        cmp     cx,0        ;Loop if mouse
        jge     loop        ; hasn't move left
        cmp     dx,0        ;Loop if mouse
        jge     loop        ; hasn't move up
        .
        .
        .
```

SET USER-DEFINED EVENT HANDLER (FUNCTION 0CH)

Call With

AX = 000CH

CX = Event mask

ES:DX = Address of the event handler

Returns

Nothing

11 The Microsoft Mouse Driver Routines

Description

Mouse driver function 0CH sets a user-defined event handler to the address passed in registers ES:DX. The user-defined event handler is called whenever one of the events specified in the event mask occurs. The event mask is passed in register CX as follows:

Bit	Event
0	Mouse movement
1	Left button pressed
2	Left button released
3	Right button pressed
4	Right button released
5	Center button pressed
6	Center button released

Upon entry to the event handler, the mouse driver will pass values to the event handler in the following registers:

Register	Contents
AX	Event flags
BX	Button status
CX	Mouse pointer's x-coordinate
DX	Mouse pointer's y-coordinate
SI	Vertical mickey count
DI	Horizontal mickey count
DS	Mouse driver data segment

Suggested Macro Definition:

```
userhandler    macro    mask,handler
               mov      cx,mask
               mov      ax,seg handler
               mov      es,ax
               mov      dx,offset handler
               mov      ax,0ch
               int      33h
               endm
```

The Microsoft Mouse Driver Routines 11

Example

The following program fragment demonstrates mouse driver function 0CH by setting a "left button pressed" event handler:

```
        .
        .
        .
        mov     cx,2                ;CX = Left button pressed mask
        mov     ax,seg handler      ;AX = Handler's segment
        mov     es,ax               ;Put it into ES
        mov     dx,offset handler   ;ES:DX = Handler's address
        mov     ax,0ch              ;Set the
        int     33h                 ; event handler
        .
        .
        .
```

11 The Microsoft Mouse Driver Routines

TURN ON LIGHT PEN EMULATION (FUNCTION 0DH)

Register Summary:

AX: | AH | AL |
BX: | BH | BL |
CX: | CH | CL |
DX: | DH | DL |

SP
BP
SI
DI

IP
FLAGS

CS
DS
SS
ES

Call With

AX = 000DH

Returns

Nothing

Description

Mouse driver function 0DH turns on light pen emulation. While light pen emulation is on, pressing both the left and right buttons at the same time will be interpreted as a "pen down" event.

Suggested Macro Condition

```
lightpenon   macro
             mov     ax,0dh
             int     33h
             endm
```

Example

The following program fragment demonstrates mouse driver function 0DH by turning the light pen emulation on:

```
             .
             .
             .
             mov     ax,0dh      ;Turn the light
             int     33h         ; pen emulation on
             .
             .
             .
```

11 The Microsoft Mouse Driver Routines

TURN OFF LIGHT PEN EMULATION (FUNCTION 0EH)

Register Summary

AX: | **AH** | **AL** |

BX: | BH | BL |

CX: | CH | CL |

DX: | DH | DL |

SP
BP
SI
DI

IP
FLAGS

CS
DS
SS
ES

Call With

AX = 000EH

Returns

Nothing

The Microsoft Mouse Driver Routines **11**

Description
Mouse driver function 0EH turns off light pen emulation.

Suggested Macro Definition

```
lightpenoff     macro
                mov     ax,0eh
                int     33h
                endm
```

Example
The following program fragment demonstrates mouse driver function 0EH by turning the light pen emulation off:

```
            .
            .
            .
            mov     ax,0eh      ;Turn the light
            int     33h         ; pen emulation off
            .
            .
            .
```

11 The Microsoft Mouse Driver Routines

SET MICKEY:PIXELS RATIOS (FUNCTION 0FH)

Register Summary

Call With

AX = 000FH

CX = Horizontal mickeys

DX = Vertical mickeys

Returns

Nothing

Description

Mouse driver function 0FH sets the horizontal and vertical mickeys to eight pixels ratios to the values passed in registers CX and DX respectively. The default horizontal ratio is 8:8 and the default vertical ratio is 16:8.

Suggested Macro Definition

```
setratios    macro    horizontal,vertical
             mov      cx,horizontal
             mov      dx,vertical
             mov      ax,0fh
             int      33h
             endm
```

Example

The following program fragment demonstrates mouse driver function 0FH by setting the horizontal ratio to 16:8 and the vertical ratio to 32:8:

```
        .
        .
        .
        mov     cx,16       ;CX = 16:8 horizontal ratio
        mov     dx,32       ;DX = 32:8 vertical ratio
        mov     ax,0fh      ;Set the
        int     33h         ; ratios
        .
        .
        .
```

11 The Microsoft Mouse Driver Routines

SET EXCLUSION AREA (FUNCTION 10H)

Register Summary:

AX: | AH | AL |
BX: | BH | BL |
CX: | CH | CL |
DX: | DH | DL |

SP
BP
SI
DI

IP
FLAGS

CS
DS
SS
ES

Call With

AX = 0010H

CX = Upper left x-coordinate

DX = Upper left y-coordinate

SI = Lower right x-coordinate

DI = Lower right y-coordinate

Returns

Nothing

Description

Mouse driver function 10H defines an area of the display screen, in which the mouse pointer is not displayed.

Suggested Macro Definition

```
setexclusion   macro   x1,y1,x2,y2
               mov     cx,x1
               mov     dx,y1
               mov     i,x2
               mov     di,y2
               mov     ax,10h
               int     33h
               endm
```

Example

The following program fragment demonstrates mouse driver function 10H by defining the right half of the display screen as an exclusion area:

```
      .
      .
      .
      mov    cx,320      ;CX = Upper left x-coordinate
      mov    dx,0        ;DX = Upper left y-coordinate
      mov    si,639      ;SI = Lower right x-coordinate
      mov    di,199      ;DI = Lower right y-coordinate
      mov    ax,10h      ;Set the
      int    33h         ; exclusion area
      .
      .
      .
```

11 The Microsoft Mouse Driver Routines

SET DOUBLE SPEED THRESHOLD (FUNCTION 13H)

Register Summary

AX: | AH | AL |
BX: | BH | BL |
CX: | CH | CL |
DX: | DH | DL |

SP
BP
SI
DI

IP
FLAGS

CS
DS
SS
ES

Call With

AX = 0013H

DX = Threshold speed (mickeys:second)

Returns

Nothing

Description

Mouse driver function 13H sets the double speed threshold to the value passed in register DX. The default double speed threshold is 64 mickeys per second.

Suggested Macro Definition

```
setdouble    macro    threshold
             mov      dx,threshold
             mov      ax,13h
             int      33h
             endm
```

Example

The following program fragment demonstrates mouse driver function 13H by setting the double speed threshold to 200 mickeys per second:

```
        .
        .
        .
        mov    dx,200    ;DX = New threshold
        mov    ax,13h    ;Set the new
        int    33h       ; double speed threshold
        .
        .
        .
```

11 The Microsoft Mouse Driver Routines

SWAP USER-DEFINED EVENT HANDLERS (FUNCTION 14H)

Register Summary

AX: | AH | AL |
BX: | BH | BL |
CX: | CH | CL |
DX: | DH | DL |

SP
BP
SI
DI

IP
FLAGS

CS
DS
SS
ES

Call With

AX = 0014H

CX = Event mask

ES:DX = Address of the event handler

Returns

CX = Old event mask

ES:DX = Old event handler's address

404

Description

Mouse driver function 14H swaps a previously installed user-defined event handler with a new user-defined event handler.

Suggested Macro Definition

```
swapuserhandler macro   mask,handler
                mov     cx,mask
                mov     ax,seg handler
                mov     es,ax
                mov     dx,offset handler
                mov     ax,14h
                int     33h
                endm
```

Example

The following program fragment demonstrates mouse driver function 14H by swapping the current event handler with a new event handler:

```
    .
    .
    .
    mov     cx,2                ;CX = Left button pressed mask
    mov     ax,seg newhandler   ;AX = New handler's segment
    mov     es,ax               ;Put it into ES
    mov     dx,offset newhandler ;ES:DX = New handler's address
    mov     ax,14h              ;Swap the
    int     33h                 ; event handlers
    .
    .
    .
```

11 The Microsoft Mouse Driver Routines

GET MOUSE STATUS BUFFER SIZE (FUNCTION 15H)

Register Summary

AX: | AH | AL |
BX: | BH | BL |
CX: | CH | CL |
DX: | DH | DL |

SP
BP
SI
DI

IP
FLAGS

CS
DS
SS
ES

Call With

AX = 0015H

Returns

BX = Buffer size

The Microsoft Mouse Driver Routines 11

Description
Mouse driver function 15H returns the size of the mouse driver's status buffer in register BX.

Suggested Macro Definition

```
getbuffersize   macro
                mov     ax,15h
                int     33h
                endm
```

Example
The following program fragment demonstrates mouse driver function 15H by retrieving the size of the mouse driver's status buffer:

```
            .
            .
            .
            mov     ax,15h      ;Get the
            int     33h         ; buffer size
            .
            .
            .
```

11 The Microsoft Mouse Driver Routines

SAVE MOUSE DRIVER STATUS (FUNCTION 16H)

Register Summary

Call With

AX = 0016H

ES:DX = Buffer address

Returns

Nothing

The Microsoft Mouse Driver Routines 11

Description

Mouse driver function 16H saves the mouse driver's status buffer in a buffer at the address specified by registers ES:DX.

Suggested Macro Definition

```
savestatus   macro    buffer
             mov      ax,seg buffer
             mov      es,ax
             mov      dx,offset buffer
             mov      ax,16h
             int      33h
             endm
```

Example

The following program fragment demonstrates mouse driver function 16H by saving the mouse driver's status buffer:

```
            .
            .
            .
            mov    ax,seg buffer      ;AX = Status buffer's segment
            mov    es,ax              ;Put it into ES
            mov    dx,offset buffer   ;ES:DX = Status buffer's address
            mov    ax,16h             ;Save the
            int    33h                ; status buffer
            .
            .
            .
```

11 The Microsoft Mouse Driver Routines

RESTORE MOUSE DRIVER STATUS (FUNCTION 17H)

Register Summary

AX: | AH | AL |
BX: | BH | BL |
CX: | CH | CL |
DX: | DH | DL |

SP
BP
SI
DI

IP
FLAGS

CS
DS
SS
ES

Call With

AX = 0017H

ES:DX = Buffer address

Returns

Nothing

The Microsoft Mouse Driver Routines 11

Description

Mouse driver function 17H restores the mouse driver's status buffer to the values in the buffer at the address specified in registers ES:DX.

Suggested Macro Definition

```
restorestatus   macro   buffer
                mov     ax,seg buffer
                mov     es,ax
                mov     dx,offset buffer
                mov     ax,17h
                int     33h
                endm
```

Example

The following program fragment demonstrates mouse driver function 17H by restoring the mouse driver's status buffer:

```
        .
        .
        .
        mov     ax,seg buffer       ;AX = Status buffer's segment
        mov     es,ax               ;Put it into ES
        mov     dx,offset buffer    ;ES:DX = Status buffer's address
        mov     ax,17h              ;Restore the
        int     33h                 ; status buffer
        .
        .
        .
```

411

11 The Microsoft Mouse Driver Routines

SET ALTERNATE EVENT HANDLER (FUNCTION 18H)

Register Summary

AX: | AH | AL |
BX: | BH | BL |
CX: | CH | CL |
DX: | DH | DL |

SP
BP
SI
DI

IP
FLAGS

CS
DS
SS
ES

Call With

AX = 0018H

CX = Event mask

ES:DX = Address of the event handler

Returns

AX = Success flag

Description

Mouse driver function 18H sets one of three alternate event handlers to the address passed in registers ES:DX. The alternate event handler is called whenever one of the events specified in the event mask occurs. The event handler's event mask is passed in register CX as follows:

Bit	Event
0	Mouse movement
1	Left button pressed
2	Left button released
3	Right button pressed
4	Right button released
5	**SHIFT** key pressed during a mouse button event
6	**CTRL** key pressed during a mouse button event
7	**ALT** key pressed during a mouse button event

At least one of bits five through seven must be set in the event mask. If the alternate event handler is successfully set, register AX will return with a value of 0018H. Otherwise, register AX will return with a value of 0FFFFH. Upon entry to the event handler, the mouse driver will pass the following values:

Register	Contents
AX	Event flags
BX	Button status
CX	Mouse pointer's x-coordinate
DX	Mouse pointer's y-coordinate
SI	Vertical mickey count
DI	Horizontal mickey count
DS	Mouse driver data segment

Suggested Macro Definition

```
setalthandler   macro   mask,handler
                mov     cx,mask
                mov     ax,seg handler
                mov     es,ax
                mov     dx,offset handler
                mov     ax,18h
                int     33h
                endm
```

11 The Microsoft Mouse Driver Routines

Example

The following program fragment demonstrates mouse driver function 18H by setting an alternate event handler:

```
        .
        .
        .
        mov     cx,22h              ;CX = Left button/Shift key mask
        mov     ax,seg handler      ;AX = Handler's segment
        mov     es,ax               ;Put it into ES
        mov     dx,offset handler   ;ES:DX = Handler's address
        mov     ax,18h              ;Set the
        int     33h                 ; event handler
        .
        .
        .
```

GET ALTERNATE EVENT HANDLER'S ADDRESS (FUNCTION 19H)

Register Summary

Call With

AX = 0019H

CX = Event mask

Returns

CX = Event mask

ES:DX = Address of the event handler

11 The Microsoft Mouse Driver Routines

Description

Mouse driver function 19H returns the address of an alternate event handler in registers ES:DX. If an alternate event handler hasn't been established or a matching event mask can't be found, mouse driver function 19H will return register CX with a value of 0000H.

Suggested Macro Definition

```
getalthandler   macro   mask
                mov     cx,mask
                mov     ax,19h
                int     33h
                endm
```

Example

The following program fragment demonstrates mouse driver function 19H by retrieving an event handler's address:

```
        .
        .
        .
        mov     cx,22h      ;CX = Left button/Shift key mask
        mov     ax,19h      ;Get the event
        int     33h         ; handler's address
        .
        .
        .
```

The Microsoft Mouse Driver Routines 11

SET SENSITIVITY (FUNCTION 1AH)

Register Summary

AX: | AH | AL |
BX: | BH | BL |
CX: | CH | CL |
DX: | DH | DL |

SP
BP
SI
DI

IP
FLAGS

CS
DS
SS
ES

Call With

AX = 001AH

BX = Horizontal mickeys

CX = Vertical mickeys

DX = Threshold speed (mickeys:second)

Returns

Nothing

11   The Microsoft Mouse Driver Routines

Description

Mouse driver function 1AH sets the horizontal and vertical mickeys to eight pixels ratios and the double speed threshold.

Suggested Macro Definition

```
setsensitivity  macro   horizontal,vertical,threshold
                mov     bx,horizontal
                mov     cx,vertical
                mov     dx,threshold
                mov     ax,1ah
                int     33h
                endm
```

Example

The following program fragment demonstrates mouse driver function 1AH by setting the mouse sensitivity values:

```
        .
        .
        .
        mov     bx,32       ;BX = 32:8 horizontal ratio
        mov     cx,32       ;CX = 32:8 horizontal ratio
        mov     dx,100      ;DX = 100 mickeys/second threshold
        mov     ax,1ah      ;Set the new
        int     33h         ; sensitivity values
        .
        .
        .
```

GET SENSITIVITY (FUNCTION 1BH)

Register Summary

AX: | AH | AL |
BX: | BH | BL |
CX: | CH | CL |
DX: | DH | DL |

| SP |
| BP |
| SI |
| DI |

| IP |
| FLAGS |

| CS |
| DS |
| SS |
| ES |

Call With

AX = 001BH

Returns

BX = Horizontal mickeys

CX = Vertical mickeys

DX = Double speed threshold

11 The Microsoft Mouse Driver Routines

Description
Mouse driver function 1BH retrieves the horizontal and vertical mickeys-to-pixels ratios and the double-speed threshold.

Suggested Macro Definition

```
getsensitivity   macro
                 mov     ax,1bh
                 int     33h
                 endm
```

Example
The following program fragment demonstrates mouse driver function 1BH by retrieving the sensitivity values:

```
        .
        .
        .
        mov     ax,1bh      ;Get the
        int     33h         ; sensitivity values
        .
        .
        .
```

SET INTERRUPT RATE (FUNCTION 1CH)

Register Summary

AX: | AH | AL |
BX: | BH | BL |
CX: | CH | CL |
DX: | DH | DL |

SP
BP
SI
DI

IP
FLAGS

CS
DS
SS
ES

Call With

AX = 001CH

BX = Interrupt rate

Returns:

Nothing

11 The Microsoft Mouse Driver Routines

Description

Mouse driver function 1CH sets the mouse driver's interrupt rate. The interrupt rate is passed in register BX as follows:

Bit	Number of Interrupts per Second
0	0
1	30
2	50
3	100
4	200

Suggested Macro Definition

```
setintrate   macro   rate
             mov     bx,rate
             mov     ax,1ch
             int     33h
             endm
```

Example

The following program fragment demonstrates mouse driver function 1CH by setting the interrupt rate to 100 interrupts per second:

```
        .
        .
        .
        mov     bx,8        ;BX = 100 interrupts/second value
        mov     ax,1ch      ;Set the new
        int     33h         ; interrupt rate
        .
        .
        .
```

SET POINTER DISPLAY PAGE (FUNCTION 1DH)

Register Summary

AX: | AH | AL |
BX: | BH | BL |
CX: | CH | CL |
DX: | DH | DL |

| SP |
| BP |
| SI |
| DI |

| IP |
| FLAGS |

| CS |
| DS |
| SS |
| ES |

Call With

AX = 001DH

BX = Display page

Returns

Nothing

11 The Microsoft Mouse Driver Routines

Description
Mouse driver function 1DH sets the mouse pointer's video display page to the value passed in register BX.

Suggested Macro Definition

```
setdisplaypage  macro   page
                mov     bx,page
                mov     ax,1dh
                int     33h
                endm
```

Example
The following program fragment demonstrates mouse driver function 1DH by setting the mouse pointer's display page to video page two:.

```
        .
        .
        .
        mov     bx,2        ;BX = Video display page number
        mov     ax,1dh      ;Set the pointer's
        int     33h         ; display page
        .
        .
        .
```

GET POINTER DISPLAY PAGE (FUNCTION 1EH)

Register Summary

AX: | AH | AL |
BX: | BH | BL |
CX: | CH | CL |
DX: | DH | DL |

SP
BP
SI
DI

IP
FLAGS

CS
DS
SS
ES

Call With

AX = 001EH

Returns

BX = Display page

11 The Microsoft Mouse Driver Routines

Description
Mouse driver function 1EH retrieves the mouse pointer's video display page.

Suggested Macro Definition

```
getdisplaypage  macro
                mov     ax,1eh
                int     33h
                endm
```

Example
The following program fragment demonstrates mouse driver function 1EH by retrieving the mouse pointer's display page:

```
        .
        .
        .
        mov     ax,1eh      ;Get the pointer's
        int     33h         ; display page
        .
        .
        .
```

DISABLE MOUSE DRIVER (FUNCTION 1FH)

Register Summary

Call With

AX = 001FH

Returns

AX = Success flag

ES:BX = Previous contents of INT 33H

11 The Microsoft Mouse Driver Routines

Description

Mouse driver function 1FH disables the mouse driver and returns the previous contents of the INT 33H interrupt vector. If the operation is successful, register AX will be returned with a value of 001FH. Otherwise, register AX will be returned with a value of 0FFFFH.

Suggested Macro Definition

```
disabledriver   macro
                mov     ax,1fh
                int     33h
                endm
```

Example

The following program fragment demonstrates mouse driver function 1FH by disabling the mouse driver:

```
        .
        .
        .
        mov     ax,1fh      ;Disable the
        int     33h         ; mouse driver
        .
        .
        .
```

ENABLE MOUSE DRIVER (FUNCTION 20H)

Register Summary

AX: | AH | AL |
BX: | BH | BL |
CX: | CH | CL |
DX: | DH | DL |

SP
BP
SI
DI

IP
FLAGS

CS
DS
SS
ES

Call With

AX = 0020H

Returns

Nothing

11 The Microsoft Mouse Driver Routines

Description
Mouse driver function 20H enables the mouse driver.

Suggested Macro Definition

```
enabledriver    macro
                mov     ax,20h
                int     33h
                endm
```

Example
The following program fragment demonstrates mouse driver function 20H by enabling the mouse driver:

```
                .
                .
                .
                mov     ax,20h      ;Enable the
                int     33h         ; mouse driver
                .
                .
                .
```

RESET MOUSE DRIVER (FUNCTION 21H)

Register Summary

AX: | AH | AL |
BX: | BH | BL |
CX: | CH | CL |
DX: | DH | DL |

SP
BP
SI
DI

IP
FLAGS

CS
DS
SS
ES

Call With

AX = 0021H

Returns

AX = Success flag

BX = Number of buttons

11 The Microsoft Mouse Driver Routines

Description

Mouse driver function 21H resets the mouse driver and returns the number of mouse buttons in register BX. If the function is successful, register AX will be returned with a value of 0FFFFH. Otherwise, register AX will be returned with a value of 0021H.

Suggested Macro Definition:

```
resetmouse   macro
             mov      ax,21h
             int      33h
             endm
```

Example

The following program fragment demonstrates mouse driver function 21H by resetting the mouse driver:.

```
        .
        .
        .
        mov     ax,21h      ;Reset the
        int     21h         ; mouse driver
        .
        .
        .
```

SET LANGUAGE (FUNCTION 22H)

Register Summary

AX: | AH | AL |
BX: | BH | BL |
CX: | CH | CL |
DX: | DH | DL |

SP
BP
SI
DI

IP
FLAGS

CS
DS
SS
ES

Call With

AX = 0022H

BX = Language code

Returns

Nothing

11 The Microsoft Mouse Driver Routines

Description

Mouse driver function 22H sets the language for the mouse driver's messages to the language code passed in register BX as follows:

Code Number	Language
0	English
1	French
2	Dutch
3	German
4	Swedish
5	Finnish
6	Spanish
7	Portuguese
8	Italian

Suggested Macro Definition

```
setlanguage   macro   code
              mov     bx,code
              mov     ax,22h
              int     33h
              endm
```

Example

The following program fragment demonstrates mouse driver function 22H by changing the mouse driver's language to Italian:

```
            .
            .
            .
      mov   bx,8       ;BX = Italian language code
      mov   ax,22h     ;Set the mouse driver's
      int   33h        ; language to Italian
            .
            .
            .
```

GET LANGUAGE CODE (FUNCTION 23H)

Register Summary

AX: | AH | AL |
BX: | BH | BL |
CX: | CH | CL |
DX: | DH | DL |

SP
BP
SI
DI

IP
FLAGS

CS
DS
SS
ES

Call With

AX = 0023H

Returns

BX = Language code

11 The Microsoft Mouse Driver Routines

Description
Mouse driver function 23H returns the mouse driver's language code in register BX.

Suggested Macro Definition

```
getlanguage    macro
               mov      ax,23h
               int      33h
               endm
```

Example
The following program fragment demonstrates mouse driver function 23H by retrieving the mouse driver's language code:

```
        .
        .
        .
        mov     ax,23h      ;Get the mouse driver's
        int     33h         ; language code
        .
        .
        .
```

GET MOUSE INFORMATION (FUNCTION 24H)

Register Summary

AX: | AH | AL |
BX: | BH | BL |
CX: | CH | CL |
DX: | DH | DL |

| SP |
| BP |
| SI |
| DI |

| IP |
| FLAGS |

| CS |
| DS |
| SS |
| ES |

Call With

AX = 24H

Returns

BH = Major version number

BL = Minor version number

CH = Mouse type

CL = IRQ number

11 The Microsoft Mouse Driver Routines

Description

Mouse driver function 24H returns the mouse driver's version number, mouse type, and mouse adapter's IRQ setting. The mouse type returned in register CH is interpreted as follows:

Contents	Mouse Type
1	Bus mouse
2	Serial mouse
3	InPort mouse
4	PS/2 mouse
5	HP mouse

Suggested Macro Definition:

```
getinfo     macro
            mov     ax,24h
            int     33h
            endm
```

Example

The following program fragment demonstrates mouse driver function 24H by retrieving the mouse information:

```
            .
            .
            .
            mov     ax,24h      ;Get the
            int     33h         ; mouse information
            .
            .
            .
```

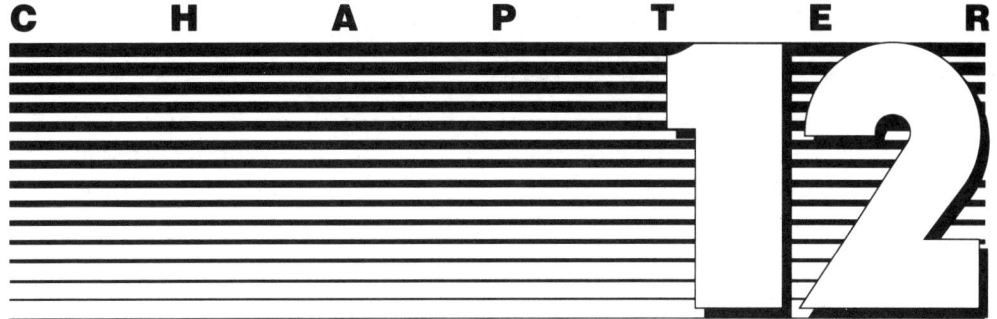

COMPILING THE GWINDOWS TOOLBOX

This chapter explains the compiling of the GWINDOWS toolbox using the Zortech C++ compiler. It also tells you where to modify the GWINDOWS programs to build the GWINDOWS toolbox when using a non-Zortech C++ compiler.

12 Compiling the GWINDOWS Toolbox

THE ZORTECH C++ COMPILER

The following listing, called **zortech.bat**, is a batch file for compiling the GWINDOWS toolbox, **gwindows.lib**. In addition to constructing the GWINDOWS toolbox, **zortech.bat** compiles and links FONTEDIT, **fontedit.exe**, and compiles the two sample font table source-code files, **sanscga.obj** and **sansega.obj**.

```
rem
rem             zortech.bat
rem             Compile GWINDOWS with Zortech C++
rem
masm /mx graphics,;
ztc -c -ml -dZORTECH lowlevel pointer windows menus popup dialog pulldown idate idollar inumber iphone issn istring
rem
rem             Build GWINDOWS library - gwindows.lib
rem
lib gwindows +graphics +lowlevel +pointer +win-
dows +menus +popup +dialog +pulldown +idate +idollar +inum-
ber +iphone +issn +istring;
rem
rem             Compile and Link FONTEDIT
rem
ztc -ml -dZORTECH fontedit gwindows.lib fgl.lib
rem
rem             Remove the Unwanted OBJ Files
rem
del *.obj
rem
rem             Compile the font files - sanscga.obj and sansega.obj
rem
ztc -c -ml -dZORTECH sanscga sansega
```

OTHER C++ COMPILERS

At the time of this writing, Zortech C++ is the only C++ compiler available for the MS-DOS operating system. Rumors abound, however, about soon-to-be released C++ compilers from both Microsoft and Borland. Accordingly, the following list of possible problem areas should help in modifying the GWINDOWS programs for use with a compiler other than the Zortech C++ compiler.

Compiling the GWINDOWS Toolbox 12

graphics.asm

Because the Zortech C++ assembly language calling conventions are identical to the calling conventions used by Microsoft's C and QuickC compilers and Borland's Turbo C compiler, modification of the assembly language functions shouldn't be necessary.

lowlevel.cpp

Uses the **fg_init_all** function to initialize the graphics mode and the **fg_term** function to restore the original video mode. Consequently, similar functions will have to be substituted to achieve correct compilation and program operation.

fontedit.cpp

Uses the **fg_drawbox** function to draw boxes, the **fg_fillbox** function to fill boxes, the **fg_drawarc** function to draw circles, the **fg_readdot** function to retrieve a graphic pixel's color value, the **fg_drawdot** function to set a graphic pixel's color, and the **filesize** function to determine if a file exists. Consequently, similar functions will have to be substituted to achieve correct compilation and program operation.

Additionally, the Zortech C++ graphics functions use a right-handed coordinate system where the lower left corner of the display screen is located at coordinate (0,0). Both Microsoft and Borland use the same coordinate system as the GWINDOWS toolbox; therefore, modification of the program's y-coordinates will be necessary to obtain correct program execution.

Other Programs

The following GWINDOWS programs should not require any modification when using them with compilers other than the Zortech C++ compiler:

dialog.cpp	pointer.cpp
idollar.cpp	popup.cpp
inumber.cpp	pulldown.cpp
iphone.cpp	sanscga.cpp
issn.cpp	sansega.cpp
istring.cpp	windows.cpp
menus.cpp	gwindows.hpp

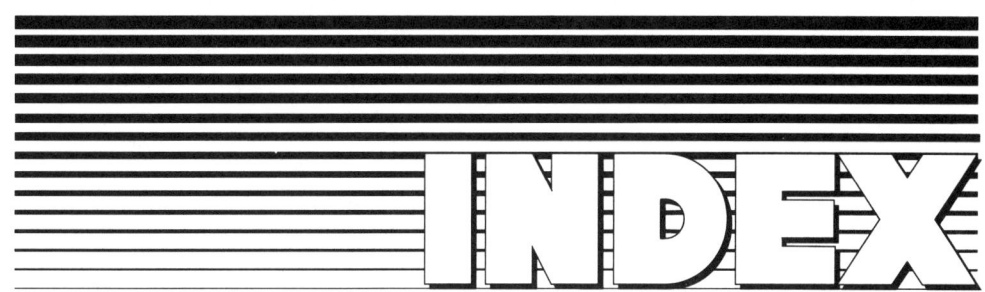

80286, 36
80386, 36
80486, 36

B

background, 216
bit_planes, 80
boolean, 209

C

calloc, 104-105
clearcolumn, 216-217
clearrow, 217-218
clearwindow, 73, 218
Color Graphics Adapter (CGA), 7-8
    bit masks, 13-14
    graphic pixels, 11-12
    resetting pixels, 15-16
    setting pixels, 14-15
    text characters, 26-29
    video memory, 11-12
    video memory offset, 12-13
cursorcolor, 71, 219
cursoroff, 71, 219-220
cursoron, 70, 219-220

D

date, 209
date_func, 150-151
date_string, 150, 220-221
delete, 103-104
dialog, 211
dialog box menus, 126-127
dialog.cpp, 127-130
dialog::get, 131-133, 221-222
direct memory access, 7
disp_char, 79-80
display coordinates, 26
display screen windows, 102-103
display_date, 152, 222-223
display_dollar, 157, 223-224
display_number, 160, 224-225
display_phone, 165, 225-226
display_ssn, 170, 226-227
display_string, 172, 227
displaycenter, 92, 228
displaychar, 71-72, 228-229
displaystring, 72-73, 229
dollar_func, 155-157
drawborder, 93, 230

E

EGA ROM BIOS video functions, 6-7
    Get Configuration Information (1210H), 358-359
    Get Font Information (1130H), 356-357
    Load ROM BIOS 8-by-14 Font (1101H), 335-336
    Load ROM BIOS 8-by-14 Font (1111H), 344-345
    Load ROM BIOS 8-by-8 Font (1102H), 337-338
    Load ROM BIOS 8-by-8 Font (1112H), 346-347
    Load User Font (1100H), 333-334
    Load User Font (1110H), 341-343
    Select Alternate Screen Print Routine (1220H), 360-361
    Select Character Generator RAM Block (1103H), 339-340
    Set All Palette Registers (1002H), 329-330
    Set Border Color (1001H), 327-328
    Set Font Table Pointer (1121H), 350-351
    Set Font Table Pointer to 8-by-14 Font (1122H), 352-353
    Set Font Table Pointer to 8-by-8 Font (1123H), 354-355
    Set Palette Register (1000H), 325-326
    Set Upper Font Table Pointer (1120H), 348-349
    Toggle Blink/Intensity Flag (1003H), 331-332
egacolor, 230-231
egamode, 68-69, 231-232
Enhanced Graphics Adapter (EGA), 7, 9
    bit masks, 20
    color planes, 17-18
    color values, 17-18
    graphic pixels, 17
    map masks, 22
    read map select, 24-25
    setting pixels, 20-23
    testing pixels, 23-26
    text characters, 26-31
    video memory, 17-19
    video memory offsets, 19-20
    write-only bit masks, 20-21
environment, 211-212
environment::~environment, 91
environment::environment, 91

F

fig_vid_ptr, 79
fillcolumn, 232-233
fillrow, 233
fillwindow, 74, 234
font, 212
font::~font, 91
font::close, 92, 234-235
font::font, 91
font::getptr, 235-236
font::open, 91-92, 236
font_tab_ptr, 79
fontedit.cpp, 174-186
free, 104, 106-107
function names, 34

G

getcurpos, 92, 237
getfontvectors, 78, 237-238
gmenu, 208
graphic coordinates, 10-11
graphic pixels, 4
graphics.asm, 36-68, 97
graphinit, 68
gwindows.hpp, 82-88, 207, 209, 211
gwindows.lib, xvi

H

hidemouse, 69, 238-239
horizontal scroll bars, 102
hotstring, 120, 239

I

idate.cpp, 148-150
idollar.cpp, 152-155
input_date, 152, 240
input_dollar, 157, 241
input_number, 160, 241-242
input_phone, 165, 242-243
input_ssn, 170, 243-244
input_string, 172, 244-245
inumber.cpp, 157-159
iphone.cpp, 160-163
issn.cpp, 165-167
istring.cpp, 170-171

K

keypressed, 78, 245-246

L

left_button, 208
local variables, 36-38
lowlevel.cpp, 88-91

M

malloc, 104-105
max, 246-247
memory-mapped devices, 7
MENU, 209-210
MENU_HEAD, 210
menucolors, 212
menucolors::color, 247
menucolors::highlight, 247-248
menucolors::setcolor, 248-249
menucolors::sethighlight, 249
menus.cpp, 120
Microsoft mouse driver functions, 96-97
    Disable Mouse Driver (1FH), 427-428
    Enable Mouse Driver (20H), 429-430
    Get Alternate Event Handler's Address (19H), 415-416
    Get Button Press Status (05H), 377-378
    Get Button Release Status (06H), 379-380
    Get Button Status and Pointer Position (03H), 373-374
    Get Language Code (23H), 435-436
    Get Motion Count (0BH), 389-390
    Get Mouse Information (24H), 437-438
    Get Mouse Status Buffer Size (15H), 406-407
    Get Pointer Display Page (1EH), 425-426
    Get Sensitivity (1BH), 419-420
    Reset Mouse Driver (21H), 431-432
    Reset the Mouse Driver (00H), 367-368
    Restore Mouse Driver Status (17H), 410-411
    Save Mouse Driver Status (16H), 408-409
    Set Alternate Event Handler (18H), 412-414
    Set Double Speed Threshold (13H), 402-403
    Set Exclusion Area (10H), 400-401
    Set Graphic Shape (09H), 385-386
    Set Horizontal Limits (07H), 381-382
    Set Interrupt Rate (1CH), 421-422
    Set Language (22H), 433-434
    Set Mickey:Pixels Ratios (0FH), 398-399
    Set Pointer Display Page (1DH), 423-424
    Set Pointer Position (04H), 375-376
    Set Sensitivity (1AH), 417-418
    Set Text Pointer Type (0AH), 387-388
    Set User-Defined Event Handler (0CH), 391-393
    Set Vertical Limits (08H), 383-384
    Swap User-Defined Event Handlers (14H), 404-405
    Turn off Light Pen Emulation (0EH), 396-397
    Turn off the Mouse Pointer (02H), 371-372
    Turn on Light Pen Emulation (0DH), 394-395
    Turn on the Mouse Pointer (01H), 369-370
mouse, 100, 208
mouse_col, 208
mouse_row, 208
mouse_x, 209
mouse_y, 209
movewindow, 77-78, 251
MS-DOS video functions, 4

N

new, 103-104
number_func, 159-160

P

phone, 210
phone_func, 163-165
phone_string, 163, 251-252
pointer, 213
pointer.cpp, 97-99
pointer::~pointer, 99
pointer::col, 100, 252-253
pointer::lbutton, 100, 253-254
pointer::off, 99, 254-255
pointer::on, 99, 255
pointer::pointer, 99
pointer::rbutton, 100, 255-256
pointer::read, 99, 256-257

pointer::row, 100, 258
pointer::x, 99-100, 258-259
pointer::y, 100, 259-260
pop-up menus, 121
popup, 213
popup.cpp, 121-124
popup::get, 124-126, 260-262
pull-down menus, 133-134
pulldown, 214
pulldown.cpp, 135-141
pulldown::display, 141, 262-263
pulldown::get, 141-145, 263-268

R

read_mask, 80
readmouse, 69-70, 268-269
realloc, 104-106
resetmouse, 69, 270
restorewindow, 76-77, 270-271
ROM BIOS video functions, 4-7
    Read Character/Attribute Pair (08H), 309-310
    Read Cursor Values (03H), 299-300
    Read Graphics Pixel (0DH), 319-320
    Read Light Pen Position (04H), 301-302
    Scroll Window Down (07H), 307-308
    Scroll Window Up (06H), 305-306
    Select Display Page (05H), 303-304
    Set Color Palette (0BH), 315-316
    Set Cursor Position (02H), 6-7, 297-298
    Set Cursor Type (01H), 295-296
    Set Video Mode (00H), 293-294
    Write Character/Attribute Pairs (09H), 311-312
    Write Character in Teletype Mode (0EH), 321-322
    Write Characters (0AH), 313-314
    Write Graphics Pixel (0CH), 317-318

S

sanscga.cpp, 192-197
sansega.cpp, 198-203
savewindow, 75-76, 271-272
setcurpos, 92, 272
setfontvectors, 79, 273
showmouse, 69, 274
ssn, 211
ssn_func, 168-169
ssn_string, 168, 274-275
stack frames, 34-35
string_func, 171-172

U

ucursoroff, 71, 275-276
ucursoron, 70, 275-276
underline, 74-75, 276

V

V20, 36
V30, 36
variable names, 34
vertical scroll bars, 103

W

waitkey, 78, 277
window, 214-215
window::~window, 113
window::close, 114, 277-278
window::clreol, 115, 278
window::cls, 115, 279
window::curcol, 279-280
window::currow, 280-281
window::draw, 113-114, 281
window::horizontal_bar, 118, 281-282
window::open, 114, 282-283
window::p_col, 283
window::p_row, 284
window::print, 116-117, 284-285
window::printat, 117-118, 285-286
window::println, 117, 286
window::printlnat, 118, 287
window::scroll, 115-116, 287-288
window::setcurpos, 114, 289
window::vertical_bar, 118, 289-290
window::window, 113
windows.cpp, 107-113
write_mask, 80

Z

zortech.bat, 440

RELATED TITLES FROM MIS: PRESS

TEACH YOURSELF C
Charles Siegel
$22.95   ISBN 0-943518-99-7

TEACH YOURSELF C++
Al Stevens
$22.95   ISBN 1-55828-027-8

X WINDOW APPLICATIONS PROGRAMMING
Eric F. Johnson and Kevin Reichard
$29.95   ISBN 1-55828-016-2
With disk $59.95   ISBN 1-55828-035-9

ADVANCED X WINDOW APPLICATION PROGRAMMING
(Includes Release 4.0)
Eric F. Johnson and Kevin Reichard
$29.95   ISBN 1-55828-029-4
With disk $59.95   ISBN 1-55828-054-5

USER INTERFACES IN C++ AND OBJECT-ORIENTED PROGRAMMING
Mark Goodwin
$23.95   ISBN 1-55828-023-5
With disk $53.95   ISBN 1-55828-037-5

OBJECT-ORIENTED ENVIRONMENT IN C++
David Hu
$29.95   ISBN 1-55828-014-6
With disk $49.95   ISBN 1-55828-039-1

EXTENDING TURBO C PROFESSIONAL
Al Stevens
$24.95   ISBN 1-55828-013-8
With disk $49.95   1-55828-038-3

USER INTERFACES IN C
Mark Goodwin
$24.95   ISBN 1-55828-002-2
With disk $49.95   ISBN 1-55828-036-7

C/C++ FOR EXPERT SYSTEMS
David Hu
$24.95   ISBN 0-943518-86-5
With disk $$49.95   ISBN 1-55828-034-0

QUICK C
Al Stevens
$24.95   ISBN 0-943518-80-6
With disk $49.95   ISBN 1-55828-042-1

TURBO C
Al Stevens
$24.95   ISBN 0-943518-35-0
With disk $44.95   ISBN 0-943518-76-8

C DATA BASE DEVELOPMENT
Al Stevens
$23.95   ISBN 0-943518-33-4
With disk $43.95   ISBN 1-55828-044-8

Available where fine books
    sold.

MANAGEMENT INFORMATION SOURCE, INC.
P. Box 5277 • Portland, OR 97208-5277
(503) 282-5215

Call free
1-800-MANUALS

PUBLISHING
FOR THE
TWENTY-FIRST
CENTURY

MANAGEMENT INFORMATION SOURCE, INC.

·ORDER FORM FOR

PROGRAM LISTINGS ON DISKETTE

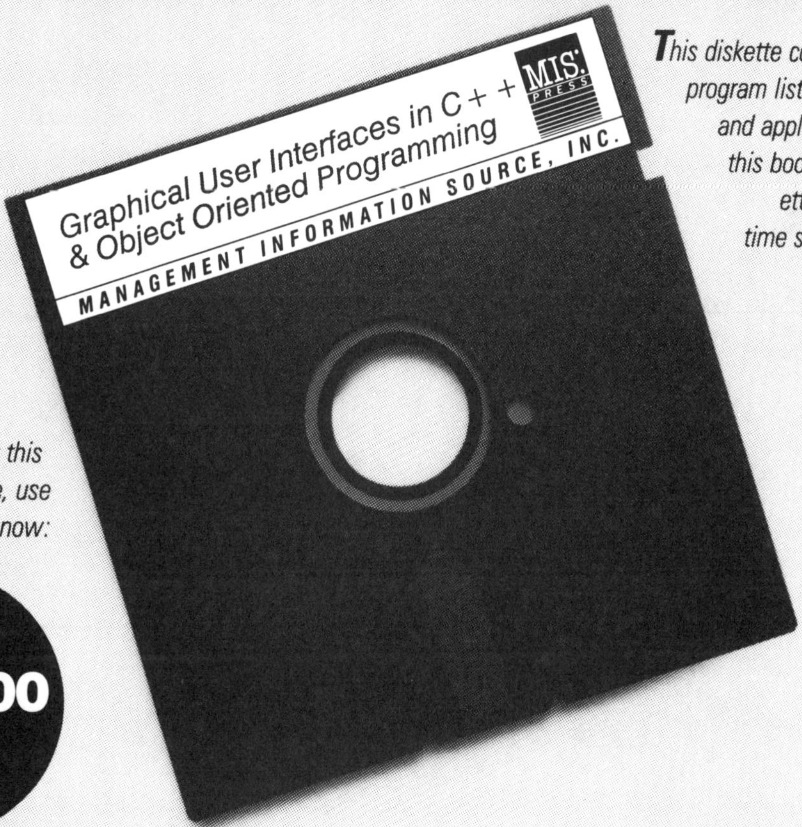

This diskette contains the complete program listings for all programs and applications contained in this book. By using this diskette, you will eliminate time spent typing in pages of program code.

f you did not buy this ook with diskette, use is form to order now:

Only:
25⁰⁰

ANAGEMENT INFORMATION SOURCE, INC.
). Box 5277 • Portland, OR 97208-5277
)3) 282-5215

Graphical User Interfaces in C + +
☐ *Diskette only, $25.00*
Please add $3.00 shipping & handling, $6.00 foreign.

Please check
☐ *VISA* ☐ *MasterCharge* ☐ *American Express*
☐ *Check enclosed $*__________

____
ME (Please print or type)

____
)RESS

____
Y *STATE* *ZIP*

____
ACCT.

____
EXP. DATE

____
SIGNATURE

all free
-800-MANUALS

MIS:
PRESS

ANAGEMENT INFORMATION SOURCE, INC.

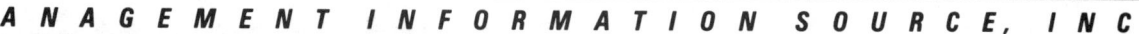